The Dirty
College Game

The Dirty
College Game

*Corruption, Gambling
and the Pursuit of Money
in NCAA Football and Basketball*

AL FIGONE

McFarland & Company, Inc., Publishers
Jefferson, North Carolina

LIBRARY OF CONGRESS CATALOGUING-IN-PUBLICATION DATA

Names: Figone, Albert J., author.
Title: The dirty college game : corruption, gambling and the pursuit
  of money in NCAA football and basketball / Al Figone.
Description: Jefferson, North Carolina : McFarland & Company, Inc.,
  Publishers, 2019 | Includes bibliographical references and index.
Identifiers: LCCN 2019027024 | ISBN 9781476671123
  (paperback : acid free paper) ∞
  ISBN 9781476634814 (ebook)
Subjects: LCSH: Sports—Corrupt practices—United States. | Football—
  Betting—United States. | Basketball—Betting—United States. | Organized
  crime—United States. | National Collegiate Athletic Association.
Classification: LCC GV718.2.U6 F54 2019 | DDC 796.04/30973—dc23
LC record available at https://lccn.loc.gov/2019027024

BRITISH LIBRARY CATALOGUING DATA ARE AVAILABLE

ISBN (print) 978-1-4766-7112-3
ISBN (ebook) 978-1-4766-3481-4

Front cover image by Sergey Nivens (Shutterstock)

Printed in the United States of America

McFarland & Company, Inc., Publishers
  Box 611, Jefferson, North Carolina 28640
  www.mcfarlandpub.com

This book is dedicated to my wife Jenifer Sara Figone,
who is my conscience, confidante, friend, communicator,
role model, listener, supporter, and lover.
She is sincere, spontaneous, and non-judgmental.

Acknowledgments

Without the assistance of the following people this book would not have been possible or written: Pete Michel, director and curator of the UNLV Archives; Delores Brownlee, Special Collections, UNLV; Diane Mizrachi, UCLA archivist; Terry Gugliotta (now retired), head university archivist, University of New Mexico. Dr. Michael Minix, ophthalmologist and former football player at the University of Kentucky, offered his insights on how Kentucky head football coach Charley Bradshaw administered and served as the head coach of the football program at the institution. David Sumner, professor of journalism and coordinator of the magazine journalism major at Ball State University, offered constant and consistent encouragement while I was writing the book. Anthony Timek, now an archivist at Rutgers, was instrumental in successfully accessing material at the University of Michigan related to the *FAB Five* while they played at the University of Michigan. Letitia Shen on several occasions assisted this author with technical computer difficulties. Haley Hicks was an invaluable digital native who offered guidance regarding technical needs, while proofreading and assisting in formatting the entire manuscript. Belinda Breyer painstakingly edited, reviewed, and suggested relevant changes and formatting for the entire manuscript in preparation for publication—a truly formidable task.

Table of Contents

Preface

The topics in this book—gambling, academic fraud, illegal booster activity, and a single-minded pursuit of television contracts—have rarely been assigned the same importance by sport historians as the other corruptive aspects of college sports. In addition, those in power positions, including commissioners and boards of trustees (BOT), tend to ignore discussions of the inconsistencies, internal contradictions, and commonly held ideological beliefs about sports in America. Such discussions are important, however, because they reveal the enormous gap between commonly held public beliefs about universities as noble places of educational opportunity, sports as an aid to physical well-being—between the idea that college sports are non-commercial and governed by a strict code of ethics—and the reality of college athletics, particularly big-time college athletics. This book shows how the regulatory agency for college sports, the NCAA, is supposed to enforce rules that maintain the principles listed above, and how often it fails to do so or inconsistently applies those rules. Public exposés about the corruptive aspects of big-time college sports have been regarded by professional owners, the NCAA, corporate sponsors, and television advertisers as threats to the bottom line. In many cases, college trustees and administrators share the professional leagues' suspicion of outsiders collecting data and conduct investigations that usually remain in-house.

Another aspect of this sidetracking of principles is the difficulty it presents student athletes in obtaining an education. Where a chance to better oneself by gaining that education seems to exist, it may be illusory. Special courses are created, transcripts faked, college credits bought. Time that might be devoted to broader scholastic and social activities is channeled into athletic pursuits. It is a great disservice to the students—and gross hypocrisy on the part of universities.

It is ironic that the culmination of the NCAA basketball season has become, in effect, one of the biggest gambling holidays ever: March Madness. Even casual fans eagerly fill out their brackets and pay into pools, and they

1

aren't alone in placing bets. The seemingly endless conference, regional, and national tournaments are a bonanza for the few institutions fortunate to advance. Often, of course, those institutions are among the largest and most commercialized in Division I basketball, and come from conferences composed of similar schools. (The same is true during bowl season and for the newly created FBS football playoffs, which is dominated by Power 5 programs.) The infrastructure of these elite conferences resembles that of professional leagues in nearly every respect except how the athletes are, or are supposed to be, compensated.

Corruption in college sports, purportedly amateur, is a direct result of gross commercialization. The emphasis on money and a "what's in it for me" attitude have opened the door for gamblers and organized crime to gain a foothold in these arenas. Corruption in athletics is about contaminating the competitive environment so whoever has a stake in the event's outcome no longer can depend on a fair result. In horse racing, the state, as part-owner of the business, has a stake in an honestly run race. The state enhances the perception of honesty through strict enforcement of the rules. The public needs to be assured that their wager will be decided fairly. In college and professional basketball from the 1940s through the 1960s, a few players were routinely assisting gamblers by playing not to beat the spread. Under these circumstances legitimate bettors had no guarantee that their bets would be consummated fairly. Stated differently, without an external monitoring organization similar to horse racing, betting on college and professional basketball was handicapped.

Two distinct forms of corruption emerge in this book. One type occurs when an institution sponsors athletic programs with the unspoken goal of generating large profits. The second form of corruption occurs when the legitimacy of contests themselves is in doubt, as when the final score is manipulated by players to favor gamblers. Any business regulated by the state has the backing and support of the government that spectators will be exposed to a "fair game" on the field or court. Any institution that sells tickets to a game is guaranteeing that the contest will be untainted by illegal gambling money. Beginning in the 1930s through the 1980s, colleges were afflicted by a small number of athletes, especially in basketball, who rigged games for gamblers. Fortunately for commercialized college basketball, spectators were more interested in watching games instead of reading about fixing games by players. Scandalized athletic programs reveal that some form of corruption has existed long enough to have spread like a disease and is adversely affecting the entire program. This can include the negative publicity that accompanies any scandal, as the public is usually offered a rare public glimpse regarding the inner workings of an institution's athletic policy. In the Jerry Sandusky scandal at Penn State, the public revelations about the scandal informed how each layer of the administration in the university was willing to cover up the egregious conduct of a public employee who was viewed as an icon in the Penn State community.

The Professional and Amateur Sports Protection Act (PASPA) makes any form of sports gambling illegal except in the states of Delaware, Montana, Nevada, and Oregon. If one peruses the internet during fall or winter seasons, numerous off-shore betting outlets can be accessed if one wants to place a bet on a specific game. Technically, these online sites are legal in the country in which they obtain a license, but are not legalized to operate in the United States in any fashion (online, via a bookie, etc.) or where the United States has jurisdictional control.

The first two chapters in this book examine the history of collegiate football and basketball, particularly their growth alongside the development of televised sports and the changing gambling habits of the public. Chapters 3, 4, and 5 present case studies of corrupt programs that flourished briefly within institutions that devoted little administrative oversight. Finally, Chapters 6, 7, and 8 delve into corrupting influence exerted by various other stakeholders, including boosters and gamblers.

1

The Historical Symbiosis
Between Corruption
and Sports

During the latter part of the nineteenth century, high schools and colleges began to spread the quasi-religion of sports by establishing interscholastic and intercollegiate competitions. Pulp fiction promoted the belief that sport was a metaphor for democracy played out on the field of amateur sports. Adopting the Protestant belief that winning enhanced the moral fiber of the individual, community, or institution, athletics at the college level quickly became commercialized (i.e., structured to generate profits) and professionalized (i.e., coaches hired to train athletes for competition).[1] Competitive sports appealed to urban audiences in the East Coast late in the nineteenth century, and gradually this appeal expanded to other areas in the United States by the mid-twentieth century. And wherever professional sports and commercialized collegiate sports existed, the shadow of illegal gambling followed.

Despite the unwanted intrusion of gambling in the beginning of professional and college sports, gambling experts, sport historians, and journalists have largely chosen to ignore how illegal gambling and professional gamblers became associated with a number of sports. The reason for this dearth of investigations may be related to sports gamblers' and bookies' reluctance to place their records in public and historical repositories because they fear prosecution and retribution. In some cases where organized crime has been involved, exposure of legal and illegal sports gambling's dark side has led to hefty fines, jail sentences, bodily harm, and death. Nearly 80 years ago, prominent sportswriter Paul Gallico observed how the singular quest for money tainted college football and abandoned his sportswriting career because he believed the sport required "too high of a price to pay for decency."[2] In the late 1800s, American colleges' commercialization and professionalization of football, and baseball put to rest the belief that such competition was pure, amateur, simple, and quaint. In 1986, *Sports Illustrated* senior writer Frank Deford described how in 1869, the first year of intercollegiate football competition between Rutgers and Princeton, the game was canceled "because the faculties [of the two institutions] feared overemphasis." Deford added, "by the turn of the century, the president of the United States was decrying the abuses of college sports."[3] The *New York Times* cited lynching and football as America's twin evils during that same time period.[4]

Sports that were bet on in the nineteenth century included track, commonly known then as pedestrianism, boxing, baseball, and college football. Track and boxing lost the public's trust because gamblers were known to fix races and boxing matches. Since an individual was easier to bribe than an entire team, people involved in organized crime preferred to gamble on a sure bet. College football was casually bet on by students, alumni, and a few serious gamblers. Professional baseball, for reasons that have puzzled baseball and sport historians, attracted and was corrupted by professional gamblers. By the early part of the twentieth century, reported and unreported game fixing had become endemic in the sport.[5] Perhaps the most infamous case was the Chicago Black Sox scandal.

The Industrial Revolution created economic, social, and political changes that included gambling on sports, stocks in mythical gold mines, and odds on not being caught in graft or fraudulent business activity.[6] Individuals transported portable bookmaking booths from one event to another during the 1870s, selling lottery tickets and taking bets on a sporting event.[7]

Early Football

The beginnings of college sports in the United States and their association with gambling paralleled the rise in social acceptance of gambling on sports activities established in the late nineteenth and early twentieth century. Except for baseball, which hid its gambling corruption from the public until the early twentieth century, dishonest competition or fixes had been the death knell of sports such as professional track, wrestling (i.e., junk sport), and— for a time—boxing. In 1880, noted Harvard physical education instructor Dudley Sargent deplored college football's trend toward commercialization and professionalization, stating, "Betting will be the bane of competitive contests."[8]

Thirteen years later, college football founder and Yale coach Walter Camp, observing the open bidding and money offered by colleges to obtain the best players, cautioned, "Playing for gamblers could be just as easy as playing for a college."[9] Deceit and excesses in college football during this time period included collegiate players competing in the nascent professional leagues for money, playing for more than one team during a season (i.e., tramp athlete), salaries for coaches that often exceeded professors' salaries, ignoring admission requirements for athletes, and direct payoffs to players. Failed institutional self-regulations led to the formation of conferences and creation of the National Collegiate Athletic Association (NCAA) in 1906. The organization proved to be as ineffective as previous efforts in curbing gambling and other abuses once money became the primary measure of a successful football program.

By the 1890s, social scientists and others were decrying the physical softness and feminization of American society because of its increasing urbanization, complexity, mechanization, and standardization.[10] Football competition provided the perfect social antidote, as it emphasized imagination, robustness, and ingenuity. Football at Yale, reported President Arthur T. Hadley in 1906, blurred the line between social classes by taking hold of the student body in such a way as to make class distinctions relatively unimportant and "enabling the students to get together in the old-fashioned democratic way."[11] In a short time, generations of young men in Pennsylvania and other coal mining states would turn their backs on the mines that employed their fathers to play college or professional football.

The annual Thanksgiving game in 1893 between Yale and Princeton created frenzy in New York among the wealthy residing on Fifth Avenue, which reflected the game's popularity and the gambling proclivities of the elites. The excitement on Fifth Avenue was evident as blue and white Yale banners were displayed at the Whitney and Vanderbilt mansions, while Old Nassau colors were hung by the Sloanes, Alexanders, and Scribners. Thanksgiving Day services were cut short by clergymen so churchgoers could attend the game.[12] Alumni of the Big Three (Harvard, Yale, Princeton) and several other schools were observed on the floor of the New York Stock Exchange—and wherever else one could tender a bet—a week before the game. The game prospered, as did a few bookies and gamblers. When Yale played Princeton in the Big Three championship at New York's Polo Grounds before a crowd of 5,000 in 1880, newspapers reported that an "unusual number of young collegians swung handsful [sic] of greenbacks in the air loudly calling for bets."[13]

Ten years later, the press reported that $4,000 was sent to Princeton with orders to bet the money on Yale at odds of five to one or better. In 1891, noted minister and social reformer Henry Ward Beecher might have found it perplexing and ironic that his grandson and former Yale football star of the same name was observed on a New York street offering an unheard-of sum of $2,000. He was betting $1,000 that Princeton would not kick a field goal and another $1,000 that his alma mater would win by more than 20 points.[14] The elder Beecher stated about gambling in 1896:

> To every man who indulges in the least form of gambling, I raise a warning voice! Under the specious name of amusement, you are laying the foundation of gambling. Playing is the seed which comes up gambling. It is the light wind which brings up the storm. It is the white frost which precludes the winter. You are mistaken, however, in supposing that it is harmless in its earliest beginnings.[15]

During its development from the late 1800s until 1930, college football would find its supporters among the constituents needed to promote the sport: college presidents, legislators, the press, alumni, coaches, businessmen, bookies, gamblers, and the public. In 1873, football's role on the college campus was temporarily derailed by Cornell President Andrew D. White's infamous remark when asked by 30 players if they could travel to Cleveland to play a game against Michigan: "I will not permit thirty men to travel four hundred miles to agitate a bag of wind."[16]

In time, Cornell, like most other colleges in America, welcomed the sport. Less than ten years later, during a seven-day period, Michigan traveled east to play Harvard, Yale, and Princeton. The land grant institutions, seeking any means to attract students, raise money, and mitigate the lack of government funding, embraced football as an important recruiting tool. With no eligibility rules, the young bachelor president of Ohio's Miami University required all capable men on the faculty to try out for the football team. The University of Oregon played against the same player in three successive contests against three different teams.[17] Excesses such as Harvard's 28-game schedule in 1882, in which 19 games were played away from campus, led to a short-lived period of student-faculty control of athletic programs in the colleges.

Football apologists were quick to mute any critics who pointed out that the game was not consistent with physical culture or training of the body. Hired by the University of Chicago in 1892 to build the institution into a football power in the Western Conference (the forerunner to the Big Ten), former Yale athlete Amos Alonzo Stagg was quick to point out how football satisfied the essential ideals of a college.[18] Stagg believed drinking had become a major college sport until intercollegiate sports were introduced. Many presidents cited football as responsible for reducing the incidents of rebellion, hazing, and rioting that occurred on many campuses before the sport was introduced.

By the late 1880s, political leaders viewed the sport as necessary in assisting America's expansionism and military aspirations and in succeeding in domestic businesses leading to corporate victories. "Courage, coolness, and steadiness of nerve, quickness of apprehension, resourcefulness, self-knowledge, and self-reliance" were attributes one might find applicable to John D. Rockefeller buying another rival company or to Admiral Dewey at Manila Bay.[19] The qualities described above were the words of a college president describing an ideal football player in the 1890s.[20] During the Progressive Era, muckraking (a term coined by President Theodore Roosevelt, referring to journalists who wrote about America's social ills) writers were deploring the game's brutality and uselessness. America's new contact sport satisfied many values embodied in TR's "strenuous life" dictum. However, the president warned that he would abolish the game by executive order unless it was cleaned up.

Wanting it both ways, Harvard President Charles Eliot, mindful of the sport's early popularity, complained that football had become a place "where young men were being instructed in driving a trade or winning a fight, no matter how." Instead, he hoped that Harvard men would shun the "reckless, unmotivated courage of football" and admire the courage that advocated "the cause of the weak."[21] The game's attraction to many gamblers was not lost on its critics. Cornell's President White observed:

> The sight of a confused mass of educated young men making battering-rams of their bodies, plunging their heads into each other's stomachs, piling upon each other's ribs, or maiming each other for life—sometimes indeed killing each other—in the presence of a great mass of screaming, betting bystanders, many among them utterly disreputable, is to me a brutal monstrosity.[22]

Thorstein Veblen, writing in *The Theory of the Leisure Class*, viewed gambling on football and other sports as "conspicuous leisure," a little-known term that was closely connected to "conspicuous consumption," a phrase used to describe the relationship between spending and social status.[23] To Veblen, participation in golf, tennis, sailing, and other sports that required money represented a gratuitous form of social status. Friendly wagering among the elites at football games was to Veblen like viewing "a one-sided return to barbarism promoting exotic ferocity and cunning."[24] He found no redeeming value in the sport.

The press' role in the development and spread of college football cannot be understated. For the first time, the American college was a source of popular news, encouraging enrollment-seeking administrators to support football. In fact, all forms of athletics began to serve the public relations functions of colleges. Seeking faculty approval for an extended baseball trip in 1879, students at Illinois College pointed out "how the publicity of such a trip would benefit the college."[25] Traveling to the east in 1895, the University of

California track team's victories were viewed as a successful public relations venture. The money-starved land-grant and state universities viewed winning in sports as more important than other activities in lobbying reluctant legislators for more money.[26]

By 1900, the relationship between football and publicity had been established. Of all the sports, football generated the most interest from students and the public. Also, the sport brought into its fold college supporters for whom the idea of attending college was out of the question but, as a matter of good business, believed in supporting a team (i.e., boosterism). Just as the college campus served as a democratizing agent and instrument for raising social status, off-campus sports fans would experience democracy by collectively consuming a new form of public entertainment.[27] Justification for the sport as a public relations tool would survive into the twenty-first century.

Once the game was validated by support from college presidents, boards of trustees, alumni, legislatures, and the press, there could be no failure. America's capitalistic system was built on business success and an expansionist economy that required the opening of new foreign markets. Militarists believed that football prepared men for combat in ways that were not possible in other forms of physical activity. Old-line professors observed and studied the newly adopted extra curriculum with indifference. Games had to be won, and organized athletics quickly formed a management alliance between students and alumni.

By the end of the nineteenth century, the structure of athletics grew too large and complex, necessitating a more formal administration of growing sports programs. The position of Athletic Business Manager was created, the forerunner of today's Director of Athletics. Observing the fine line between legal tactics and foul play that had been established by the titans of industry during the Gilded Age, these men administered sports programs as a business. The colleges had discovered an instrument for teaching students what their peddler parents may have taught them a generation before.[28] Viewing the meteoric rise of the game's popularity, one critic commented:

> Men trained in such methods through all the years of school and college life may become future leaders, but they will be leaders in the art of evading taxes, manipulating courts, and outwitting the law of the land[29]

Observing a void that student inefficiency and faculty indifference created in athletic administration, alumni jumped at the opportunity to create football and other sports programs in their image, receiving the blessings of administrators and faculty. The older alumni who had witnessed nothing more than straightforward competition for boosting enrollment quickly embraced football as a new source of loyalty. Younger alumni, some of whom had played the game, became the game's most vocal supporters. One graduate stated in a national magazine in 1890, "You don't remember whether Thorpwright was valedictorian or not, but you can never forget that glorious run of his in a football game."[30]

Achieving total domination of college athletics, alumni filled their school's financial vacuum as far they were able and willing to do so. Total mobilization for victory required money for recruitment, training, feeding, salaries of coaches, and special care of athletic heroes.[31] Many commentators, administrators, and coaches linked football with capitalism that made rationalizing its development more compatible as a commercial enterprise in the rapid industrialization of the United States in the late nineteenth and early twentieth century.[32]

The possibility that the game would be returned to the students was lost in 1915 when the University of Pittsburgh introduced the placing of numerals on the backs of its players to promote the selling of programs.[33] This tragically symbolic event illustrated how control over the sport had been transferred from those who played it to the paying customers, alumni, and treasurers of the athletic associations.[34] Colleges introduced colors in which to encase their football players accompanied by songs, posters, banners, music, and other carnival-like displays, enabling the public to identify institutions and football teams by their hue. It was not long before spectators, the press, and gamblers believed the main purpose of American colleges was to field a winning football team.

The development of intercollegiate sports benefited a minimal number of people in a college community. Thirty years before the turn of the century, the rich sent their sons and daughters to colleges, expecting the newly created physical culture departments to provide wholesome exercise that was believed to cure infectious diseases (penicillin and other antibiotics had not yet been discovered). By 1904, the football craze at the University of California prompted one student to complain, "Athletics as conducted now in our larger universities is but for the few picked teams while the very students who most need physical development become stoop-shouldered rooting from backless bleachers."[35]

The undergraduates wanted fun and exercise. Finding a place for men and women who found competition unappealing, the colleges introduced intramural sports. The movement created a double standard in college athletics that troubled critics of intercollegiate sports. The expert athlete was elevated to celebrity status and achieved a near-professionalized standard of play through sacrifice and hard work. In contrast, the majority of undergraduates viewed participation in intramurals as simply exercise for fun.[36] Not unexpectedly, coaches began to view intramurals as tryouts for their teams.

The football coach emerged as a cultural hero because he provided the victories needed to justify money obtained from the colleges, alumni, and private businessmen who promoted the sport as a profit-making venture. Invariably, former players or professional trainers who had played the game well under less than amateur conditions were selected as coaches. Before long, they became more visible and perceived as more important to a college than its president. The Big Three introduced expenses-only appearances of former captains as coaches for games during a season.[37] When as many as 30 ex-captains appeared to coach a team, athletics administrators saw the inefficiency of the practice and abandoned it. The hiring of Stagg at Chicago, Bill Reid at Harvard, and Fielding "Hurry Up" Yost at Michigan marked the beginning of contracting full-time coaches. In the early 1900s, the football coach was the only person who could share in the profits resulting from his labors. As the only money-making activity on campus, football supported the coaches' salaries, which in many cases were disproportionate in comparison to administrators and professors.[38] Professional coaches' personal stakes in winning escalated the need for brawn instead of intellect, which met with alumni favor.

In a short time, the game had been taken away from students and became a contest between two alumni groups and rival coaches for job security.[39] Michigan's Yost had played for the Allegheny Athletic Club of Pittsburgh, Lafayette College, and the University of Virginia. Before arriving at Michigan in 1900, he had coached at Ohio Wesleyan, the University of Nebraska, and Stanford.[40] During the 1890s, the Allegheny Athletic Club and Pittsburgh Athletic Club were part of the club movement that was theoretically under the auspices of the newly formed Amateur Athletic Union (AAU). Because of the money bet on the games, the clubs began to recruit college players under assumed names and offered to pay the players' salaries and traveling expenses. Gate receipts generated as much as $1,200 a game, meanwhile affording the opportunity to bet on the games, violating the spirit of amateurism.[41]

After a 4–0 Allegheny win (a touchdown was worth four points), Pittsburgh refused to pay off their bets, alleging that three Chicago Athletic Club players, including All-American tackle Pudge Heffelfinger, were offered twice their traveling expenses and money to play in the game. The local newspapers referred to both teams as amateurs while printing allegations of their professionalism. Disputes of this nature were commonplace in college football from the game's beginnings well into the 1920s.[42] By the mid–1890s, Midwestern colleges agreed to allow no more than two paid or professional players on a college team.

The transformation away from playing the game for enjoyment was not entirely attributable to coaches. The alumni expected money given to the football program to generate victories, creating an enthusiasm for spectacles of barbarism that were favored by the public. Faculties had become powerless in supervising college football. The early beginnings of football and later basketball created a stage for the endless and redundant debates between academicians and athletic apologists involving the manner in which commercialized college sports undermined an institution's academic integrity. There was never really any competition.

Three early-twentieth century events refined football's commercialism, which did not escape the attention of bookies and gamblers: World War I, intersectionalism, and the construction of cement and steel stadiums. Horse racing was shut down by the government after America's entry in the Great War in Europe in 1917.[43] In response, bookies migrated to college football games during the war, booking bets in unofficially designated wagering sections in stadiums. The invention of phone and wire service in the late 1800s allowed for a wider distribution of betting odds and sporting events' results. This added a measure of sophistication to bookmaking.[44]

When America joined the allies in defeating Germany in 1917, America's military success was believed to have resulted from participation in competitive sports. With more than half of the country's youth living in rural communities, physical educators were stunned by the high rejection rate of draftees.[45] High schools and colleges dismissed the notion that competitive sports excluded those who needed physical activity the most. Military preparation for World War I included football and other games. According to sport historian Patrick Miller, the stadium-building orgy of the 1920s represented the foremost patriotic symbols of the decade, "solidly establishing the bonds between muscular and martial values, cementing the relationship between the war effort, between Mars and Minerva."[46]

Capitalizing on a spectatorship that welcomed competition, college football employed new ways to publicize their programs—intersectionalism and the emerging medium of advertising.[47] In the beginning of the twentieth century, private promoters proposed an "intersectional Saturday every fall [where] four of the big eastern teams will go west for a game and four of the best western teams will travel east to do battle."[48] Motivated by profit, the big-city promoters and administrators rationalized staging intersectional games between the mythical top teams in the country as educational opportunities for the players (e.g., seeing the United States from a train) and good for ticket sales.

Journalists and colleges did not miss the open season on gambling on college and professional sports that was sweeping the country.[49] Two intersectional games in 1926 were harbingers of how commercialized college football would grow alongside illegal wagering in the twentieth century. The annual Army-Navy game was staged in Philadelphia or New York (except in 1924, when Baltimore was awarded the game). In 1926, Chicago outbid the other three cities. With only 40,000 available seats, the promoters received an unheard-of 600, 000 applications for tickets. The sale of tickets at Soldier Field banked $800,000 for the promoters. After paying $600,000 for travel, housing, food, and game-related expenses, the $100,000 checks paid to each service academy and the economic benefits to Chicago businesses, including illegal drinking and gambling, were not lost on promoters in other cities.[50]

The Notre Dame–Southern California intersectional game began in 1926 and was played at the recently constructed and privately financed Los Angeles Coliseum. The moneyed promoters who financed the construction were looking to bid for the 1932 Olympics. An estimated crowd of 75,000 was reported at the inaugural game. Subsequent games in 1927 and 1929 at Chicago's Soldier Field attracted crowds of more than 115,000. Estimated gate receipts in 1927 were more than $350,000, with the profit to each school approximately $50,000. In 1929, just before the burst of the "manic football bubble," *New York Times* sportswriter John Kieran foresaw an increase in intersectional games, predicting, "As passenger planes increase in size, the teams will be scooting around the country and back in big passenger planes—it is bound to come the way football and aviation are growing."[51]

College football historian Michael Oriard cited the Harvard-Centre game in 1921 as the decisive event launching the age of intersectionalism.[52] A school of just 270 students, Centre College in Danville, Kentucky, embarked on one of the most bizarre schedules in the history of college football. Undefeated in 1919 and losing only to Harvard in 1920, the team returned to Cambridge in 1921. According to the *Associated Press*, "the greatest upset of the century" was recorded as they defeated the Crimson, 6–0.[53] The Praying Colonels barnstormed from coast-to-coast as the players routinely wagered on their own team. Returning home the night of the Harvard upset, Earl Ruby of the *Louisville Courier-Journal* reported that All-American Alvin "Bo" McMillen had more folding money on the night of October 29, 1921, in a lower berth on a Pullman than could normally be found in a lot of small-town Kentucky banks.[54] That a prestigious college like Harvard would schedule an opponent with fewer than 300 students illustrated that what mattered the most to colleges that sponsored big-time football programs was providing money to pay football players. In an era without any formal organizational

George Gipp, legendary running back for Notre Dame. When asked by famed coach Knute Rockne at halftime in 1920 if "he had any interest in the game," Gipp responded, "Look Rock, I've got $400 bet on this game and I'm not about to blow it" (courtesy Notre Dame Archives).

structure including NCAA divisions, small colleges could compete with the elites in the sport.

The use of public stadiums, such as the Polo Grounds, Yankee Stadium, and the Los Angeles Coliseum, for intersectional play, including the ones used by the Jesuit institutions for regular season games, created problems for college officials. The flagrant commercialized and professionalized atmosphere at these venues included widespread gambling, drinking, and scalping of tickets.[55] Curley Grieve, a sportswriter from San Francisco, after observing a game at the Polo Grounds between St. Mary's (California) and Fordham in November 1932, stated, "There's an utter lack of color and atmosphere at the football encounters with rooting sections obscured behind goal posts; the cheer leaders like so many wooden soldiers.... College football is handicapped under these conditions."[56]

Gamblers had been known to bet openly on baseball games at Braves Field, which hosted the Boston College–Holy Cross rivalry in Boston, and at St. Louis' Sportsman's Park, the home field of the St. Louis University Billikens. Neighborhood bookies welcomed the college football business. Players at these venues routinely reported offers as high as $1,000 to throw a game. At most meetings of college officials during the 1930s, discussion on how to deal with gambling and drinking in college football produced no practical solutions to the two problems that had grown unchecked since the game's beginnings. In 1936, an editorial in the *Saturday Evening Post* reminded its readers, "Professional gamblers are now brazen enough to get their information from the players themselves and from undergraduates working on college newspapers."[57]

In 1929, the *Carnegie Report* cited gambling on football as an unsavory part of the game. Yet the report was conspicuously silent about addressing the attraction of the sport to gamblers—money. Since basketball players were not officially subsidized and the sport had not captured spectator and gambler interest, the report offered no commentary about that sport. Football's commercial transformation continued during the Depression, and cutting non-revenue sports was one strategy implemented to avoid reducing football budgets.[58] Gambling on college football and basketball during that period lagged behind other sports such as horse racing, boxing, and baseball in terms of total money bet.

Working on the same side of law enforcement during Prohibition (1919–1931), business-by-intimidation rackets included prostitution, illicit liquor, and bookmaking on all forms of illegal and legal betting. The repeal of Prohibition cut into the illegal liquor profits. However, bookies were increasingly prominent as local businessmen. Needing a reputation for honesty and quick

payoffs to winners, these individuals cultivated a trust among their clients as their profits soared.[59] Many of their clients were attempting to recoup their financial losses from the 1929 stock market crash. Ironically, bookies had become the professionals' and collegians' best defense against a rigged game, as they were usually the first ones to detect a fix and remove the game from their boards.

Early Basketball

From its beginnings in the early 1890s, manipulation of final scores in basketball was easier because players and coaches controlled the financial and organizational aspects of the sport. When the YMCA determined that young players preferred competition, rather than the exercise benefits intended by the game's founder, Dr. James Naismith, it discontinued its support of games and tournaments. Those who wanted to continue in the sport were temporarily forced to practice and play as professionals, occasionally attracting large crowds.

Barnstorming teams such as James Furey's Original Celtics and the New York Whirlwinds, managed by Tex Rickard, earned the most money. In 1921, a best two-out-of-three series between the Celtics and Whirlwinds was scheduled in New York. After splitting the first two games, the third game was inexplicably canceled. According to Robert Peterson, in *Cages to Jump Shots: Pro Basketball's Early Years*, and the *Reach Guide,* the game was not played because "the series created so much interest that certain gamblers tried to connect in the fixing of one of the games."[60] The total attendance for both games was 18,000. By 1905 the colleges had incorporated basketball into their intercollegiate programs. Professional leagues, especially in the Northeast quadrant of the country, proliferated.[61] How many college athletes played for money in these leagues has rarely been recorded in basketball literature. Reluctantly, coaches accepted this practice, often with a stipulation that a player not play with the professionals on weekends.

By the mid–1930s, doubleheaders in public arenas provided bookies and a few colleges paydays they otherwise would not have seen. In 1938, Ned Irish introduced the National Invitational Tournament (NIT) at Madison Square Garden (MSG), followed by the NCAA finals tournament in 1939. In the 1940s, radio and television followed college basketball. By the time the colleges, NCAA, and legislators understood how gamblers could fix games with offers equal to those of recruiters, payoffs to players, and lack of institutional supervision, it was too late. Many bookies refused to do business on certain college basketball games in the 1940s when the wagering pattern or word on the street was that one or both teams were playing for gamblers.

World War II and the Rise of Gambling

During World War II, declining unemployment, rising incomes, and expansion of war production industries caused an increase in all forms of gambling nationwide. Fearing legal action against themselves and their employers, sportswriters who followed college football and basketball ignored writing about the illegal gambling, point shaving, and fixing offers.[62] Professional basketball had generated little public interest, as the owners had yet to develop the organization necessary for financial stability. For the college game, it was the appearance of players as tall as seven feet (individuals over six-foot-six were exempt from the military draft) that ushered in the era of pivot play, or shooting close to the basket, which became the dominant form of scoring and elevated the caliber of play.[63] Large crowds, especially when big men such as Bob Kurland of Oklahoma A&M (now Oklahoma State) and DePaul's George Mikan squared off, were common.

In football, some colleges dropped the sport for a year or so. Colleges with naval training programs were allowed to field strong teams, while those with army training programs were not (drafted players were expected to devote all their time to their studies). War powerhouses included the service academies at West Point (Army) and Annapolis (Navy) and military teams comprised of former collegians and professionals.[64] The final 1943 AP Top Ten poll included Iowa Pre-Flight, Great Lakes Naval Training Center, and Del Monte Pre-Flight. All three trained on college campuses.[65]

Prewar horse racing attendance revenues before 1941 had averaged $15 million; by 1944, it surpassed $17 million. On-track nationwide betting totaled $1.5 billion that same year, while in 1943 it was slightly over $700 million.[66] At least twice the latter amount was bet through off-track bookies. "America was off on the damnedest gambling binge in its history," wrote Dan Parker, sports editor of the *New York Daily Herald*. "Almost everyone was playing the horses."[67] In 1945, even though the government ordered the tracks closed for more than four months, betting numbered $1.4 billion and attendance was 17 million. If horse players wanted to bet on human sports during the brief track closing, their working capital allowed them to do so. With money to spend and little to spend it on, people sought to make even more money via various forms of sports and other gambling. Law enforcement's attention and resources were focused on the war effort. The FBI would investigate "suspect" games only in the course of investigating other aspects of illegal gambling connected to organized crime.[68]

Postwar gambling proliferated along with the prosperity that normally accompanied a country that remained unscathed from major enemy attacks. Commercialization and professionalization of college football and basketball followed as a slew of older athletes entered college under the GI Bill.[69] In 1946, estimates of betting on college football were reported at $100 million. Wagering on the "Game of the Century" between Notre Dame and Army that year approached an unheard-of $5 million. Gamblers had contacted coaches and players at each institution by phone and were seen at the teams' hotels, ostensibly to bribe players and coaches or seek inside information, a problem more than likely encountered by other football and basketball teams. Athletic officials canceled the annual series after the 1947 game because of the wagering and ticket scalping.

The postwar crime scare created a public uneasiness that moved some newspapers to publish series of articles linking organized crime to all forms of gambling. *Brooklyn Eagle*'s Ben Gould penned a series of articles in 1950 that specifically targeted the rigging of basketball games that included "one big-time basketball coach."[70] For his consistent scoops (exclusive news stories), the writer was awarded the Polk Plaque "for an amazing series of articles that opened up the shadowy backgrounds of gamblers, fixers, and players who were their dupes," and the revelations were "far in advance of official disclosures of the District Attorney."[71] The widespread fixing of college basketball games in the late 1940s was the worst-kept secret on the streets of New York.[72]

In 1950, the Kefauver Committee reported that organized crime's cut of the nation's gambling pie was between $15 and $30 billion, equal to ten percent of the gross national product. According to Richard Sasuly, the author of *Bettor and Bookies: Two Hundred Years of Gambling*, the committee's assumption was inaccurate.[73] Their hearings did not uncover any reliable evidence that a nationwide organized crime ring was involved in fixing boxing matches, professional and college football and basketball, and major league baseball games.[74] The committee was seeking to expose a well-organized national crime syndicate's bookmaking profits from other forms of illegal gambling. In fact, sports betting, then illegal, registered merely a blip on law enforcement's radar. The reason was simple: spectators' interest in professional and college sports was less than in major league baseball.[75]

Occasionally, writers wrote columns about what most gambling cognoscenti knew. Gambling in professional tennis, boxing, and professional and college football and basketball was a small part of the vast illegal bookies' business.[76] Assuredly, some of the bookies' profits were funneled to several groups loosely defined as organized crime. Most bookies handled bets on sports as a favor to their best customers, who usually preferred horse racing and fixed boxing matches. In certain sections of football stadiums and indoor venues, bookies could easily be spotted accepting bets.

Contrary to media reports, books, and other scholarly reports on the 1951 college basketball scandal, the New York County District Attorney's Office and district attorneys in other jurisdictions did not actively investigate the widespread problem of fixed college basketball games in the 1940s. Assuredly, local law enforcement, through wiretaps, bookies, and newspaper writers, had been aware of the behind-the-scenes gambling and fixed games that had taken place for years.

It was the work of *New York Journal-American* sports editor Max Kase, who brought two years of investigative reporting to the attention of New York County District Attorney Frank Hogan in January 1951.[77] Hogan and the New York County detectives initiated a one-month investigation on gambling in college basketball, confirming that Kase's evidence was on the mark.[78] One month later, the first arrests in the first major college basketball scandal hit the papers. The scandal shocked college officials and the public only because they refused to acknowledge and believe what bookies knew: fixing of games in college basketball was as common as a two-handed set shot in the 1940s and early 1950s.[79] Kase was not an outsider to college and professional basketball. A lifelong New Yorker, he almost succeeded in bringing professional basketball to the Big Apple. The organizers of the Basketball Association of America (BAA) owned indoor arenas and franchises in the National Hockey League (NHL) and viewed professional basketball teams as potential tenants to fill open dates.[80] Ned Irish's management of Madison Square Garden provided the edge over Kase in securing a franchise for the city.[81]

The widespread fixing of college basketball games uncovered in 1951 did not curtail the fixing of games in the sport. In fact, twice the number of players fixed games in the 1961 scandal in comparison to the 1951 scandal. Basketball audiences were not interested in reading about fixed games and scandals as attendance proliferated in the sport. By 2017, the sport has grown to a level where fixing of games is virtually impossible because of video technology.

2

Changing Mass Media Viewing Demographics and Attitudes Towards Sports Gambling

In 1960, few television network executives envisioned how college football could be converted into "entertainment sports" without a written script. If the networks did carry a sporting event, it was as a leftover. Most viewers wanted programs such as *The Loretta Young Show*, *You'll Never Get Rich*, *Name That Tune*, *Gunsmoke*, and an occasional live drama, *Studio One*, *the U.S. Steel Hour*, and *Playhouse 90*.[1] The networks' chieftains found live TV too unpredictable. The ideologically unsound, the uncensored, and the unexpected were too possible.[2]

Television's move away from live programming toward a pre-packaged mass entertainment mode like the movies reflected the networks' preference for the controlled, prearranged, and predictable.[3] Except for baseball, cautious network executives may have sensed that sporting contests stirred some primitive nerve endings or uncomfortableness in the psyches of television audiences.[4] Boxing had self-destructed in the 1940s and 1950s. College basketball had demonstrated a propensity for allowing gamblers to influence players in the 1940s, 1950s, and 1960s. Would college football players be vulnerable to organized crime's obsession with any form of illegal gambling? Appetites that yearned for *White Rain Shampoo* and *Speedy Alka-Seltzer* might be disturbed with a steady diet of television sports programming, worried network executives[5]; and they were right.

The next generation of TV executives focused on college and professional football, the Olympics, *Wide World of Sports*, and auto racing. They intuitively sensed that TV would foster a growing public interest in sports.[6] A few outsiders from advertising were hired, including A. Craig Smith and Edgar Scherick.[7] These two advertising mavericks would harness young human forces and create fortunes for ABC, CBS, and NBC. The three networks added professional and college football and basketball to their telecasts and presented them as entertainment sports. Games that once may have stood as a celebration of youth and vigor now became the subject of TV money and its misuse.

The sources of greed were legion, and the scandals in college football and basketball forced the NCAA to perennially write its infractions manual as a tome that only attorneys could understand. The organization has repeatedly penalized most elite athletic programs and in some cases even shut down a football program like Southern Methodist University (SMU). Boards of trustees, college presidents, and boosters at these colleges and wanna-be elite programs fought each other for a place in line for the money. Unscrupulous agents, academic cheating, player payoffs, recruiting violations, gambling scandals and performance-enhancing and

Sportscaster Red Barber from his broadcasting days, 1955 (photograph by Al Ravenna, New York World Telegraph and Sun Collection. Copyright Library of Congress).

recreational drug scandals became the legacy of a few money-hungry programs.[8] The professional franchises and commercialized college programs bear most of the responsibility for the dollar-obsessed corruption of sports from the middle of the twentieth century and into the twenty-first century.

Before ABC programmer and southerner Tom Moore came on board, college football was televised using three still cameras, laced with statistics and boring commentary about weather, upcoming comedy shows, and news. Roone Arledge and a group of young producers at ABC—Jim Spence, Chuck Howard, and Chet Simmons—were responsible for college football's conversion to entertainment and show business. The transition was instant and successful.[9] The newly created Area of Dominant Influence (ADI) metric was implemented by the network for football. The ADI allowed ABC to determine where they could deliver games to audiences that had rarely seen their favorite football team on TV. College towns like Baton Rouge, Auburn, Tuscaloosa,

Little Rock, Columbus, and Corvallis were eager to have their games appear before viewers in Butte, Fargo, Sioux City, or Salt Lake City. Subdividing audiences by age, income, sex, and occupation, and by employing the science of demography (i.e., Designated Market Area or DMA), ABC learned that many young viewers under the age of 40 were not loyal to any network. ABC set out to become the "Network of the Young."[10] The catalyst for the transformation would be sports. When NBC and CBS affiliate managers in Austin, Texas, Columbus, Georgia, Lexington, and other college towns saw that they could obtain ABC football for their football-crazed viewers, many dumped their staple programs like *Gunsmoke* and *The Lawrence Welk Show*.[11]

Julius Barnthan, ABC's demographic researcher, stated, "If you have the NCAA in the South, it's like God."[12] Arledge's vision of how to take a fan to a game reflects what Scherick, the advertising turned television executive, labeled his "will to power."[13] Each time audiences viewed a football game in the last part of the twentieth century, the genius of Arledge's vision was experienced.[14] There was also Arledge's vision and unyielding conviction that TV in the 1960s could use previously unheard-of techniques to bring entertainment sports into households: "Heretofore television has done a remarkable job of bringing the game to the viewer, we will now bring the viewer to the game. In short, we are going to add show business to sports," stated Arledge.[15]

In one of Arledge's early telecasts of college football, the producers filmed the pregame activities at Penn State by roaming the streets in University Park with portable cameras. Entering the restaurants, bars, hotel lobbies, and student hangouts, interviewers captured the moods and predictions of the Nittany Lions' supporters and followers of Ohio State, that day's opponent. Aerial shots of a long line of cars streaming into Happy Valley, including

Roone Arledge, president of ABC Sports and one of the most influential figures in developing sports on television, 1969 (Everett Collection—courtesy Alamy.com).

the surrounding farming landscape, were designed to bring the viewer to the campus and stadium. Handheld cameras filmed the opposing team arriving at the stadium and walking to the locker room, capturing the players' faces from the ground up, a reflection of youthful idealism and exuberance. Arledge stated:

> We must gain and hold the interest of women and others who are not fanatic followers of the sport we happen to be televising—-women come to football games not to marvel at the adeptness of the quarterback in calling an end sweep or a lineman pulling out to lead play, but to sit in a crowd, see what everyone else is wearing, to watch the cheerleaders—incidentally, few men have ever switched channels when a nicely proportioned girl was leaping into the air.[16]

During a game, the faces of women were shown as a team scored a touchdown. Close-ups of a coach's wife with their child, as his team marched for a touchdown with the score tied, were videotaped. Cameras captured the cheerleaders during timeouts, a pretty girl's face after her hero caught the winning touchdown, or two romantic students sharing a blanket late in the game on a cold day in Pullman, Washington. All images were replayed for home audiences. Arledge wrote:

> Instant replays and microphones from different angles and parts of the venue were inserted. Referees were mic-ed so fans and viewers could hear their calls. Cameras were positioned to follow the spiral of a fifty-yard pass into a receiver's hands and showed the key blocks that sprang a ball carrier for a 105-yard kickoff return. The handheld cameras beamed the happy face of the speedster who returned the kick as he came off the field and showed the frustration on the opposing coach's face. Images of the players, enthusiastic college kids, the pride of America, were repeatedly shown during the game on the sidelines.[17]

Arledge's strategy memo was distributed to advertisers to generate sponsorships. The sales pitch included how this new way of presenting sports would appeal to wider and more diverse audiences. In reality, Arledge produced college football backwards from what he envisioned; he took the game to the fan.

The fast, eclectic, and intimate barrage of images came at such a volume that no fan could ever hope to duplicate it by actually going to the game. By garnering almost all of college football's audiences because of Arledge's prescient genius in the 1960s, networks in the future could charge higher advertising fees.[18] The money began to roll in to the colleges. The postgame shows were refined, expanded and provided an early Sunday edition for bettors. Gambling on human sports was made popular by television's appeal to a new generation of fans and technology's ability to make results available in real time. Weekly, ABC aired and kept tabs on up to 65 to 70 games.[19] Thirty labeled as the most critical to gamblers were posted as soon as they became available. By the standards of the 1960s, betting on college sports in the media was viewed by the networks as part of entertainment. Unabashedly, CBS hired noted Las Vegas gambler Jimmy "The Greek" Snyder, and NBC signed betting expert Pete Axthelm, as "touts," or predictors of game outcomes, in the 1970s.[20]

In 1970, the NFL and TV launched another delight for bookies and gamblers.[21] After NBC nixed carrying Monday night football games because of Johnny Carson's objections to giving up a time slot, ABC and Roone Arledge were there to scoop it up.[22] *Monday Night Football* became a TV staple created in the style of producer Arledge and director Chet Forte. For gamblers, the added game might allow them to recoup their weekend losses. Subsequently, professional and college sports would make their way into American homes during prime time, producing billions of dollars in profits for the gambling and advertising industries.

CBS became embroiled in a gambling scandal in the 1970s with its coverage of tennis. In May 1977, Neil

Howard Cosell, pictured here in 1979, along with Frank Gifford and Don Meredith, launched the era of "studio or television sports" on ABC in 1970. By bringing home audiences to the game and adding show business to the telecasts during prime time, advertisers could be charged higher fees, and future television contracts would become the biggest source of revenue for the colleges and professionals (Zuma Press—courtesy Alamy.com).

Amdur of the *New York Times* reported that three of CBS's four heavyweight tennis matches had been fraudulently advertised as winner-take-all.[23] This became the first instance in which TV coverage of tennis promoted the payment of "guarantee" money to top players, assuring players of rich payments regardless of their performance.[24] Around the world, many tournament directors took up the practice officially outlawed by tennis associations. Guarantee or appearance money had been offered to the stars.[25] But it also opened the floodgates to gamblers who were in on the deception the whole time.

Players either lost on purpose (i.e., dumped) or withheld their peak performances. This was for the purpose of hurrying off to the next tournament and its guarantee money.[26] Before a congressional subcommittee had completed sifting through a grab bag of TV sports abuses and excesses, CBS President Robert Wussler resigned.[27] The subcommittee rebuked his denials about knowledge of appearance money in the winner-take-alls by stating, "The conduct cannot be excused, considering the weight of evidence, by suggesting it was all a mistake."[28] The enormity of CBS's self-destruction was obvious as the possibility of betting on players to lose or not play their best was more than a passing possibility.

As damning as Wussler's testimony under oath was for CBS, additional deceptions were uncovered. The network's visual depictions while holding the matches at Caesars Palace intrigued a Federal Communication Commission (FCC) staff member as he reviewed the videotapes, compiling how many times the announcers voiced the winner-take-all claims.[29] Moreover, the FCC official counted 57 visual depictions and mentions, or *pops*, of Caesars Palace without any reference that the casino had paid for promotional consideration.[30]

From its inception in 1906, the NCAA had been created as a rules-making body with no real enforcement mechanisms. The colleges' inability to adhere to the basic tenets of amateurism in football led the organization to consider becoming more regulatory in the early 1930s. At its annual convention in 1940, the Executive Committee of the NCAA assumed legislative and judicial powers. The committee was authorized to investigate alleged violations and issue interpretations related to rules violations in admission requirements, athletic scholarships, and academics.[31] Following World War II, advances in air travel, expansion of recruiting from regional levels to national levels, and the addition of post-season bowl games in football had increased the number of programs willing to sacrifice the perception of amateurism for money.[32]

In 1945, the association created a set of rules, the *Principles for the Conduct of Intercollegiate Athletics* (an earlier version of these principles was labeled the *Purity Code* by the media).[33] The adoption of the *Sanity Code* in 1948 was an extension of these principles and included: adherence to the definition of amateurism, student-athletes' commitment to maintaining the same academic standards as the student body, awarding of financial aid without consideration of athletic ability, and prohibiting a coach from recruiting prospective student-athletes with offers of financial aid or similar inducements.[34] In 1951, the *Sanity Code* was repealed because many institutions believed they could not live by it.[35]

One year earlier, the Association's compliance committee had cited seven institutions (Virginia, Villanova, Virginia Tech, Maryland, Boston College, The Citadel, and VMI) for code violations and possible expulsion from the

NCAA. The vote of 111 in favor of expulsion to 93 opposed fell 25 votes short of the needed majority to expel the *Sinful Seven*. The vote reflected an unwillingness of many institutions to issue a "death penalty" to its fellow members. Colleges in the South and Southeast had previously indicated that they would not follow the short-lived code.[36]

The 1984 Supreme Court ruling indicating that the NCAA could no longer negotiate TV contracts on behalf of all its members was a hollow victory for the College Football Association (CFA).[37] The resultant glut of football and basketball games on TV decreased the amount of TV money distributed to conference members. For the next decade, it was a buyer's market for advertisers.[38] Television contracts for MLB, NFL, and NBA events more than doubled in comparison.[39] Before college football and basketball could negotiate contracts for the Bowl Championship Series (BCS) and basketball playoffs (March Madness), there were legal and economic complexities that had to be addressed. Big TV money brought perennial in-fighting, legal challenges and disorganization in NCAA head Walter Byers' television committee. Byers' spread-the-wealth mentality frustrated the elite football schools and their moneyed boosters, who did not want to share with less successful programs.[40]

Inviting the networks to take over Ann Arbor, Baton Rouge, or South Bend was similar to an army occupying a conquered city for three days. These programs were spending too much to share their hard-earned, in many cases scandal-ridden, money in hosting them.[41] The creation of three NCAA divisions had been designed to stop the sharing of money from Division I football and basketball programs with other colleges less able to invest millions into their programs. In the early 1990s, a new group of CFA conference commissioners, at the behest of the boards of trustees, presidents, and boosters of the super football and basketball colleges, began to talk about and conceive of a few elite conferences. One division was not enough for the largest athletic programs who ultimately created the most elite of all NCAA divisions, the College Football Association, the forerunner to the BCS.[42] The most commercialized divisions in the history of the organization, including the Pac-12, Big Ten, Southeastern Conference (SEC), Atlantic Coast Conference (ACC), and Big Twelve, were officially in business.

With TV money flowing like a spigot, why not add games to football's and basketball's regular season schedules and create conference championship games and tournaments?[43] The possibilities for making money on college sports as entertainment had increased exponentially for the colleges and bookies, but so had the expenses and gambling on sports. Deregulation began in earnest in the 1990s as the SEC, ACC, Pac-12, Big Ten, with the exception of the Big Eight (still ten teams), morphed into 12-team conferences divided into two six-team divisions. A championship game was added as TV revenues created realigned conferences to attract advertisers, who were ever mindful of where the best markets were located.[44] The rounds of musical chairs continued into 2012 as the mid-majors (e.g., Conference USA, Mid-American) scrambled to find a home to scoop up whatever TV revenue was left over from the big-time program.[45] ESPN rescued the mid-majors by signing contracts to televise their games.[46]

Anyone following college football and basketball over the past half-century could not have missed the ever-increasing dollar value that the major conferences, bowl committees, and NCAA placed on telecast rights for the two sports.[47] Nor can anyone paying attention fail to connect the perennial descending morass of gambling, recruiting, and illegal payoff scandals that have become as much a part of what is presented as commercialized college sports as the forward pass or jump shot.[48] The pursuit of TV money by a few of the most commercialized programs included a reflexive lowering of academic standards for athletes, an abiding mood of shame, bitter cynicism from critics and the public, and an atmosphere of distrust. About 65 institutions have created a caste system (i.e., five elite Super Conferences) in sports heretofore unseen in the history of college athletics.[49]

Television-driven entertainment sports are designed to engage the widest possible audiences, who purchase products ranging from iPhones to high-priced vehicles. Game analysts dissecting the action on the field, such as legendary Oklahoma coach Bud Wilkinson in ABC's inaugural telecasts with Chris Schenkel in the 1960s, would be regarded as too bland or boring today. The new breed of game analysts, many of whom are ex-coaches and players, in the studio and at the game site present the intricacies of the game in a language understood by TV audiences. Just as important are the countless human-interest stories, replays of games, game highlights, and rehashing of just-completed games. The analysts who feed the gambling enthusiasts are expected to predict outcomes ranging from final scores to which players, including those returning from an injury, will most influence a team's chance of winning.

By the early part of the twenty-first century, TV and the Internet have saturated the public with all forms of entertainment sports events. Incidents such as an NBA referee consorting with gamblers, or college players investigated for fixing games, were overshadowed by 24-hour programs presenting nonstop sporting events seven days a week.[50] Advertisers have avoided alienating potential buyers by sponsoring television programs that display the internal contradictions and inconsistencies while publicly avowing ideological beliefs regarding sports.

In TV negotiations involving colleges, never have the players (the income producers) been considered in terms of their commercial value.[51] Or maybe they have—but only by boosters … illegally.[52] Creating football and basketball as entertainment sports has reached such a fever pitch in the early twenty-first century that rendering a set of workable NCAA rules for revenue sports has become a nightmare.[53] The convergence of sports as entertainment in venues like Las Vegas has attracted more middle-class gamblers, and off-shore wagering has soared.[54] The point spread and different ways (i.e., over/under, quarter and halftime scores, individual performances, etc.) to bet have created more opportunities for illegal bookie operations to profit as they funnel profits to the higher echelons of worldwide organized crime. The FBI estimates that 97 percent of the estimated volume in sports betting in the United States is illegal.[55]

Regardless of increased and greater sources of TV revenue, most BCS football and Division I basketball programs continue to fall short of expected profits. Spiraling costs outstrip revenue streams even as boosters' payments and influence remain an increasing and necessary presence. Financial sustainability for the majority of all collegiate commercialized athletic programs remains razor-thin as the largest athletic programs realign themselves to garner the most lucrative TV markets.[56]

3

Kentucky Football, 1962
Scandal and Cover-Up

If one wanted to produce a movie that characterized all the sordid elements of college football and basketball in the early 1950s and 1960s, one need go no further than the University of Kentucky (UK). Adolph Rupp, Paul "Bear" Bryant, and Charlie Bradshaw had created programs that even by the standard of the times would be sure-fire entries into college sport's corrupt "Hall of Fame." By 1952, UK's basketball program, including its coaches, players, and boosters, could boast of a gambling scandal including point shaving and the basketball team traveling to away games in the company of the country's leading college football bookmaker, Ed Curd.[1] Curd's headquarters was upstairs in the Mayfair Bar, located two blocks from Rupp's office in Alumni Gym. The shutting down of the basketball program for the 1952–1953 season, now more commonly referred to as the "death penalty," had been mandated by the SEC and NCAA. This unprecedented penalty made clear that UK's NCAA violations were deep, widespread, and long-standing.

The football program under Charlie Bradshaw at the University of Kentucky continued to ignore the policies of the SEC and NCAA, not to mention the health and safety of its athletes. Up to the early 1960s, reporters from Louisville and Lexington had successfully shielded UK's repeated violations from the NCAA and the rest of the college sports world. With the hiring of Bradshaw in 1962, UK's moneyed boosters, Board of Trustees, athletic board, president, and athletic director would repeatedly be called on to defend Bradshaw's coaching methods until 1968, when he was forced to resign.

Before sentencing the players involved in the 1951 college basketball scandal, New York General Sessions Court Judge Saul S. Streit conducted his own research on the corruption in college football and basketball programs. The resulting 6,000-word essay detailed the widespread corruption in big-time college sports that had intensified in post–World War II America. It remains one of the earliest and most scathing indictments in the history of

Adolph Rupp (center) pictured with Bill Lickert (left) and Dick Parsons (right) in 1959 (courtesy of University of Kentucky Archives).

commercialized college sports. During Streit's sentencing of UK's players, 15,000 words were devoted to its athletic program. After labeling Rupp "the Frank Erickson [gambling kingpin of New York City] of Kentucky with an ear to the betting odds," Streit's cautionary warning to the administrators of college sports included:

That not many more storm flags would be hoisted to alert intercollegiate groups to rid themselves of the disintegrating influence of money mad athletics … Intercollegiate basketball and football at Kentucky have become highly systemized, professionalized, and commercialized enterprises … with covert subsidization and ruthless exploitation of players, cribbing on examinations, illegal recruiting, a reckless disregard for players' physical welfare, matriculation of unqualified students, demoralization of athletes by the coach, alumni, and townspeople, and flagrant abuses of athletic scholarship (an acme of professionalization).[2]

Judge Streit's description of Kentucky's football and basketball programs characterized the SEC's money-making programs. The SEC's and NCAA's decisions to prohibit UK's basketball team from conference and nonconference games during the 1952–1953 season resulted from Rupp's repeated violations of conference regulations since 1932. Bryant's cheating in football since 1946 was equally serious. Newly appointed NCAA head Walter Byers, after reading UK's infractions self-report, stated he had never seen "so many [con-

Kentucky basketball team photograph, 1947–1948 season, including the "Fabulous Five": Wallace "Wah Wah" Jones (27), Alex Groza (15), Cliff Barker (6), Kenny Rollins (26), Ralph Beard (12); coach Adolph Rupp seated far left and assistant coach Harry Lancaster seated far right. Beard and Groza would be barred from the NBA for their involvement in the 1951 gambling scandal (courtesy University of Kentucky Archives).

Kentucky coach Paul "Bear" Bryant (center) with Vito "Babe" Parilli (left) and Doug Moseley, team captains, 1953. Kentucky's 1952–1953 "death penalty" in basketball was because of the program's excessive number of SEC and NCAA violations. Although the football program in all likelihood had committed as many if not more violations, the NCAA did not consider shutting down two programs (courtesy University of Kentucky Archives).

ference and NCAA] rules violations in one report." NCAA investigators reported that Ohio State coach Ernie Godfrey cited UK's football recruiters for attempting to buy Ohio's best high school prospects with money. In one instance, they left $1,000 in $20 bills at the doorstep of a prospect's home where he lived with his widowed mother. After Bryant signed a 12-year contract extension with UK, he decided to move to Texas A&M. President Herman Lee Donovan had assured him that Rupp would be fired for violating a number of SEC and NCAA rules. When Bryant discovered that Rupp was also receiving a contract extension, he bolted for Texas A&M, believing the president had lied to him.[3] More than likely, booster pressure forced Donavan to renege on his promise.

In Bryant's memoirs, he pointed to the numerous players, coaches, and people who were influenced by Total Football (a euphemism used to describe the excessive psychological and physical demands coaches imposed on players, designed to weed out quitters) throughout his iconic career. Because of his success at Alabama, he had earned a platform on which he could confess to his personal and professional shortcomings. At every step in his career, Bryant admitted to allowing boosters to pay his players, a practice he would repeat as "a young coach 28 or 30 years old and just starting out … if the competition was paying the boys and I felt I had to meet the competition."[4] In describing his reputation for brutality and driving players out of football, his explanation for doing so at UK in 1946 was that he inherited a team of underperforming, pampered stars:

> We ran off a few and worked some of them extra hard, and they quit too, and I probably made more mistakes and mishandled more people than anyone has. But we got the rest of them motivated, and they started winning that first year.[5]

However, as Michael Oriard, a former college and professional football player and academician at Oregon State, stated, "his [Bryant's] coaching style hovered over the football world of the 1950s and 1960s."[6] Paul "Bear" Bryant's Total Football was popularized in 1954, when, in his first year as Texas A&M's head coach, he transported two full busloads of at least 100 Aggies players to isolated Junction, Texas. Returning to College Station after a ten-day, brutal, pre-season regimen with 29 players, the survivors were immortalized in the 2002 movie *Junction Boys*. The movie was based on the 1999 book of the same title, written by Gene Stallings and Jim Dent.[7]

In seven seasons at UK, Charlie Bradshaw was immortalized, but for different reasons. During that period, the football program would become embroiled in scandals that included allegations of brutalization, illegally revoking athletic scholarships, male prostitution, game-rigging, and cover-ups by the university and the Lexington and Louisville media. Ten years after Judge Streit's words, UK was still not listening. By some accounts, Bryant's and Bradshaw's methods were not extreme cases in Southern football. "It was Eastern Mississippi's junior college coach 'Bull' Sullivan who perfected Total Football.[8] If a player is going to quit, I want him to quit in practice" was an oft-repeated Bryant quote.[9]

In 1962, it was Bryant's eight-year, 60–23–6 record at UK that persuaded UK to hire Bryant's assistant Charlie Bradshaw to restore the glory years of football at the institution. Bradshaw mimicked "The Bear" precisely, saying all the right things with the same inflection, tone, and verbiage as his mentor.[10] Bradshaw had been a reserve player for Bryant at UK for three years until SEC Commissioner Bernie Moore declared him ineligible after he started three games as an end in 1949. The technicality that ended Bradshaw's senior season involved veterans who had lost years to military service during World War II. If a player had entered the military before 1947, he was granted three years of eligibility. Those entering after 1947 were granted four years. Bradshaw had entered in the service in 1942.

In 1951, the Wildcats met Santa Clara in the Orange Bowl and lost to the Broncos, 21–13. Before the game, UK's players spent two weeks in two-a-day practices similar to pre-season workouts. The following season, the Wildcats finished 3–3 in the SEC, 7–4 overall, and received a Cotton Bowl invitation. The players did not vote to play in the Cotton Bowl until they were assured there would not be a repeat of the previous year's Orange Bowl practices. Bryant acceded to the player's wishes, and Kentucky defeated TCU, 20–7.

In 1954, UK head coach Blanton Collier hired Bradshaw as an assistant. He stayed with the program until Bryant moved to Alabama and called Bradshaw to join him in Tuscaloosa. In 1961, the 36-year-old Bradshaw was widely credited with designing the offense for an Alabama team that went undefeated and won the national title, defeating Oklahoma in the Orange Bowl.[11] After Kentucky jettisoned Collier, the UK Athletic Board hired Bradshaw at $50,000 a year for four years. The powerful 16-member Athletic Board had been formed in 1946 to keep pace with other SEC members, paying football and basketball coaches salaries commensurate to what other colleges paid their head coaches. In Kentucky, the state legislature had mandated a salary cap of $5,000 a year for state employees, including coaches. The Athletic Board, composed mainly of moneyed boosters, not only skirted the state law but, also the legislature and governor, who theoretically represented the citizens of one of the poorest states in America. Lexington legislator John Brown, Jr., the future fried chicken magnate, proudly stated: "The King is dead. Long live the King. I am a Charlie Bradshaw man."[12]

Bradshaw's coaching staff consisted of a mix of Bryant apostles, who dispensed excessive brutality, and a group of young coaches looking to make their own mark in the coaching profession. However, their methods eventually got them fired. Bradshaw at UK never grasped that the young men who refused to accept his brutalization mentality were more capable than he and the Bryant disciples on the staff. The players refused to act like the abusive coaches because it was not the "right thing to do."[13]

Bradshaw's NCAA-prohibited winter conditioning program began in four racquetball courts with 88 players in January 1962. Common sense dictated that the drills should have been football-skill related. Instead, they were designed to weed out unwanted players on four-year guaranteed scholarships, remove every ounce of football self-confidence from the players, and reassemble the players' technical execution in a way that suited the coaching staff, essentially expecting the players to become human robots. In the words of Bradshaw: "We are trying to break [down] your attitudes and strip you down so we can build you back up."[14]

Players were subjected to physical abuse that would have violated state laws outside of UK's racquetball courts. The "forearm shiver" was used regularly on hapless players.[15] An exception was Homer Rice, who remained with Bradshaw as the offensive coordinator and would have been named head coach if Bradshaw had been fired in 1965.[16] George Boone and Leeman Bennett were too young and inexperienced to mitigate the abusive behaviors. The rest of the coaching staff fed off Charlie Bradshaw and Bob Ford. Non-screamers became screamers, pulled players off piles, slammed them into walls, and regularly struck them. Dr. Michael "The Missile" Minix, a survivor of the workouts, stated:

> The final court was for "feature bouts." Teammates lined the four walls and two players were called-out. They entered the center of the mat-covered ring. Often they were mismatches on purpose (i.e., backs vs. linemen). They were forced to repeatedly wrestle until they pinned their opponent. Players admitted later they had whispered to their hapless buddy to stay down so his teammate could catch a rest. Many lost as much as an alarming sixty pounds during the "conditioning."

By the start of spring practice in April 1962, 70 players remained of the original 88. Bradshaw falsely believed the 70 "would stick it out" and the dead weight was gone. He was wrong. Center Randy Beard was repeatedly winning the war in a three-on-three blocking drill. After one failed block, Bradshaw jumped on the prostrate Beard and screamed, "I'll send your ass back to Alabama to eat grits if you don't do better than that." A bright and introspective person, Beard saw the hypocrisy of Bradshaw's methods, immediately quit, returned to Alabama, and became a successful attorney.

Beard concluded that Ford and Moore were just "goons" brought in for attrition purposes, a Bryant strategy that Beard believed the two had mastered. Beard reasoned that Bradshaw never found his own personality, and his failed attempts to emulate Bryant by using meaningless violence, brutality, and hypocrisy eroded whatever respect, if any, the players had for the coaching staff. It was an undoubtedly regrettable experience that plagued many coaches at all levels of the sport. Total Football had been a powerful tool in the eyes of Cold War militarists who saw interscholastic and intercollegiate competition sweeping the country at the time.[17] Athletic preparation and participation were considered essential training for entering the military.

The exodus from the Kentucky program continued as the level of emotional and physical brutality increased, including academic exploitation of some players. Dr. Minix was enrolled in a botany class with labs in the afternoons. Bradshaw wanted all players enrolled in a physical education class that was, in essence, football practice with full gear. Minix left the team, continued his pre-med major studies, and became an ophthalmologist. He later co-authored a mortality and morbidity study of the players at UK in 1962 that is cited in the endnotes. Some players left the program for personal reasons and could articulate to Bradshaw, "I'm opposed to your program and don't want to be a spokesperson for this program."[18] One player, Larry Schad, who had played for Blanton Collier the year before and contemplated quitting, sought advice from the gentle coach. Collier told him, "I'll be proud of you regardless of your decision."[19] Schad left the program, later served in Vietnam, and became a lawyer. During spring practice, the shift of power from the coaches to the players planted the seeds of destruction for Bradshaw and UK's football program.

In one incident, a player who refused to pummel a ball-carrier friend in an 11-player gang tackling drill incurred the wrath of Ford. Kicker Clarkie Manfield carried the ball against 11 minus his close friend, "Jock" Seward. When Ford saw this, he acted like an enraged bull and headed for Seward. Most of the time it was the players' unreadiness that made the coaches' forearm shivers or some other "cheap shot" effective.[20] Players were now determined to be the punishers. When Seward heard Ford's cussing as he moved toward him, he readied himself in a football position (ready to execute a tackle or block). As Ford prepared to deliver a blow, Seward elevated up in a spring-like action and put the assistant on his back. After he collected himself, Ford responded, "That's the way I want to see you hit someone."[21]

In another incident involving Bradshaw, who favored the peel-back, blind-side block as his favorite "cheap shot," Elmer Patrick purposely moved slowly to the next drill, dragging behind as the last player. Knowing this would aggravate the smaller Bradshaw to attack him, Patrick planted his left foot, making that side of his body as solid as a brick wall. At contact, Bradshaw fell to the ground as if he'd struck an immovable object. The head coach had to be carried off the field. It was inevitable that the physical superiority and conditioning of the players would humiliate the coaches in any one-on-one physical confrontation.

For players like Jim Bolus, leaving the program was an agonizing decision. The freshman high school standout studied game films in high school and was a coach on the field. After he turned his back on Bradshaw's program, he became a sportswriter, traveling the country and covering many football games. The exodus of players was an open secret among the UK hierarchy of boosters, athletic administrators, Board of Trustees, Athletic Board, President's Office, and regional media. It was similar to what had occurred in the Rupp and Bryant programs. The two coaches annually over-recruited and expected the most talented and toughest ones to stay.[22] Opposing coaches complained loudly and often to the SEC and NCAA about Rupp's and Bryant's rules and recruiting violations.

One of Bolus's high school classmates was David Hawpe, an aspiring undergraduate writer, who would ultimately become a newspaper journalist and editorial board head. His other three friends from Louisville's Male High in UK's football program regularly informed Hawpe about the brutality of Bradshaw's illegal, secret winter practices and closed spring workouts.[23] Bradshaw's methods went national after he was interviewed by Carl Modecki, the sports editor of the *Kentucky Kernel*, the university's student newspaper. The article's headline in April 1962, *37 Quit Football Squad*, was a blockbuster because it exposed the brutality and rules violations in the program. Modecki was well-informed by Hawpe, and Bradshaw's responses reflected the head coach's attempts to deflect the real issues in the program. In doing so, he was less than truthful by stating: "There have [sic] been some [physical] contact, but there won't be anymore. We're not proud of it and it won't happen anymore." The squad now numbered 51, prompting the coach to state, "we'll play with ten and a coach if we have to."[24]

In August 1962, *Sports Illustrated (SI)* writers Morton Sharnik and Robert Creamer spent several days in Lexington following the coaches, and they had complete access to their meetings, including time spent at the Bradshaw home. They were gathering information for an article on UK's football program titled: *Rage to Win*. The unsuspecting Bradshaw expected an article that would exalt him for cloning Bryant's methods, even though he had not coached a regular season game. *Atlanta Journal-Constitution* college football cynic and writer Furman Bisher interviewed three players for the article:

Minix, Shelby Lee, who transferred to play at Arkansas State and later earned a Ph.D. in English, and Louis Owen, who earned a degree in architecture at UK after refusing to give up his scholarship.[25] Each player's comments were only mildly critical of Bradshaw's methods. In the environment created by Bradshaw, retribution (pulling a scholarship) or ostracization by the coaching staff were always possibilities. The local media interpreted the players' comments as supportive of the program. All three players later left the program.

To the players, the article, published on October 8, 1962, was accurate in every respect as it laid bare all of the brutality that was commonplace in UK's program. The photos included Bradshaw barking orders and a player on the same page ankle-deep in muddy water as he worked on isometric bars. Two illegal practices were exposed: the winter workouts and the pulling of scholarships. Ten years earlier, had not New York Judge Streit observed the same practices in Bryant's and Rupp's programs ("a reckless disregard for players' physical welfare and flagrant abuses of athletic scholarships")?[26] The article quoted Coach Bob Ford, who stated, "It was an accident" when he blindsided converted defensive back Louis Owen. Owen had not seen the coach coming because his back was to him, but he did not miss Ford's open hand to his jaw.[27] The player lost a tooth.[28] The program's "lean and mean" coaching style also included compromising players' long-term health. One of the coaches referred players to a motel on the outskirts of Lexington to purchase amphetamines for weight loss.[29]

The article reported that in Ford's office, pictures of Robert E. Lee and Stonewall Jackson were proudly displayed. The magazine's readers were led to believe that Ford sounded crazy. But to some players, the coach's behaviors were more sadistic than crazy.[30] Pointing to Jackson in one of the photos, Ford stated to the *SI* writer, "You see this man here. He was a real Christian gentleman. He taught a Sunday school. But, he went out and killed, didn't he?"[31] That Bradshaw and other coaches could stand up on a Sunday in church and preach commitment, pride, and duty was all music to the ears of the 1960s establishment. Deeply religious players would be in church on Sundays and see the Bradshaws of the world stand up in front of children and humbly state: "Come to Jesus. He loves you, little boys."[32] The *SI* article was noted by the NCAA, which placed UK's football program on probation in 1964. "We have done nothing wrong of which we're ashamed," Bradshaw was quoted in the article as saying.[33]

Bradshaw's only choice was to deny the accusations, as would the local media in the win- and money-driven culture of the SEC. In the *Lexington Herald*, Ed Ashford's column after the *SI* exposé was titled, "UK is Victim of Hatchet Job."[34] Ashford recounted in the article that Sarnick and Creamer, while in Lexington, did not observe that the UK football workouts were any more strenuous than others they had observed at other colleges. The players, according to Ashford, were made to sound critical of the program in the *SI* article, when in fact they were not. And the illegal scholarship ruse was defended by Ashford, who explained that the ones who gave them up did so "voluntarily."[35] In response to others' accusations, including allegations of brutality, Ashford's defense was weak and self-serving. He, like anyone else associated with the corruption in Kentucky's athletic program, had one choice. The *Herald's* editors, as they did before the 1951 gambling scandal, were not going to lay bare before a national audience UK's legacy of athletic scandals; that would come in the 1980s.

In the cut-throat world of the SEC, other coaches would openly talk to reporters about the cheating they knew existed in the conference. Ole Miss football coach Johnny Vaught, in September 1962, had read the papers and knew about the "Bradshaw Purge." In the course of an interview with legendary *Louisville Courier-Journal* sportswriter Earl Ruby, Vaught openly wondered how UK could bypass NCAA regulations:

> If I could dispose of them [Ole Miss's 26 redshirts] as easily as Charlie Bradshaw got rid of 30 or 40 boys at Kentucky, you wouldn't see 26 redshirts on my squad. I'd like to know how Bradshaw did it. I think the NCAA might like to know.[36]

Speaking on behalf of the players, Vaught issued a salvo that must have been music to the ears of the recently appointed head of the NCAA, Walter Byers[37]:

> Don't those boys who got chased off know that under the [NCAA] rules they are entitled to four full years of room, board, tuition, and books whether they lay a hand on a football or not? That's the law as I understand it. What does Bradshaw know that the rest of us don't?[38]

The methods Bradshaw and his staff employed for coercing athletes out of their scholarships were reprehensible. Most of the players who left the team were summoned to Bradshaw's office "for two one-hour career subversion and ultimatum meetings."[39] Others were chased down by an assistant and coerced into signing a voluntary waiver. If the release of something of value was voluntary, why didn't the players come to the coaches on their own volition to sign their waiver of that benefit? Bradshaw's scheme of running off inherited players who did not fit the new regime's criteria was to brutalize, humiliate, and shame them into quitting.[40] With their football self-confidence and passion for the game shattered, signing a release waiver was coercion and not voluntary by any reasonable legal standard.[41] Athletic Director Bernie Shively's response to the scholarship abuses was typical of the cover-ups at UK:

All football players who gave up the sport, but who stayed in school voluntarily, signed statements that they were giving up their scholarships.[42]

Two weeks later, Shively reinstated the scholarships of four players, who were not publicly identified "to avoid embarrassing the boys."[43] Also, John Helfers and six others, including future horse-racing author and Louisville sportswriter Jim Bolus, wanted their scholarships back. Before the hearing with UK President Frank G. Dickey, David Hawpe, the student writer at the *Kentucky Kernel*, rebutted the local sportswriters who characterized the seven as quitters who had given up the right to be on campus for free. Bradshaw was described as magnanimous simply because he attempted to persuade the seven not to give up the "free ride" by sacrificing 45 (in reality it was 90) minutes a day for the illegal winter workouts.[44] On September 21, 1962, the day of the hearing before the UK Board of Trustees and Dickey, the *Kernel* published Hawpe's column, which has been repeated by thousands of big-time college sports critics since the 1960s.

Hawpe had it right, but was not taken seriously by the few UK boosters in Lexington who wanted winning football and basketball programs at any cost. "College was about education first and athletics second," reasoned Hawpe, the very thing that Bradshaw and his staff told parents but did not practice. With brutal practices, some of which were over three and a half hours long, how could even the finest scholar on the planet muster the energy to study? Those from Bradshaw's original 88 who chose academics over football and became professionals in fields other than sports had shown how warped commercialized college sports at UK had become.

It was all there on that day at the hearing. The president's hands were tied as well. With the Board of Trustees present, how could he hint that the players' scholarships were rightfully their property? Dickey, like many presidents before and after him, chose the path that the Board of Trustees more than likely advised, displayed and read the standard athletic department release that Shivley had approved: "This is to notify you that I am, of my own volition, giving up my football grant-in-aid and releasing the university from its obligations. I intend to remain in school and pay my own expenses."[45]

Every player who quit the team was rightfully allowed to finish his education if he chose to do so—on UK's money. As the first game of the season, against Florida State, approached in mid–September, the squad had been reduced to 30 from the original 88. Certain positions were without a single experienced player; Bradshaw and his staff had to convert and prepare players to fill new positions. Most of the starters would have to go both ways, as platoon football was impossible. Larry Boeck, UK beat writer for the *Courier-Journal*, named the Wildcats "The Thin Thirty."[46] Before spring practice ended the previous April, his choice for the team title was "The 49ers." The Thin Thirty referred to both the team's roster size and the unsafe weight loss of some players. In some cases, players had shed more than 70 pounds. Bradshaw's practices included no water and a steady diet of full-speed contact drills.

Louisville and Lexington sportswriters had little choice but to write about Bradshaw's methods as solid preparation for games. In fact, games would feel like a "cakewalk" in comparison to the practices. The *Lexington Herald's* Ed Ashford fed the belief in Bradshaw's program by pointing out that Bryant's Junction experiment had reduced the squad to 29 yet had finished first in the SWC. The journalist believed, based on what he had observed regarding Bradshaw's methods, that UK fans might expect an SEC title one year earlier than expected. A second coming, a Bryant disciple was in their midst. However, Ashford failed to remind his readers that Bryant's Texas Aggies could not appear in the Cotton Bowl because of a two-year bowl ban for paying players and other widespread rules violations.[47] The writer was also aware that the SEC and NCAA, because of the astounding number of rules violations and point shaving, had shut down UK's basketball program. A week before the first game, Ashford wrote what the boosters and UK administrators wanted to hear. According to UK's top cheerleader, the Wildcats could win if The Thin Thirty were SEC-caliber players. In fact, in any game the year before, Collier had never used more than 37 players.[48]

Ashford may have been correct if he was writing to inspire local fans to attend a home game in the 1950s. One-platoon football used as a cost-cutting measure had come and gone. College football was on the cusp of specialization in 1962. Two-platoon football, kicking specialists, and situation substitutions would soon become commonplace in the sport.[49] The columnist's misinformation also implied that Bradshaw's conditioning and long practice sessions during the playing season were standard preparation in football. The practice sessions were in fact risking serious injuries to players.

In the *Lexington Herald's* "Pressbox Pickup" column, Billy Thompson informed his readers that Bradshaw's practices were no more demanding or strenuous than those he had observed at "Eastern [Kentucky] or Western [Kentucky] or anyplace else."[50] On game day, it was not unusual for Thompson to write poetically to please the Board of Trustees and their booster friends:

> You are few in quantity, 'tis true, but long in quality. The cream of the crop is left and on your broad shoulders will rest the hopes for glory of the State of Kentucky. Let's hope the backfield gets off on the right football and that the line makes big holes, not semi-holes, in the Seminole line. We're banking on you for the biggest massacre since Sitting Bull.[51]

In the win-at-all-costs environment in Lexington and the SEC, the medical professionals who took an oath "to do no harm" chose to avoid the wrath of their bosses at the expense of the health of UK's athletes, including risk of death or catastrophic injury. Money trumped the health and safety of UK's football players. Possibly because of "inside pressure" from the Board of Trustees, or some other booster-related reasons, team doctors George Gumbert, O. B. Murphy, and R. J. "Bob" Angelucci issued the following statement before the first game of the season against Florida State: "Films have been made of the controversial football procedures at the University of Kentucky and will disprove allegations of oppressive techniques against the players."[52] The statement was hollow and false, as it appeared more of a preemptive move in telling the outside world, "If you intend to sue us, we'll fight it."[53] At UK, it was Bradshaw's no-water policy that the doctors believed was backward thinking. "Don't deny a football player fluid during practice or a game. His body needs water to function properly, particularly under the stress of football."[54]

The Florida State game ended up as a tie (0–0) despite the Seminoles' numerical roster advantage, as did the game against Georgia (7–7). UK's losses would come against Ole Miss (which did not lose a game in 1962), Auburn, LSU, Miami, and Xavier. The wins were against Detroit, Vanderbilt, and, incredibly, Tennessee in the last game of the season, 12–10. No opponent blew out UK despite its brutal and long practices. After UK's 7–0 loss to LSU in Baton Rouge, Bradshaw ordered a team practice in Lexington after the plane landed.

As the sun rose and coaches continued to exhort the young men to hit harder, the unnecessary and dangerous practice session was brought to an end by one of the smallest guards and linebackers in the country. As Bradshaw headed for 180-pound Vince Semary to slap him on the helmet for a technical mistake, Semary raised his good arm and defiantly neutralized Bradshaw's arm. Incensed, the coach raised the other arm to strike Semary, who raised his permanently injured arm and held both of Bradshaw's arms as the players surrounded the two. Semary's arm had been injured in an earlier practice.[55] Bradshaw, completely humiliated, reacted in the only way he could ... practice was over. The Thin Thirty had won again.

On October 20, 1962, veteran Atlanta sportswriter Furman Bisher wrote a blistering indictment of Bryant's and Bradshaw's style of football in the *Saturday Evening Post*. The article gained further notoriety in 1963 when Bryant filed a $10.5 million lawsuit against Curtis Publishing, the *Post*'s parent company.[56] The brutal methods of some college football coaches became scandals in themselves, similar to what had occurred in college football in 1905 and

1931. Bisher referred to a new term, "hard-nosed," which had replaced "finesse" as a way to win. The latter style characterized Bud Wilkinson's Oklahoma Sooners in the 1950s and 1960s, relying on speedy backs, hit and run, and brush blocking as a formula for winning.

When the Sooners played Notre Dame in 1957, they lost 7–0 to a bigger and slower, meat-grinding team. The loss ended the Sooners' 47-game winning streak. The legendary and gentlemanly Oklahoma coach, who later became a football analyst with play-by-play announcer Chris Schenkel, vowed to never again allow his players to suffer the humiliation of a physical pounding by a bigger and better-conditioned team. Wilkinson countered Notre Dame Coach Frank Leahy's success by recruiting bigger and more rugged players and conditioning them well beyond what was needed on the field, more akin to taking a beachhead. Soon the Bisher-labeled "roughness model" was refined and practiced beyond recognition by the Bryants, Bradshaws, and Jim Owens of the college football coaching world. "Riffraff" became the new term describing football players who were mistakenly given a four-year, guaranteed scholarship but had to be brutalized into giving them up. In reality, Total Football had been modernized to appeal to a new generation of television viewers.[57]

Invariably, some of the players in these programs played an excessively physical style of football that was illegal but rarely penalized by officials because it was increasingly accepted as part of the game. "Hard-nosed" football was almost indistinguishable during that period from dirty football. In some instances, the injuries were serious and fatal. In 1959, California halfback Steve Bates, after a 15-yard gain, was knocked out of bounds and landed on his back. The films showed USC's Mike McKeever moving toward the prostrate ball carrier and landing on him with the full weight of his body, intentionally striking Bates' face with his elbow. The player's face was badly damaged with a broken nose, cheekbone, and jaw.[58]

A similar incident in 1961 involved Georgia Tech's Chick Graning and Alabama's Darwin Holt. With Alabama leading, 10–0, Tech punted to the Crimson Tide, whose receiver signaled a fair catch. Graning was Tech's outside contain man, and he slowed up when he saw the fair catch signal. Presumably, an official's whistle had not been blown. Holt veered off his course to the bench and delivered a forearm shiver under the unsuspecting Graning's face bar, causing massive facial injuries.[59] Four days earlier, Bisher had been to an Alabama practice and saw Holt practicing, but not in full gear like the other players. Bryant explained, "He's so tough we don't let him scrimmage during the week. He's liable to hurt someone."[60] After the game, Bryant subtly defended the player by commenting, "Holt came up to me after the game," stated Bryant, "and told me he had hit this Tech player. He's all broken up about it. He said he did not know why he did it."[61]

In the article, Bisher pointed out that there were 20 football fatalities in 1961. Six in college football were as a result of football injuries or complications directly associated with football injuries. More disturbing was the change in high school coaches. Many had played in college programs where maiming a ball carrier, head-butting with plastic helmets, and use of the forearm as a weapon were common. Hence, "smash mouth" football became a staple in many secondary school programs. Fifty-six years earlier, during the college football crisis, Harvard President Charles Eliot made a prescient observation: "Death and injuries are not the strongest argument against football. That cheating and brutality are profitable is the main evil."[62] If injuries occurred when players employed "knock his head off" techniques, coaches praised and awarded helmet stars to players like McKeever and Holt. This kind of play, by all accounts, produced a later generation of players, especially at the college and professional levels, who prematurely suffered various forms of brain disease.

The scandalous nature of the UK's football program was not limited to its activities on the field. Legendary *Louisville-Courier* sports editor Earl Cox reported a conversation with Bradshaw after he was hired involving male prostitution in Lexington:

> He [Bradshaw] said that Dr. Ralph Angelucci, the team physician and a member of the UK trustees, told him the first thing the coach had to do was to run off the gays, including actor Rock Hudson, who was seeing some of the football players.[63]

Angelucci's statement was on the mark. In August 1959, two gay men in a new convertible Cadillac cruised the streets of Lexington. One was Jim Barnett, who was openly gay and a big-time promoter of professional (the oft-labeled "garbage sport") wrestling.[64] Barnett and his partner, Lonnie Winter, were asking young men, who just happened to be football players, if they wanted to ride in the Cadillac. Ostensibly, they were seeking dates, prospective prostitutes, or both. Ultimately, they established an illegal prostitution business involving wealthy and gay clients, including Hollywood actor Rock Hudson. By all accounts, the venture involved some of the UK football players until Bradshaw ended the illegal business in 1963.[65] Moving from the plush downtown Lexington Lafayette Hotel, Barnett purchased a large home at 1729 North Lakewood Drive, a street in a less populated section of Lexington. The home was large, but not overly ostentatious, and situated on a large parcel of land with a lavish pool.

Barnett by this time was wealthy and considered one of the biggest promoters of professional wrestling. The matches were staged, but during the early years of television, professional wrestling as a spectator sport was a TV staple. Barnett's fortune came from his idea to hold matches inside a television studio, which invariably made the matches more fixable and a boon for wrestling fans and gamblers. A match in Omaha could be viewed and wagered on in other parts of the Midwest. The small TV screens of the 1940s and 1950s required promoters to stage more exaggeration, showmanship, histrionics, and acrobatics in the sport. Interviews were included in the production, and characters such as Gorgeous George were crowd favorites. The wrestler demanded that if touched by a referee, he was to be dusted off by his valet.[66] His followers loved it. Barnett's setting up of a business in a small city like Lexington in 1959 was understandable. From there, he could manage and promote his wrestling business in the South, Midwest, and other parts of the country.

Although wrestling was becoming redefined as entertainment, promoters like Barnett still wanted the sport to be associated with elements of athleticism: masculinity, virility, toned bodies, and rugged attractiveness. Barnett was also aware that the religious and moral teachings of small communities in the Southern Bible Belt did not accept homosexuality as a lifestyle. In each community where he did business, he was successful at ingratiating himself into powerful political, legal, and civic organizations such as police departments and judges' circles.[67] His money-based strategy was to keep the athletic commissions of each state from regulating the "garbage sport" that was making the Chicago native rich. The erudite and wealthy patron of the arts had what most people of influence wanted … money, parties, attractive women and men, the choicest foods, liquor, clothes, and pornographic films.

The connection between Hollywood heartthrob Rock Hudson and Barnett may have begun when Hudson visited the film site of *Raintree County* in Danville and other central Kentucky locations in 1957. The movie featured alleged gay actor Montgomery Clift and Elizabeth Taylor. It's unknown how Hudson and Barnett met. Lexington's gay men frequented the Gilded Cage, where they connected socially and professionally.[68] It was the place to hang out, party, and connect with other gay men, attractive women, and businesspeople. Hudson was often at Barnett's home on Lakewood Drive.

For many of Lexington's citizens, the hook was Hudson, who was well known in Hollywood as a homosexual while simultaneously starring in many movies as a stereotypical heterosexual man. After 1959, the Lakeside address became a place for some of UK's football and basketball players to visit, freely eat and drink, earn extra money, and possibly enjoy sex with women. The other "hook" was for the players to serve as prostitutes for Hudson or other male homosexuals, including Barnett. The UK cover-up machine had to be on full alert, as any exposure of such an arrangement would have caused a national public relations disaster for the university and college sports.

Board of Trustees member Dr. Angelucci had cautioned Bradshaw about the gay parties and Hudson's association with UK athletes in 1962. By inference, everyone from the coaches to the Board of Trustees was aware of the gay issue at UK. Author Shannon Ragland recorded voluminous retrospective oral interviews, including players' recollections of the sex scandal. The weight of evidence pointed to a small number of UK football and basketball players' involvement in the prostitution scandal that had existed in Lexington since 1959.[69] Bradshaw had no choice but to end UK's athletes' visits to Barnett's home in the spring of 1963. Proof of his motivation to do so suffers from the lack of official documentation by the police, state, and U.S. Department of Justice files and primary sources from UK's archives. On Bradshaw's staff, George Boone and Leeman Bennett, as former UK players, knew about Lakeside Drive, and it's inconceivable they were not asked about it by Bradshaw or did not inform him of the activities at the residence. Bennett believed that Boone encouraged Bradshaw to act on the homosexual issue in 1963.[70]

UK's performance in a 14–9 loss to Xavier would require additional covering up. Author Shannon Ragland alleged that some UK players were paid by gamblers not to cover the 21-point spread by which UK was favored against lowly Xavier.[71] Evidence on balance has suggested that the game was not rigged except for three events, which remain mysterious.[72] One incident involved the ball on Xavier's 18-inch line and with just seconds left in the first half. Quarterback Jerry Woolum called a pitch-option play that required a read by the quarterback as he placed the ball in the belly of the running back. If he saw the hole closed for the back to score, the quarterback had to pull the ball out of the back's belly and pitch it to a running back if he was charged by the defensive end. Or he could have kept the ball and stepped into the end zone. There were three possible decisions and two possible exchanges of the ball, not a typical goal line play. The pitch was mishandled, fumbled, and kicked, and the ball was spotted on Xavier's 29-yard line as time expired in the first half.

Plays requiring multiple choices for the quarterback, even if he was a three-year starter, were normally not called 18 inches from paydirt.[73] A Bradshaw staple would have been a quarterback sneak or a running back straight ahead that assured a 14-point lead. The errant play was called by Woolum. This perhaps can be seen as casting suspicion on him as being involved in the game rigging when accounts of his second half, subpar performance are considered. In the second half, the senior quarterback repeatedly did not move the offense and missed his receivers. Despite the spectators' calls for a backup, Bradshaw played Woolum the entire game. The head coach was rightfully livid about Woolum's poor choice at the goal line.

Bradshaw's next decision was disastrous as he ordered the team to practice its goal line offense during the entire halftime break. The incident involving linebacker Jesse Grant's inferior second half defensive play may have pointed to his participation in the fix. Defensive coordinator Ford wanted to modify his scheme or prevent Grant from repeatedly being blocked or removed from the play. Ford could not communicate his adjustments to the player on the field, which suggested inept coaching and not a fixed game. A comment by one player that it "looks like we're throwing the game" is not the same as reporting to someone that he was in on the fix or saw players receiving money from gamblers or a student.[74]

If Woolum had been one of the stars frequenting Lakeside Drive and developed a working relationship with Barnett for delivering players to the residence, the likelihood of his conspiring with Barnett to rig the game seems plausible. Did the game films show certain players deliberately committing mistakes? The coaches would never reveal such a possibility, especially knowing the bitterness the players felt toward them, or their friends who left the team would have leaked the accusations to David Hawpe. In the spring of 1963, Bradshaw decided to enlist the assistance of Tommy Bell in shutting down the Lakeside Drive parties. Since Bell was an NFL referee, attorney, and respected booster with legal connections in Lexington, this may have been because of pressure from various boosters and Board of Trustees' members that the sex and fixing rumors might be reported outside of Kentucky. A scandal involving Barnett and gamblers conspiring to fix a UK game may have brought a death penalty ruling to UK's football program.

Bradshaw's brutality softened in subsequent seasons for economic and publicity reasons. He witnessed the near-death of Giles Smith in the spring of 1963. Surgeons had to perform an emergency craniotomy to repair the blood vessels and stop the bleeding. Smith was comatose for a long period and suffered long-term effects from the injury.[75] Of course, Bradshaw's critics would at first allege brutality as the cause of Smith's condition. From all accounts of players and others present at the practice, the injury's direct causal effect could never be ascertained.[76] Total Football at UK reached its finest moment on September 26, 1964, when UK upset three-point favorite and the No. 1 team in the country, Ole Miss, 26–21 in Oxford. Bradshaw's methods were vindicated in the media but not in the players' minds. After he was carried off the field, Bradshaw's two comments about his methods spoke volumes about his belief in Total Football: "If 'ol Bear could see me now," he said.[77] He also asked the players rhetorically, "Let me ask you, was it worth it?"[78]

That question was answered by Bradshaw's nemesis, David Hawpe. Then a senior and still writing for the *Kentucky Kernel*, the young editor answered Bradshaw's question with an indictment of Total Football. With questions that would be asked by countless commercialized football and basketball cynics and reform groups over the next 60 years, Hawpe posed and answered the following questions with reasoned evidence:

> Is this victory worth the heartbreak and anguish suffered by those who found Total Football too much to endure? Is it worth the loss of numerous fine athletes who might have profited by attending this university and who might have established proud records as alumni? Is it worth the embarrassment of censure by the NCAA? Was it worth it to betray principles and break the rules? Can men be expected to learn honor and sacrifice when inconvenient rules are bent? Did the decision to take scholarships flow from Bradshaw? Was it worth it to put these boys out on the street and take what was rightfully theirs? Was it worth it to not just take scholarships, but also to take their books? What did the success really mean?[79]

On the same editorial page, *Kernel* cartoonist Sid Webb echoed Hawpe's questions by asking in the cartoon's headline, "Is It Worth It? ... Yes Sir!"[80] Below the headline, a caricature of Bradshaw's face appeared on a large, dark figure with a megaphone resembling a coach barking orders that dwarfed a small figure representing education.[81]

The words of Judge Saul S. Streit had been ignored in UK's 1962–1968 football program.[82] Kentucky's legacy of sports scandals continued under Bradshaw. In a Tallahassee game on October 10, 1964, against Florida State, led by quarterback Steve Tensi and future Pro Football Hall of Fame receiver Fred Biletnikoff, the fifth-ranked UK Wildcats were humiliated, 48–6. One year later in 1965, after Bradshaw's 6–5 season, his job was offered to Homer Smith. But Smith had seen enough of Total Football and moved to Cincinnati as the head coach. The boosters were stuck with Bradshaw for three more years. He announced his resignation late in the 1968 season.

The Thin Thirty's last official reunion in Lexington was in September 1992, where they were introduced at halftime. Bradshaw was not invited. The ones who left the program, contrary to Bradshaw's wisdom that "winners eat steak and quitters eat hamburger," had eaten their fair share of steak. They would organize their own reunions and celebrate their families and their own professional successes. But the UK brutality was etched in their memories for life. When has it been legal or moral to intentionally brutalize another person on or off the football field? In the 1960s, the quest for a winning college football program justified the Bradshaws of the world. In 1990, Brad-shaw was reunited with one of his favorite players, Tommy Simpson, in Lex-ington. "I'm sorry if I mistreated you. If I did anything to you, I'm sorry."[83] Unfortunately, the unfairness, harsh measures, and other barbaric practices left a countless number of victims with no spokesperson. But even if the vic-tims had a spokesperson, would the university's powers and athletic boosters have listened?

4

The Butts and Bryant Phone Calls, 1962

More Than Social Conversations

One NCAA weakness was in its memberships' history of never voting at a national convention to suspend a program. Kentucky sportswriter Ed Ashford crowed, "So Kentucky basketball fans now can quit worrying about the possibility of any immediate punitive action by the NCAA."[1] In one of Walter Byers' first moves as the newly appointed NCAA head and Enforcement Committee chair, he persuaded the committee to craft a measure uniquely designed for UK. It was based on an NCAA bylaw that in part stated, "NCAA members had agreed to schedule games only with colleges that had agreed to abide by the organization's rules."[2] Hence, to remain in good standing with the organization, any member scheduling a basketball game with Kentucky would be subject to a suspension. UK representatives Leo Chamberlain and Abe Kirwan appeared before the enforcement committee proceedings in Chicago and accepted the one-year shutdown pending the approval of UK President Herman L. Donovan.

A faction of the UK boosters vehemently argued for a legal challenge to the actions of the SEC and NCAA. If UK had forced an NCAA membership vote to shut down the basketball program for one year, it's unlikely that two-thirds of the membership would have voted to pass such a resolution.[3] Donovan and UK decided to accept the one-year penalty following the recommendation of UK's two representatives in Chicago. Kirwan was later named the NCAA's first enforcement committee head. New York County District Attorney Frank Hogan's shutting down of the college basketball investigations in the early 1950s left more questions unanswered than answered related to gambling in college football and basketball. Clearly, sports gamblers were moving from horse racing to professional and college sports in the early 1940s.

Paul "Bear" Bryant's coaching record is intermingled with his public reputation and testimony from players who survived his programs' excessive demands. Many of the players in his programs suffered the ignominy of being labeled "quitters" because they did not believe in his system. On balance, it may have been Bryant's realization that in the world of commercialized college football, winning and profits justified his methods of weeding out or pulling scholarships.

During Bryant's eight years in Lexington (1946–53), the football program remained unscathed from NCAA scrutiny. The winning of six national titles and a 323–85–17 overall record places him among the all-time leaders in the sport. Payoffs to UK players and many UK recruits were well known among his competitors.

In 1975, after twenty-nine years as a head coach, Bryant turned any semblance of college football reflecting anything less than paraprofessional status on its head by stating:

I used to go along with the idea that football players on scholarship were "student-athletes," which is what the NCAA calls them. Meaning a student first, an athlete second. We are kidding ourselves trying to make it more palatable to the academicians. We don't have to say that and we shouldn't. At the level we play the boy is really an athlete first and a student second. He's there as an emissary of the school, paid with a scholarship to perform a very important function. He represents students, the administration, the alumni, everybody. Sometimes before millions of people, the fact that he's a student, the second part of the deal, is the only meaningful way we have to pay him.[4]

After Alabama (UA) went undefeated in 1961, including a 10–3 win over Arkansas in the Sugar Bowl, Bryant's coaching style added to the controversy that had followed him at Maryland, Kentucky, and Texas A&M. Most people who knew him attributed his coaching success to an extraordinary capacity for hard work, efficient use of his time, a flawless memory, and a preoccupation with thoroughly preparing his team for its next opponent.[5] Former NFL coach and Bryant assistant Bum Philips stated:

Coach Bryant doesn't coach football. He coaches people. When I went to work for him—and I say for him because you sure don't work with him—the feeling was he could get more out of people than anybody. Others might know more about football, but I think, I know, I've never been around anyone who knows as much about people. Like Jake Gaither used to say, Bryant could take his'n and beat your'n, and take your'n and beat his'n. He could win with either group."[6]

In 1960, Wally Butts had been pressured to resign from coaching despite one year earlier leading the University of Georgia (UG) to a 9–1 record, capturing a SEC title, and beating Missouri in the Orange Bowl.[7] The reasons for the external pressure to resign were his conservative offense, a six-year record from 1955 to 1960 of 29–34, and perhaps most importantly, the deterioration of his personal life. UG University President O. C. Aderhold knew about Butts' excessive drinking in Atlanta nightclubs with his booster buddies, public displays of intoxication, and his highly visible sexual affair with 32-year-old Evelyn Lindsey.

His behavior had become common knowledge among the region's junior college and high school coaches, compromising his ability to recruit in the Southeast. Aderhold stated in a memo about Butts' reputation: "The deterioration of Butts' personal life involved excessive drinking in public and frequent out-of-town trips and night-club appearances in the company of a young mistress."[8] Butts' resignation was publicly attributed to health reasons. Later events would reveal that the decision to give up the head's coach position was hardly voluntary, as his personal financial life was also in a downward spiral. Reportedly, Butts was on the verge of insolvency, borrowed money from his gambler friend Frank Scoby, and had lost money on risky investments. To maximize his retirement benefits, Butts requested to remain as the director of athletics and was scheduled to retire from the university on June 30, 1963.[9]

On March 22, 1963, the *Saturday Evening Post* published a story titled: "The Story of a College Football Fix," accusing Butts of sharing UG's offensive and defensive game plans and other inside information with "Bear" Bryant. The substance of the story involved a phone conversation between the two coaches overheard by a 41-year-old Atlanta life insurance sales manager, George P. Burnett. The sales manager had been hooked up to the two coaches' conversation by a cross-connect. On the morning of September 13, 1962, nine days before the Crimson Tide would meet the Bulldogs in the season opener at Birmingham's Legion Field, Burnett attempted to call a friend at Communications International, an Atlanta public relations firm.[10] After calling his gambler friend Frank Scoby in Chicago, Butts called Bryant in Tuscaloosa at the same time Burnett was attempting to reach his friend. The phone connection to Communications International proved hard to establish until Burnett heard the operator say, "Coach is out on the field now, Coach Butts, but he is on his way to the phone. Do you want to hold, or do you want him to return the call?" Butts informed the operator that he would hold.[11]

When Bryant came on the line, Burnett heard, "Hello, Bear," to which Bryant answered, "Hi, Wally, what do you have for me?" Knowing UG and UA would meet in nine days, Burnett surmised that Bryant was expecting the call and it was for his benefit. During the 15-minute call, Butts relayed a number of UG's specific offensive and defensive individual and team schemes, which would be valuable to any opponent playing its first game of the season. Alabama offensive coach Charlie Bradshaw had scouted the Bulldogs' spring game. But in an opening season game, any new defensive or offensive plays might upset a team that had won the national title a year earlier.[12] Burnett recorded seven pages of notes during the conversation. Burnett heard Butts respond to a number of Bryant's questions by saying, "I don't know" followed by Bryant's, "Can you find out for me?" "Well, wait until I see the scrimmage Saturday, I'll probably have something more for you," responded the "little round man."[13] The two agreed to talk again via phone that coming Sunday.

When UG's youngest assistant, Johnny Griffith, was hired to replace Butts in January 1961, he publicly stated there would be "no connection between his program and Butts." The former head coach publicly hinted during Griffith's initial 3–7 season that the new staff was not obtaining maximum performance from the players, and he was publicly critical of the team's play. "He was actually proving a detriment to the program because of his criticism of Coach Griffith, the University, and Athletic Board," wrote UG President Aderhold.[14]

Butts attended the Saturday scrimmage despite the president's orders to disassociate himself from the football program. The planned call was made on Sunday, September 15. Butts and Bryant more than likely did not talk "about football in general" during the 67-minute conversation. More plausibly, they talked about any new "wrinkles" the UG staff had inserted in preparation for its first game in 1962, and Butts' scouting report from the Saturday scrimmage.[15] Any newly inserted play would certainly be of interest to Alabama's staff.

The *Saturday Evening Post* story hit the newsstands on March 22, 1963. The byline was especially ominous if the allegations stated in the article proved to be true:

> Not since the Chicago White Sox threw the 1919 World Series has there been a sports story as shocking as this one. This is a story of one fixed game of college football. Before the University of Georgia played the University of Alabama last September 22, Wally Butts, athletic director of Georgia, gave Paul (Bear) Bryant, head coach of Alabama, Georgia's plays, defensive patterns, all the significant secrets Georgia's football team possessed.... How prevalent is the fixing of college football games? How often do teachers sell out their pupils? We don't know—yet. For now we can only be appalled.[16]

The story's shock value in the SEC and the rest of the country was predictable and expected by the magazine. Most coaches and Georgians believed Butts was perfectly capable of selling out UG's coaches and players. In Alabama, one would have been hard-pressed to find a single person who believed Bryant needed any assistance in defeating UG, which the Crimson Tide crushed, 35–0.

Regardless of public opinion, the inflammatory nature of the headlines would undoubtedly force the publisher into court with Butts and Bryant to defend its accusations. Bryant's lawyers were already preparing to sue the *Atlanta Constitution*'s (Furman Bisher's "Football Has Gone Bezerk" article) and the *Post*'s parent company, Curtis Publishing. A week later, Butts filed a $10 million cause of action for libel against Curtis Publishing.[17] Within days, Bryant's lawyer filed a similar case in Birmingham's federal court against Curtis for $10.5 million. The Butts court case involved four fundamental questions that were related to the possibility of Butts and Bryant conspiring to fix a college football game in 1962:

1. Did Bryant intentionally request from Butts UG's offensive and defensive game plans before UA's first game of the 1962 season against UG?
2. If so, was it for gambling or other reasons, such as avoiding a season-opening loss?
3. Did Wally Butts share UG's defensive and offensive game plans with UA and other UG opponents during the 1962 season?
4. Was Wally Butts persuaded by at least three of his gambling and business friends to share information about UG's game plans with its opponents' staffs in 1962, enabling him and his friends to bet money on the favorable side of the odds?[18]

The last question is best understood by examining Bryant's decision in the 1962 Alabama-Georgia Tech game, won by the five-point underdog Yellow Jackets, 7–6. In what he would describe as the "dumbest decision of his career," Bryant ordered UA's quarterback to pass on first down with the ball on Georgia Tech's 14-yard line in the closing minutes of the game. The pass was intercepted, sealing the upset. Why did Bryant not run the ball for three downs and kick a chip-shot field goal? It was commonly known that Bryant coached to cover the spread so UA's booster-gamblers won big money.[19] A 13–6 win would have covered the five-point spread; a 9–6 win did not. This was UA's only defeat during the 1962 season, which concluded with a 17–0 victory over Oklahoma in the Orange Bowl.

In the UG game, the spread favored UA from 14 to 17 points. In playing an unknown team from a strategic perspective, was Bryant seeking to secure bets for his boosters, or defeat UG by covering the spread? Facing UG as its first opponent in 1962, Bryant's staff was not able to ascertain if the Bulldogs had added new offensive and defensive schemes before its first game. The UA team returned several starters from the 1961 roster, and UG was fielding a team of mostly sophomores. What motivated Bryant to seek UG's game plan from the disgraced ex-head coach? Traditionally, season-opening games are strategically the most difficult to map. The Crimson Tide was returning almost all of the undefeated 1961 team, with sophomore quarterback Joe

Namath a notable exception. Sportswriters had rated the Bulldogs as a much-improved team from the previous year. Bradshaw, now at UK, had reported a bigger, faster, and more talented team than the previous year after scouting Georgia in its spring game.[20]

The weight of the evidence points to Bryant as the aggressor in seeking UG's game plans from Butts. Bryant's powerful will to win was well known and documented by his self-admitted acceptance of booster payoffs at UK and Texas A&M. In his fifth year at Tuscaloosa, he was not as financially secure as he would be in the 1970s, when he was more likely to admit to recruiting violations, payoffs to players, and brutality. The following April 9, 1963, FBI memo documented that Bryant had bet on college football at Texas A&M:

> Denver [FBI office] received information alleging that Bryant placed bets on Texas A&M football games in 1957 ... Denver has set out leads to locate and interview original sources of this information, as well as bookies with whom Bryant allegedly placed bet [sic].[21]

In this report, we can only speculate as to why the FBI was tracking Bryant's betting. Could it have been that illegal bookies or organized crime figures with whom he placed his bets were not reporting their incomes? To be sure, big-time gamblers' knowledge of how the football coach was betting would have caused them to bet the same way on Texas A&M. In another memo reported by the FBI, Bryant bet on his own team not to cover the spread:

> New Orleans bookmaker [redacted] ... advised he specifically recalled that Bryant had bet on the outcome of the Texas A&M-Tennessee game, which was played at the Gator Bowl in Florida in December 1957, and Bryant reportedly took the 4-point spot given to the underdog Tennessee team."[22]

Bryant won his bet as Texas A&M failed to cover the spread as they lost, 3–0. The only people who would have benefited from knowing how Bryant bet on his team not to cover the spread would have been gamblers and bookies. A bookie might have shared or sold how the coach bet with a number of bettors. Bryant's betting on college football did not prove he and Butts rigged the UG-UA game. There was no evidence of his betting on the game.

In two separate letters (the first one on February 28, 1963) to Alabama president Frank A. Rose, why did Bryant falsely indicate that the conversation Burnett overheard did not occur? Instead, Bryant said in one letter that the conversation involved Butts describing passing plays later used to defeat Tennessee. In this case, why was Butts assisting Alabama in defeating another team in the same conference? Was it for gambling reasons? In the second letter to Rose, Bryant denied that the first conversation was about passing routes. Instead, in a letter dated March 6, 1963, Bryant wrote that both conversations centered around the NCAA's concerns about officials not enforcing unsportsmanlike conduct rules (i.e., piling on, roughing the passer, rule changes, etc.).[23] And how they would penalize "smash mouth" football programs like Alabama's. That explanation strains credulity.

Why would an opposing AD want to inform an opponent about how his team would be penalized for its style of playing football? More importantly, why would any coach not properly instruct players on how to execute within the framework of the rules to avoid costly penalties, especially, a coach of Bryant's caliber? Also, the official head of the SEC had visited Tuscaloosa to explain how the rule changes would be interpreted one week before the Butts-Bryant conversations.

None of the items about Bryant's gambling on his team to cover the spread or his contradictory letters to the president in isolation point to two coaches colluding to win a bet. But when all the Bryant and Butts evidence is examined, the likelihood of the two coaches conspiring to ensure that Alabama would cover the spread against UG seems likely.[24]

Butts' motivations to assist Alabama were most likely related to his personal indiscretions, financial distress, and involuntary removal from the head coach and athletic director positions. Despite his financial losses and mounting debts, Butts continued to see and travel with his mistress, Evelyn Lindsey, to Georgia's away games and to the Caribbean on vacations. Many of his travel expenses, gifts, and expenses involving Lindsey were placed on the university's credit card. He was later asked to repay the debts to the university. When he was pressured to give up the athletic director's position, he met with UG President Aderhold, who noted: "I got the impression that he [Butts] may owe more than $100,000. It is inconceivable that a man can get so financially involved as Coach Butts is at the present time."[25]

Records uncovered by attorney James Kirby, who was assigned to cover the trial for the SEC, demonstrated that Butts had created "a financial house of cards" by investing in a number of shady ventures, including Florida's citrus grove industry.[26] Big-time coaches have often been targets of business offers, including stock at discounted prices, restaurants bearing their names, land investments, and partnerships in business ventures. Part-owner Lewis Tose of Tose Trucking in Philadelphia endorsed a loan for Butts and brought him in on a Coca-Cola distributorship in Pennsylvania.[27] Tose's brother, Leonard, had purchased the Philadelphia Eagles in 1969 and was well known for accumulating big debts from gambling losses. Ultimately, he was forced to cede control of the franchise to his family after accumulating $25 million in gambling losses at Atlantic City casinos.[28] Many of Butts' business associates, such as Frank Scoby, were heavy college football gamblers.

The pattern of Butts' phone calls to Scoby in 1962 included none in April and May, five in June, two in July, four in August, and 14 in September. The September 13 call was made immediately before the call to Bryant overheard by Burnett. Also, phone records revealed that Scoby and Butts had conversed at least six times before the UG-UA game. For this game, bookies had been offering UA with a spread that varied from 14 to 17 points. It was not unusual for big-time gamblers to call a number of bookies nationwide, seeking to bet their money where the best odds were offered. Scoby may have been attempting to find out how secure a bet on Alabama would be. Finding out that Butts had passed vital strategic information to Bryant was vital knowledge for gamblers.[29]

It's naive to believe that as close friends and business associates, Butts and Scoby were not aware of each other's gambling habits. Under oath, each would admit to such knowledge. Also, did Butts' business-associate gamblers cut deals with him to forgive debts in exchange for inside information to ensure the success of their bets involving UG's games? Butts testified that when the *Post* article was published, Scoby was planning to offer him a distributorship for a new Scotch whiskey in Georgia.[30] Besides Scoby, two other gamblers were identified by Curtis' investigators as Butts' associates. The ex-coach's betting on UG's games was substantiated by another FBI memo, dated April 20, 1963:

> Denver [FBI office] is continuing to receive information concerning the betting activities of BRYANT and also former University of Georgia Athletic Director, Wally Butts, [Redacted], [redacted], and [redacted] advised SA WILLIAM J. MALONE on 3/11/64 that had lunch with JACK FAULKNER, head coach of the Denver Broncos of the American Football League on 3/9/64, and that Faulkner, who had just returned from a trip throughout the southwest part of the United States, told him that he had picked up information during his contact with coaches and their associates that WALLY BUTTS had been, while both Coach and Athletic Director at Georgia, betting on the outcome of some of the Georgia games.[31]

One of Butts' consistent defenses was that "he would never do anything to hurt Georgia." On January 30, 1963, while attending the funeral of business associate Lewis Tose, Butts was informed that Burnett had shared the notes with UG Coach Griffith. To Carmichael, the notes appeared serious enough to inform Butts of their existence at midnight before the day of the services.

In late February 1963, Butts was invited to meet with the UG hierarchy in Atlanta, including UG President Aderhold, attorney Cook Barwick, representing the executive committee of the UG Athletic Board, and SEC Commissioner Bernie Moore. Barwick was chosen to investigate the matter and serve as the board's counsel. By now Butts was aware of the Burnett notes. Besides repeating several times that he "never would do anything to hurt Georgia," Butts spent the rest of the meeting dancing around the substance of the notes and changing the focus to the common practice of two coaches "talking general football."[32] Moore, a former football coach, was not convinced. In fact, because of other evidence, the commissioner believed the conversations did occur as reported. It is also very likely that Moore had known about Butts calling other SEC coaches and offering to assist them in defeating UG. But to release that information to the media without a solid legal footing would have risked at least an investigation into the SEC's corrupt practices and would create a public relations disaster. Butts resigned as the UG athletic director the following day, five months prematurely.[33]

Another FBI memo revealed that Butts had engaged in a 52-minute telephone conversation with Florida State Head Coach Bill Peterson titled: "With reference to Butts' telephone call to Coach Peterson at Florida State University," an inquiry conducted by (redacted) in April 1963 revealed:

> Peterson had received one telephone call from Wally Butts the week before the 1962 FSU-Georgia game which FSU won in Athens, Georgia, by a score of 18–0. According to [redacted] this conversation was 52 minutes long, and Peterson took the call at a coaches meeting.... When Peterson received the call he had [redacted] [redacted] on other extensions and that [redacted] actually diagrammed the plays on a blackboard as the information was received from Butts.[34]

In a later deposition, Coach Bill Peterson testified that Butts shared only two of UG's plays with his staff during Butts' 52-minute presentation, and the plays did not affect Florida State's 18–0 shutout of UG. The FBI memo also indicated that three assistant coaches diagrammed UG's offensive and defensive schemes. Peterson's deposition was clearly not truthful. For him to admit that Butts' information was useful would put him in a conspiracy with Butts to ensure that Florida State won by more than the spread. We are led to believe that the entire 52-minute conversation was spent on diagramming two plays by three coaches. At the least, the phone call points to Butts' willingness to sell out the UG players and complicity of an opposing coach to win a game by any means.

Saturday Evening Post author Frank Graham, Jr., in *A Farewell to Heroes*, confirmed that Butts was more than "capable of hurting UG and head coach Johnny Griffith":

At least three or four other Southern coaches confided to newspapermen that the embittered old coach had called them to give away Georgia's secrets, hoping that after a succession of bad beatings, the university would give him his job back. But none of the coaches was willing to testify for the *Post*.[35]

If Graham's observations are accurate, Butts appears to have lied to the three or four coaches referred to in the sportswriter's memoirs about reasons for "selling out" UG. It appears very unlikely that Butts would have been appointed UG's head coach had the college jettisoned Griffith. In the Southeast and nationally, his flawed reputation was well known inside coaching circles, and he was not in contention for a coaching position at any college or professional team. Was Butts offering valuable information to UG's opponents to ensure that he and his gambling friends won their bets on those games?

Former University of Georgia football coach Wally Butts, ca. 1950. In 1962, he allegedly shared Georgia's game plans with Alabama's Paul "Bear" Bryant when the two teams played against each other. Later evidence revealed Butts' close relationship with Frank Scoby, who was known to bet heavily on college football, as the reason for sharing the vital information (courtesy Hargrett Rare Book and Manuscript Library/University of Georgia Libraries).

The most persuasive evidence that Burnett's notes were strategically related to UG's preparation for the first game of the season came from the investigation by Georgia's Attorney General, Eugene Cook. After viewing the notes, Cook was understandably concerned that Butts may have shared plays with UG opponents which he observed at closed practices during the 1962 season. Closed practices are designed to install any new offensive or defensive changes for which an opponent has shown an apparent weakness (i.e., an inability to cover specific pass routes or an outside pass rush). In fact, former governor and Butts drinking companion Marvin Griffin had lobbied to build a fence around UG's practice field before Butts' resignation. Cook's investigation included six UG coaches who signed an affidavit that stated:

> After viewing the notations made by George Burnett while listening to an alleged conversation between Wallace Butts and Bear Bryant on September 13, 1962, it is my opinion, as one of the coaches of the University of Georgia football team, that giving of such information to Coach Bear Bryant before the opening game of the season conveyed vital and important information that could have been of value to the University of Alabama football team and could have affected the outcome of the game on September 22, 1962.[36]

One of the assistant coaches who signed the affidavit testified on Butts' behalf at the trial. Asked by Curtis Publishing's attorney why he had signed the statement, John H. Gregory's response was that he did so fearing Griffith would fire him if he did not. But there is no evidence that such pressure was put on him. However, Griffith did fire Gregory the following day because of his damaging testimony.

In a stunning decision on August 20, 1963, an Atlanta jury found that the *Post* story libeled Butts and awarded him $3 million in punitive damages and $60,000 in general damages. In the case, Curtis Publishing did not have to prove that all the facts Graham alleged were true, only that "the sting of libel" was true. This meant Curtis had to prove that Butts rigged and fixed the 1962 UG-Alabama game by giving Bryant information calculated to or could have affected the outcome of the game—that could have caused one team to win or that could have increased the number of points by which the game was won.[37]

For this game, did Butts provide UA with UG game plans to ensure they won the game and covered the spread (winning by at least 15 points)? Without understanding how a football win was dissimilar to a gambler's win, the jury unanimously agreed that Butts did not provide UA with vital and strategic UG plans to ensure that UA won the game by covering the spread. General damages were awarded because the jury believed the *Post* article had defamed Butts in his profession and was libelous per se (i.e., on its face) and presumed to have injured him. Later, the judge reduced the punitive damages from $3 million to $400,000.

Legal scholars believed the Atlanta jury was upset at Curtis Publishing for its lack of a comprehensive investigation and sloppy preparation. The $3 million in punitive damages, according to court observers, was designed to send a message to the publisher, as the government stood to take a healthy share of punitive damages. Curtis's lawyers unsuccessfully appealed the lower court's decision three times to trial judge Lewis R. Morgan. They followed with an appeal to the U.S. Fifth Circuit Court of Appeals, where the three appellate judges voted 2–1 to uphold the lower court's decision.[38] That court's decision was appealed to the U.S. Supreme Court. The court, in a close 5–4 decision, agreed that the article's content, including its title and sidebars, constituted "libel." Justice John Harlan, in speaking for the 5–4 majority opinion, stated, "the *Post's* story was highly unreasonable conduct constituting an extreme departure from the standards of investigation and reporting ordinarily adhered to by responsible publishers."[39]

Evidence in James Kirby's *Fumble*, this author's *Cheating the Spread*, and Ball State communications professor David Sumner's forthcoming *Fumbled Call* about the Butts-Bryant conversations in September 1962, strongly suggests that Butts shared information not only with Bryant, but with at least five other UG opponents in 1962.[40] There was Butts' alleged sharing of UG's game plan via phone with UA's "Bear" Bryant, and with Bill Peterson of Florida State. And there are three or four other possible conversations Butts had with other SEC coaches that Frank Graham, Jr., reported in *A Farewell to Heroes*.

Bryant testified at the trial about one of the conversations with Butts. His precise recollection of one or both calls was never clearly established despite his reputation for possessing a flawless memory. Bryant's testimony was also laden with football terminology that was likely not understood by the Atlanta jury. He repeatedly denied asking for game information and implied that if given specific information as alleged by Burnett were true, "a hole should be bored in his head." That and other similar self-deprecatory statements were "all showmanship" and obfuscation of the facts.[41] The calls did not convincingly prove that Butts was providing information so that he, opposing coaches, and his gambling-business associates could secure their bets, assuming they bet on UG's opponents to cover the spread. They demonstrated only that Butts was calling and coaches were willing to listen to possibly obtain vital game information without any compunction in doing so. That appeared to be the nature of big-time college football in the 1960s.

Since 1962, this story, more than any other in commercialized college sport, refuses to be relegated to the heap of forgotten college football and basketball gambling scandals. In 2013, the *Saturday Evening Post*'s archivist, Jeff Nilsson, stated: "It's a story that refuses to lie down and be quiet, even a half century later. Over the past fifty years journalists who have revisited this case wonder how the *Post* managed to lose this case."[42] The *Post*'s editors believed they had a breakthrough story that would have uncovered college football's corruption. It is unlikely that a different trial outcome would have dampened the ever-elusive quest by big-time football and basketball programs for money. But the trial exposed how coaches, athletic directors, and game officials may be just as likely to play for or consort with gamblers as any other individuals in positions to affect final scores.

College football survived the Butts-Bryant scandal and repeated scandals, including the Sandusky scandal at Penn State in 2012. Almost all writers in 1963 refused to believe Bryant would sell out one group of young people for money. On the other hand, most writers who covered the trial believed Butts had exchanged game strategy to ensure UA would win and cover the spread. The trial was followed by little in-depth critical analysis by the involved colleges, the NCAA, or legislators of each state. The exception was an article in the September 2, 1963, issue of *Sports Illustrated* titled "Rx: Preventative Medicine." Butts' victory, according to the writer, did not vindicate college football:

> Vindicated? College football itself was not charged with anything. Only Butts and Bryant were directly accused. Even so, the coaches were quite right in feeling that their sport would have been grievously injured if Butts had lost his suit. The whole is never unaffected by what happens to one of its parts. Some of the mud would have been splattered on the football jerseys of boys as far as Oregon. But, if the coaches had good reason to feel uneasiness during the trial they have no reason to feel utter relief now. Conditions remain as before. The sport is a multi-million-dollar business and a subject of absorbing interest to vast numbers of book-makers and heavy gamblers. Money of this magnitude makes for greed, and greed often makes for crooked dealing. Yet the colleges have done precious little to protect themselves against scandal. Their recruiting practices have, in fact, stretched the moral principles of amateur sport beyond recognition. And, it was shocking to learn that the major effort of the Southeastern Conference to investigate the Butts-Bryant allegations was to assign one man to attend the trial.[43]

Not only did Professor Kirby attend the trial, but he meticulously recorded, commented on, and provided an extensive and objective analysis of how the Curtis lawyers should have prevailed in the *Butts v. Curtis* trial. Commissioner Moore and the SEC's lead investigator also spent significant time in seeking the truth about the scandal. The *Post* article stated that the NCAA was also planning to investigate, but was moving at its "usual slow pace" and deferred to the SEC."[44] The *Post*'s lawyers, in preparation for Bryant's lawsuit, had collected substantial evidence from Bryant's and UA President Rose's files in Tuscaloosa. The trial would have been lengthy and costly, and it would have publicized a number of Bryant's personal and professional indiscretions and placed college football in an unfavorable legal spotlight again. The most controversial coach in college football settled with Curtis Publishing for a reported $300,000, substantially less than the $10.5 million he was seeking from the publisher.[45]

Kirby submitted a report unfavorable to Butts and Bryant to the SEC, but the conference's hands were tied. In face of the Butts verdict and Bryant settlement, sanctions against the two programs would not have prevailed in a legal forum. Hence, Butts and Bryant received unmerited public and media vindication. Although there have been numerous books on the life and coaching career of Bryant, none delves into the Butts-Bryant scandal as objectively and comprehensively as Professor Kirby's.

His little-known book, *Fumble: Bear Bryant, Wally Butts and the Great College Football Scandal*, persuasively argued that Butts and Bryant had betrayed the very sport they publicly espoused. Moreover, the legal system, media, and college sports fumbled in their attempts to expose the corruption and hypocrisy in commercialized college football.[46] By all accounts, the voluminous mistakes of the Curtis lawyers before and during the trial were significant factors in the lower court jury's verdict in favor of Butts. Had the *Post* prevailed in an appeal for a retrial and argued that the *New York Times Co. v. Sullivan* ruling should apply, they may well have prevailed in a retrial. This federal ruling prohibits public officials from recovering damages for a defamatory falsehood relating to official conduct unless the plaintiff proves that the statement was made with actual malice—that is, with knowledge that it was false or with reckless disregard of whether it was false or not.[47]

5

The University of New Mexico Gambling Scandal of 1979

"As Bad as It Ever Gets!"

During the latter part of the 1960s, college football and basketball appeared to have successfully addressed many of the problems that led to NCAA infractions, including the repeated gambling scandals that had plagued basketball since the 1930s. The NCAA had solidified its oversight mandates, attendance dramatically increased in football and basketball, and television emerged as a revenue producer in the two sports. This era of self-congratulation was also remarkable for its absence of any systematic study of commercialized college football and basketball. Scattered voices from a small group of faculty and ex-athletes included Harry Edwards' seminal book on the exploitation of black athletes, Dave Meggyesy's accounts of athletic excesses at Syracuse, Gary Shaw's *Meat on the Hoof*, which documented the brutality in the Texas football program, and Jack Scott's anthology, *The Athletic Revolution*. These voices were effectively muted by the popularity of college sports and the alliance formed between the athletic establishment and the conservative right in rebutting the counterculture attacks on athletics in the 1960s.[1]

Student unrest during the 1960s, a sagging national economy, and declining state revenues prompted a series of studies on higher education. Beginning in 1968, *The Carnegie Commission on Higher Education* and the *Carnegie Council on Policy Studies in Higher Education,* chaired by noted scholar Clark Kerr, enlisted scholars from all disciplines to scrutinize higher education. Interestingly, the ensuing studies avoided any analysis of college sports.[2] Although many college presidents had devoted significant time to athletics, they were not viewed as worthy of serious study and were immune from budget cutting and ground rules applicable to other academic units.

Longtime NCAA Executive Director Walter Byers' observations about the vulnerability of colleges related to the gambling problem meant that professional and college sports were increasingly relying on the FBI and state governments to detect, investigate, and prosecute game fixing. The longtime head of the NCAA stated in *Unsportsmanlike Conduct: Exploiting College Athletes*, "Point shaving and fixing are threats to which colleges are most vulnerable and to which they give occasional attention. This is not due to lack of concern but a sense of helplessness about how to deal with the problem successfully."[3] The gambling scandals at Boston College and New Mexico in the late 1970s alerted the public and athletic officials to what bookies already knew. Legal and illegal gambling on human sports had become the largest sector of wagering worldwide.[4]

The scandal at the University of New Mexico (UNM) provides insight into how college basketball's past had escaped any serious attention from reform groups, inter-institutional studies, or the colleges themselves. This lack of inquiry arguably led to more scandals, FBI investigations, and NCAA penalties. The scandal at UNM came to represent a system in which big-time college basketball had assumed an existence apart from the university, which undermined the academic future of the institution. Corruption in college sports had reached a level where it no longer could be ignored in any dialogue involving the administration of an institution.

The Boston College scandal achieved more media notoriety than the UNM scandal because it involved three members of the Lucchese crime family: Henry Hill, James Burke, and Richard "The Fixer" Perry. Hill was the central character in Nicholas Pileggi's nonfiction book, *Wiseguys*,[5] the basis of director Martin Scorsese's film, *Goodfellas*. On September 6, 1961, Oregon defensive halfback Michael Bruce reluctantly identified professional gambler Frank "Lefty" Rosenthal before a Senate committee that was investigating organized crime's involvement in illegal gambling. Bruce fingered Rosenthal as the person who offered him $5,000 to fall down a few times in covering Michigan's receivers during the 1960 season.[6]

In 1931, UNM was a member of the Border Conference, which included the University of Arizona, New Mexico A&M (now New Mexico State University), Texas Tech, Texas Mines (now University of Texas, El Paso), Arizona State Teachers-Tempe (now Arizona State University), Arizona State Teachers-Flagstaff (now Northern Arizona University), Hardin-Simmons, and West Texas Teachers College (now West Texas A&M). In 1951, UNM joined the Skyline Conference; in 1962 it switched to the Western Athletic Conference (WAC). In 1999, the university again changed conferences, joining the Mountain West Conference (MWC), the conference to which it belongs today.[7]

In the fall of 1979, an investigation involving three basketball coaches at UNM implicated them in a series of activities that involved the forgery of players' transcripts for admission into the university, and a booster club not under the auspices of the university. Although 20 athletic boosters had regularly bet on UNM's basketball team, it was impossible to determine for how long and on which games. The FBI and state investigators could not put together enough evidence to link the gamblers to game fixing.[8] The gambling issue arose in the course of an investigation related to a gambling ring in Albuquerque that used a computer belonging to a manufacturer of military weapons employed by the Department of Energy (DOE).

In September 1979, the NCAA charged UNM with 57 violations. After additional private investigations were completed, the athletic program was found to have a total of 92 violations of NCAA regulations.[9] In October 1979, during the university's football homecoming week, the school's president, Dr. William E. Davis, reassigned Athletic Director Lavon McDonald to duties outside the athletic program. According to McDonald, the reassignment was involuntary and resulted in angry words, threats, and ill feelings toward the president from the Lobo Booster Club. The organization had been supporters of McDonald.[10] One month later, two dozen FBI agents descended upon UNM's athletic complex, armed with search warrants for athletic department records. The FBI also wanted to question Head Coach Norm Ellenberger, Assistant Coaches John Whisenant and Manny Goldstein, current basketball players, administrators, and the university president.[11]

Ellenberger and Whisenant would be tried by the federal government for wire and mail fraud. Ellenberger and Goldstein were also indicted and tried by the state of New Mexico for fraud and theft committed in conjunction with operating the basketball program. The scandal that became known as "Lobogate" was reported daily in Albuquerque newspapers and throughout the state of New Mexico.[12] The scandal had so many sordid elements that even the NCAA was shocked, if that was possible. From all indications, if the football program had been included in the investigation by the FBI and law enforcement agencies, the scandal may have reached levels unforeseen in the history of college sports. Fortunately for UNM, the authorities did not investigate the football program. Even so, state newspapers and radio subscribers to *United Press International* voted the UNM scandal as the top news story of 1979.[13]

The unsavory events had been part of the UNM basketball program since Ellenberger replaced Head Coach Bob King in 1972. Ellenberger had been hired as an assistant to King in 1967 after coaching at Monmouth College in Illinois. He became the Lobos' head coach when King moved to Indiana

State. "Stormin' Norman," a nickname he earned because of his natty and flashy attire, fiery coaching style, and flamboyant personality, brought to the university and its supporters exactly what they wanted: a record of 134–62 over seven years, WAC championships in 1974 and 1978, rankings in the nation's top 25, and near-capacity crowds at the University Arena.[14] Ellenberger was suspended in December 1979 and later forced to resign because of his involvement in the scandal. Included among the alleged violations were Ellenberger's and Whisenant's involvement in gambling on football and basketball games, players receiving payments from boosters, and academic fraud.[15]

The University Arena had been built 45 rows below ground level, held slightly more than 18,000 spectators, and was commonly known as The Pit. From its opening in 1966 until the 2001–2002 season, UNM was ranked in the top ten nationally in college basketball attendance. Within the state of New Mexico, every television station, university supporter, and media outlet

Bob King Court on the University of New Mexico (UNM) campus. From its opening in 1966 until 2002, attendance at the arena commonly known as "The Pit" ranked in the top ten nationally despite a scandal in 1979 that included UNM's boosters gambling on the team and payoffs to players (University Arena, The Pit, 1970, Facility Planning Records, UNMA 028 Box 5, Center for Southwest Research, University of New Mexico Libraries).

followed the basketball program.[16] For many of the state's citizens, the program's success was a source of regional and national identity and pride. Similar to other winning big-time football and basketball programs, UNM's basketball success was built on the backs of Ellenberger's and his coaching staff's blatant ignoring of NCAA rules and their involvement in criminal activities.[17] The lack of oversight by the athletic director, college president, and Board of Regents (BOR) permitted Ellenberger and his assistants to operate a program that had not yet caught the attention of the NCAA. The events that revealed the program's corrupt aspects became national news and were featured in *60 Minutes, The Chronicle of Higher Education, Newsweek, U.S. News & World Report, Time,* and *Sports Illustrated (SI)*.[18]

UNM's president in 1979 was William E. "Bud" Davis, an ex-football coach who had graduated from the University of Colorado with the avowed goal of becoming the "world's greatest football coach."[19] In 1961, the University of Colorado was forced to fire Head Football Coach Sonny Grandelius for violating a number of NCAA rules. Davis was appointed as the interim head coach, given the opportunity to carve his path toward college football greatness. During the 1962 season, Davis was hung in effigy after he coached the team to blowout losses against Iowa State (57–19), Oklahoma (62–0), and Missouri (57–0). He compiled a record of 2–8, which probably convinced him not to apply for the head coaching position.[20] Davis became UNM's president in 1975 in the midst of university turmoil with an athletic department that had been perennially disorganized and without adequate university oversight. The athletic program had received significant money from the Lobo Booster Club, which was known to hand out cash to football and basketball players, but was not officially connected to UNM.[21]

Ellenberger's recruiting style was similar to Jerry Tarkanian's at UNLV. Paid scouts and UNM coaches combed the inner cities, where underprivileged youngsters found an outlet and possible vehicle to escape their environments. Ellenberger would bring to UNM a number of talented basketball players that more prestigious Division I teams refused to recruit.[22] Backed by a booster club, the basketball recruits entered the university under special admission procedures. Eligibility was maintained with easy courses, available to any student, but especially created for the athletes. Many of UNM's athletes received bogus grades and unearned credits. For a period of time, Ottawa University in Kansas and Rocky Mountain College in Montana became known as institutions where an athletic program could buy transfer credits for instant eligibility.[23]

Typically, the two institutions would hire agents across the country who would certify that a non-attended course had been completed, such as

"Coaching Problems and Strategies for Solutions." In many cases, when ineligible athletes were asked how they suddenly became eligible, they truthfully
did not know.[24] At UNM, such practices were shielded from UNM's administration because the athletic department historically had never been accountable to any central administrator, including the president. To identify the
"hired hands" that created revenue for the college, the basketball coaches
required the players to wear T-shirts emblazoned with the words "I Are a
UNM Student." The graduation rate of players during Ellenberger's regime
was a dismal 25 percent.[25] Predictably, many of UNM's players had run afoul
of the law. Offenders were usually remanded to their coaches by lenient
judges.[26]

Five months before Ellenberger's program was exposed, one basketball
player was convicted of misappropriating city funds and another of credit
card fraud. A third was charged with armed robbery and aggravated assault,
but had not yet been to trial.[27] Kenny Page, who was on the 1979–1980 team
and had entered UNM as a freshman, removed a Cadillac from an Albuquerque showroom and drove it to Columbus, Ohio, to check out Ohio State's
basketball program. He returned the vehicle to Albuquerque for repairs and
was given a loaner that he did not like.[28] Returning the loaner to the dealer,
he proceeded to switch its plates to a Seville, which he drove back to Columbus to play on Ohio State's freshman team. Placed on probation during the
season for undisclosed reasons, Page returned to Albuquerque with the stolen
car and returned it to Sales Manager Alan Summers. The Sales Manager was
a member of the Lobo Booster Club and canceled the police report.[29] Page
then joined the Lobos' basketball program.

Wil Smiley had played center at UNM in 1976–1977 and 1977–1978. The
6-foot-10-inch Smiley had never graduated from high school and spent time
in several reformatories in New York City. The Bronx native found his way
to Scottsdale Community College and was convicted of rape while at the two-
year school. After his release from an Arizona prison, Smiley enrolled at
UNM to play basketball. Stated Smiley in an *SI* interview, "The man [Ellen-
berger] just used me because I was a tall dude. If I ain't six feet ten inches,
I'm back in jail and they throw away the key."[30]

Any local investigative journalist who wrote about the program's NCAA
infractions would be quietly ignored. Or the story might not even be published. From a political perspective, President Davis and the BOR had been
placed in a powerless predicament. To rein in the deeply corrupt basketball
program would have been the "kiss of death" for the president and BOR.
Publicly, Ellenberger's power outweighed the president's and that of the BOR.
A few faculty members had been caught up in the basketball frenzy that the

team created throughout the state. The majority were uninterested in athletics.[31] Many were alarmed that the citizens of the state were identifying the university as a "basketball school," with a healthy portion of resources and attention devoted to the program. The perception was that UNM was sacrificing academic programs in favor of filling its basketball arena. William Dowling, a former literature professor at UNM who moved to Rutgers, cited studies demonstrating that the state's top high school students were migrating to out-of-state institutions, as most of them viewed the university as a glorified high school. The average ACT score for incoming freshmen at UNM in 1975 was 18, and to raise the bar to 20 would have eliminated 65 percent of the state's high school seniors. An ACT score of 20 represented the 29th percentile nationally.[32]

The first evidence of wrongdoing in the basketball program was uncovered by Dr. Charles Coates, a faculty member in the Journalism Department. Dr. Coates had flunked a basketball player in summer school and wondered how the player mysteriously became eligible to play for the 1979–1980 season. Coates wrote to President Davis:

> Now I read that Mr. Belin is among six returning basketball lettermen preparing for the nineteen seventy-nine nineteen eighty season. Were the eligibility rules changed? ... Has a grievous clerical error been discovered? I took the liberty last August of bringing Mr. Belin's plight to your attention. I was distressed by the thought that the university and the athletic department might be shirking their moral obligation to the scholastic under-achievers they invite to attend the university and represent it in athletic contests. Now I am distressed by a different possibility. Could you set my mind at ease?[33]

President Davis reported to the Athletic Council that he did not respond to Dr. Coates's letter because of the "press of other duties and events confronting me at the time. I referred the memo to my administrative assistant, Tony Hillerman, for action."[34] Coates received an answer from Hillerman that Belin had earned [bought] three units from Ottawa University for a correspondence short course. When Coates asked for an investigation of the transcript, Hillerman refused and was later quoted as saying that "his brain was not turned on" when Coates asked to see the transcript.[35] Later, Coates became aware that Belin's transcript had arrived 15 days after he had been declared ineligible, and he was not planning to complete additional courses. The transcript also revealed that the player had attended a school in California simultaneous with his enrollment in Coates' summer school course.

The investigation of Belin's transcript and revelation that Ottawa University was selling course credits resulted in UNM declaring six basketball players and three football players immediately ineligible. The local newspapers and some members of the BOR excoriated President Davis for ignoring the Belin eligibility question. Stated the *Albuquerque Journal*, "The standards of behavior sunk to their lowest depths in the University of New Mexico Athletic Department under the administration of Davis. And until the cat was let out of the bag by the FBI, Davis failed in raising those standards…. It's time for someone else to have a crack at it."[36]

The Lobo Booster Club had operated outside of NCAA rules because the football team's record warranted little, if any, scrutiny, and the basketball program appeared clean. It's not known if the president of the university, the athletic director, or the NCAA had investigated this illegal association. A lack of control of any booster club by an institution could result in severe penalties. At the University of San Francisco, the president shut down the basketball program because of booster payment and improper sexual conduct by one of its players. Southern Methodist's football and Kentucky's basketball programs received a death penalty for repeated NCAA infractions, primarily involving boosters.[37] In the case of UNM, the presence of bookies and gamblers in the booster club and close interaction with basketball players was clearly illegal.

The incident that led to the UNM basketball scandal in December 1979 was uncovered by accident. When the New Mexico Organized Crime Task Force (NMOCTF) discovered that bookmakers and gamblers had been using a computer for business that was owned by a company hired by the federal government, the FBI become understandably concerned.[38] The NMOCTF was created in the spring of 1979 to investigate illegal gambling and bookmaking in Albuquerque, including ties to organized crime. The contractor that housed the computer was Sandia National Laboratories, a super-secret company located near Albuquerque that manufactured nuclear weapons. The DOE had subcontracted the company to supply the weapons it needed.[39]

In the course of the gambling investigation, the phone of a known Albuquerque bookie and gambler named Robert McGuire was tapped. The phone monitoring involved no ear listening. One of McGuire's electronically encoded messages had been sent via portable terminal and was received by a computer at Sandia. The subject line was "Data about Gambling."[40] The investigators discovered that Sandia Mechanical Engineer Jerry Shinkle did the local gambling syndicate's homework (predicting the probability of winning a bet on a game given the posted odds, posting spreads, maintaining records, etc.) using the company's computer. Shinkle had a security clearance, but according to Sandia's head of security, the computer accessed by him contained only unclassified material.

FBI and DOE officials wanted to find out how an employee and outsiders could easily access a company computer that had been used by the DOE.[41] A week later, the official in charge of security at Sandia indicated that he had set up a revamped security system that monitored and restricted access to all of the company's computers. Following a period of more wiretaps, officers at the Albuquerque police department, representatives of the State Attorney General's office, and members of the NMOCTF raided 13 Albuquerque homes and businesses, seizing betting slips, sports-line sheets, computer printouts, telephone scramblers, phone lists with coded names, a slot machine, $85,000 in cash, telephone bills, and a safe-deposit box.[42]

The local gambling organization's business operation was not small. During the 1979 NMOCTF's investigation, James Blackmer, a former member of the State Attorney General's staff, testified he had overheard wiretapped conversations between Dr. Lee Farris and Ellenberger. In one conversation, the retired gynecologist-bookmaker-gambler read a list of six football games to the coach, who placed a bet on one or more of those games.[43] Ellenberger and Dr. Farris were close friends, and the former doctor was given a special parking place in the athletic department complex. He also had unlimited access to the Lobos' locker room and was often listed as the official team physician when the team traveled although his specialty was not sport medicine.[44]

Through the Albuquerque police department's continued tap on Dr. Farris' phone, officer Larry Bullard overheard a conversation between Ellenberger and his chief recruiter and assistant coach, Manny Goldstein. The conversation resulted in the eventual downfall of UNM's basketball program.[45] By all accounts, Ellenberger liked Assistant Coach Manny Goldstein's style of high-pressure urban recruiting. Ellenberger sought junior college transfers to maintain the success his predecessor had attained and to fill The Pit with spectators. UNLV's Tarkanian had shown that recruiting African Americans could propel a basketball program to instant renown. Before arriving at UNM, Goldstein had played at Pan American University in Texas, until his eligibility ran out. He then recruited for a year and half at the college and later moved to the University of Southwestern Louisiana (today University of Louisiana, Lafayette). In 1973, the college received a death penalty for committing more than 100 violations, primarily in recruiting. UNM Athletic Director Lavon McDonald indicated that he had checked with the NCAA regarding Goldstein's background before hiring him, specifically involving recruiting violations, and was informed that he was "clean."[46]

Before the beginning of the 1979–1980 season, Ellenberger received a call from Goldstein on Farris's phone regarding the eligibility of Craig Gilbert. The junior college transfer from Santa Barbara, California, did not possess the requisite 48 transferable units and 2.0 grade-point average to be eligible to play (NCAA junior college transfer provisions at the time). Gilbert had been admitted to the university with 40 units accumulated at Santa Barbara City College and Oxnard Junior College.[47] Thus, his basketball scholarship from the university was in violation of NCAA rules. In the wiretapped call, Officer Bullard heard:

> GOLDSTEIN: I got him a degree, an A.A. (Associate of Arts).
> ELLENBERGER: You got him a degree?
> GOLDSTEIN: Yeah, they're gonna put sixteen more hours on the transcript. This is the way they want it…
> ELLENBERGER: And he'll do that?
> GOLDSTEIN: Yeah, he's doing that. I mean we got to give him a little money, but he's doing it.
> ELLENBERGER: Yeah.
> GOLDSTEIN: You know I bought him a degree and that's it.
> ELLENBERGER: Who was that, this Maruca?
> GOLDSTEIN: No, this is Dr. Wooley, the head guy.
> ELLENBERGER: Uh huh.
>   (a bit later)
> GOLDSTEIN: I'm leaving for a recruiting trip. I'm going to be in New Jersey Monday, get an envelope, and mail it myself, special delivery, airmail, and it's being shipped out there … but everything is okay the way I handled them.
>   (Then)
> ELLENBERGER: Ah, yeah, whatever you know, you know.
> GOLDSTEIN: Yeah, I told you, I'm protected.[48]

To clarify the conversation, Goldstein was informing Ellenberger that he'd pulled "the strings" so Gilbert would be awarded an Associate of Arts degree from Oxnard Junior College (out there). The head guy (Registrar Dr. Wooley) needed to be bribed with money to ensure that 16 course units from another college (Mercer Community College in West Windsor, New Jersey) would be transferred to Gilbert's Oxnard transcript, allowing him to obtain a bogus A.A. degree stamped on his transcript that was submitted to UNM's registrar. Goldstein's recruiting trip was in part for the purpose of mailing, with a New Jersey postmark, a stolen transcript, so Oxnard's registrar could include the bought 16 units for the A.A degree. The cost for the forgery was $400. When Goldstein asked Robert Maruca, Oxnard's athletic trainer and soccer coach, why it was so much money, he responded, "It's not for me. It's for Wooley. He has a cocaine habit."[49]

Following the conversation, the FBI obtained a search warrant for Goldstein's East Albuquerque apartment, where they found a folder of academic transcripts, including one for UNM basketball player Andre Logan.[50] An official seal for Mercer Community College that Goldstein had purchased from an Albuquerque printer for creating the embossed imprints seen on players' transcripts were also seized.[51] As the NMOCTF and the FBI continued to investigate Ellenberger, Whisenant, and Goldstein, they remained focused on what had been revealed by wiretaps about drugs and gambling in the basketball program. Subjects of the continuing probe included: the relationship between UNM's coaching staff and local gamblers, Ellenberger's and Whisenant's betting habits, including the head coach's possible indebtedness to bookies, overt use of drugs by UNM's basketball players and the identification of the supplier, the relationship between local gamblers and players, and were the gamblers close to UNM's team connected with organized crime in Las Vegas?[52]

According to Whisenant, it was no secret that gamblers associated with the players and coaches. The assistant coach readily admitted in the *SI* interview with Robert H. Boyle in June 1980 that he estimated 20 or so gamblers, some of whom belonged to the Lobo Club, as his friends, and that "I play golf with them." Asked if he discussed UNM basketball while on the course, Whisenant responded, "I talk with them about anything."[53] Money had steadily flowed from the boosters to the players and typically included amounts of $100 for a good game, $20 for a made free throw, and $20 for a rebound. An informal scale had been created for players to receive money by achieving certain performance goals.[54]

The boosters with access to inside information on UNM's basketball team could make a lot of money on a New Mexico game depending on how their bets were placed. The FBI had not officially investigated Ellenberger's teams for rigging games before the taped Ellenberger-Goldstein conversation. Some of the players, according to Whisenant, were "like alley cats around to get something to eat. I heard they would go out and put the touch on five boosters and end up with one hundred dollars or more in a short time. I tried to stop it by telling those guys not to give money to players unless I okayed it as a legitimate expense … like the dentist."[55] The inference was clear. Was it possible the boosters who gambled on the Lobos were passing part of their winnings to the players? If so, this more than likely blurred the difference between being paid to attend and play at UNM and receiving money from gamblers. In contrast to Ellenberger, Whisenant had been candid about his betting, admitting he regularly wagered with bookies on college and professional football. When asked about Ellenberger's gambling, Whisenant only acknowledged that he and Ellenberger talked about it.[56]

A booster had reported that Whisenant bet about $100 a week, while Ellenberger was known to have bet as much as $700 a week. According to one gambler, Ellenberger's gambling debts ran as high as $4,000.[57] Coaches directly betting with bookies could alert other gamblers about how to bet on a game in a certain way. There was always the possibility of a bookie contacting the university or the media.[58] A former member of the athletic department stated that it was an open secret that Ellenberger and Whisenant were betting on football. Apparently, their betting was so blatant that some university authorities were aware of it. The former member of the department also stated, "We heard about it when Ellenberger was slow to pay a bookie and a couple of boosters came up with cash to square the debt. But Norm stiffed the boosters. Then the word really got around."[59] If boosters were loaning Ellenberger money, the possibility of fixing a game by his coaching strategies was possible. A debt to a gambler or bookie could be forgiven by a winning bet on the Lobos. State investigators and the FBI were also interested in determining whether an Albuquerque politician was supplying drugs to UNM's players and uncovering any relationship between the gamblers and some New Mexico players. Boyle, in the *SI* article, described boosters and players attending a Christmas party at Ellenberger's home in 1977. A guest at the party alleged that a person laid cocaine on a living room coffee table that players freely snorted, similar to what he'd observed after a game.[60] Players in Ellenberger's program reportedly smoked marijuana on a regular basis.

Boyle interviewed Ellenberger, who claimed afterwards that the FBI had exonerated him of any involvement in drugs and betting, a claim that was disputed by the FBI. In fact, an FBI spokesperson reported that nobody in their office had hinted publicly or privately that Ellenberger had been cleared, and they were intensifying the fixing aspect of their investigation. Assistant coach John Whisenant stated in the interview with *SI*, "The prosecution is trying to show the use of cocaine, betting, and point shaving by players and coaches."[61] Ellenberger told Boyle, "The FBI and Grand Jury are all around— in the trees, everywhere—I'll bet they're watching now."[62]

A sportswriter reported that after the Lobos defeated UNLV in January 1979, he observed one of Ellenberger's good friends (possibly Dr. Lee Farris) hand out several $100 bills to Lobo players.[63] If Dr. Farris was distributing the cash as the head of the local gambling ring, the possibility of players playing for gamblers became more of a reality. Cash payments to prospective UNM players were substantiated by Goldstein's testimony in the federal trial involving the three basketball coaches. The assistant admitted under oath that recruits were given $700 to agree to attend UNM and another $700 after their enrollment in the institution (both in violation of NCAA regulations).[64] When a writer approached Ellenberger about the illegal payments, he reportedly "acted dumb about them."[65]

In January 1980, New Mexico's attorney general announced that he was investigating the participation of some coaches in point shaving and gambling involving UNM's basketball team. Michael Francke, deputy attorney general, stated that his office was not "ruling out any games that have been played as far as point shaving is concerned."[66] The FBI and state investigators were closely scrutinizing three games. The first was a 90–85 loss to Cal State Fullerton in the NCAA tournament's first round in 1978, which was played in Tempe, Arizona. UNM was favored by 16 points.[67] Any bet on New Mexico not to cover the spread or to lose would have been a winner.

Michael Cooper, who went on to star with the Los Angeles Lakers, played on the 1978 Lobos team and was suspicious of Ellenberger's coaching during the game. He recalled:

> The substitution was kind of funny. Marv Johnson and me were the leading scorers on the team, and between us we only got four points in the second half of the game. I figured at the time, Norm didn't think we're playing up to our potential, although he never said anything. He had us in and out, in and out, like a yo-yo thing. I'd go in, he'd yank me out. Same with Marv. It was like he didn't want us to get warm. And then there was Jimmy Allen [the starting center]. The first ten minutes of the game he was dominating. The next thing I knew he was sitting next to me. After the game he [Norm] didn't feel nothing, and that was strange too. We were thirteen and one in the conference, and when we lost to Utah—after we had the thing all wrapped up—he was in tears. After the Cal Fullerton game, he gave us a long story, but I could feel he did feel nothing. I mean so many things about it were funny.[68]

Ellenberger responded to Boyle's interview about the Cal Fullerton game by stating he did not believe Cooper said those things. Whisenant also believed the loss was attributable to both his and Ellenberger's underestimating Cal Fullerton and the subpar performance of Cooper and other players on the team. However, neither coach discussed his rationale for the jerking, in-and-out substitutions of Cooper and Johnson and the reasons center Jimmy Allen was removed from the game. Also, there was no evidence the three players were talked to by the coaches for purposes of correcting strategic mistakes and giving reasons they were not inserted back into the game quickly.

Another suspected fixed game was the 78–58 loss to San Diego State in January 1976. The play of one of UNM's best players, according to a university official, was atrocious. The *San Diego Union* reported in 1978 that the FBI was investigating possible point shaving in that game and had interviewed former San Diego State Coach Tim Vezie. The third suspected game involved the favored Lobos in February 1997, when Ellenberger ordered his team into a ten-minute slowdown in a game they lost 94–84 to Utah. A UNM official indicated that Ellenberger's reason for the strategy was to slow the tempo of the game. According to the official, that seemed "like bullshit."[69]

The state investigators, NMOCTF, and FBI did not publicly release any information involving collected evidence of fixed UNM games and ties to organized crime in Las Vegas or elsewhere. However, it would be expected that anyone who was interviewed about fixed UNM games would not readily implicate others and face the possibility of testifying in court about any connection to organized crime. That might lead to a quick and unannounced burial. The FBI most likely had not collected enough evidence involving UNM's team in the act of fixing a game to bring charges to a grand jury.[70] In December 1979, President Davis dismissed Ellenberger, stating that the coach's actions constituted "willful and grossly incompetent conduct injurious to the University of the New Mexico basketball program," the rationale for the dismissal.[71] Goldstein submitted his resignation through his attorney, who sent President Davis a letter. Whisenant had already resigned.

Davis' statement that Ellenberger injured only the basketball program was conveniently self-serving. It was during Ellenberger's seven years at UNM that the student enrollment was decreasing, as pointed out by Regent Calvin Horn in his book on the history of UNM.[72] The inference underlying Davis's rationale for firing Ellenberger was that he was a "good university watchdog," and it was the coach's "crookedness" that was responsible for his dismissal and any collateral damage to the university. But it was the president who had not placed any controls or oversight on the athletic program that enabled Ellenberger and the two coaches to conduct criminal business in addition to committing 92 NCAA violations. Davis suddenly developed temporary amnesia when he was hired at UNM in 1975. In 1961, he had witnessed how Sonny Grandelius and his staff at the University of Colorado had committed so many NCAA infractions that the university had no choice but to fire him.[73]

The experience at Colorado placed Davis squarely in the middle of a scandal that should have at least alerted him to Ellenberger's misdeeds. The president had attended most of the home basketball games. It's naive to believe that when he observed players running up and down the court at The Pit, it did not cross his mind that some of them may not have been qualified to enter the university. Later, at a state trial involving Ellenberger, deposed Athletic Director McDonald testified that Davis would regularly meet with the president and discuss which NCAA regulations were being violated in UNM's basketball program.[74] The sheer number of violations would hardly be a mystery to anyone with inside knowledge of UNM athletics. After finding that the Lobo Club lacked oversight and institutional control and that some gambling members were cozy bedfellows with basketball players, could President Davis not have put an end to the activities of the booster club? A short walk from his box at The Pit to the locker room would have exposed the president to activities that even a casual observer could not miss. During Ellenberger's trials, Davis pled ignorance of any wrongdoing in the most visible public program in the state of New Mexico.[75]

Ellenberger's and Whisenant's federal trial began in June 1980 in Roswell, New Mexico. The federal grand jury had indicted Ellenberger of plotting with Whisenant and Goldstein to use the telephone and United States mail to provide phony transfer credits to two UNM basketball players, Andre Logan and Craig Gilbert. The scheme included counterfeiting transcripts from New Jersey's Mercer County Community College. Ellenberger was also accused of sending Goldstein to Los Angeles for the purpose of bribing employees at Oxnard College. According to the grand jury, "all this constituted an attempt to defraud the NCAA, Western Athletic Conference, and New Mexico's Admissions Office concerning the eligibility of two players."[76] Ellenberger was indicted on five counts of wire fraud, one count of mail fraud, and one count of interstate travel in aid of racketeering enterprises—a total of seven counts. Whisenant was charged with four counts of wire fraud. Goldstein had turned state's evidence and admitted to one count of wire fraud. Albuquerque printer William Blackstad pled guilty to one count of mail fraud for embossing the Mercer Community College seal.[77]

Assistant coach and head recruiter Manny Goldstein was the trial's star witness. His testimony began by describing how Ellenberger, Whisenant, and he met at an Albuquerque pancake house to solve the eligibility problems of Craig Gilbert and Andre Logan. At the meeting, Goldstein showed both coaches a blank Mercer Community College transcript that he'd stolen from the college. Ellenberger pointed out that the transcript needed the seal that Blackstad could make at his printing company. The forged transcript was given to Ellenberger, who in turn delivered it to the Registrar's Office at UNM.[78] Logan became instantly eligible in November 1978.

At the trial, Goldstein recounted the process involved in converting Gilbert into an eligible player for the 1979–1980 season. The maneuver required some traveling, first to Oxnard College (north of Los Angeles) to determine if the institution's registrar would accept the Mercer Community College's bogus transcript with the fake embossed seal. After receiving assurance from the college's trainer and soccer coach, Robert Maruca, that it would be accepted, he flew to New Jersey to ensure that the transcript's envelope would bear that state's postmark. The recorded conversation between Ellenberger and Goldstein was introduced into evidence and played for the jury three times. Goldstein also admitted under oath that he offered one player $700 who chose to attend UNM and the same amount when he enrolled.[79]

Next on the witness stand was Ellenberger. Defense attorney Leon Taylor's goal was to convince the jury that the head coach had been unaware of academic matters related to eligibility, credits for courses, transfer units, academic majors, transcripts, or the academic progress of the players. In essence, academic matters were not his responsibility. According to Taylor, academic policies at UNM, Mercer Community College, and Oxnard College were not set by him (Ellenberger).[80] Under questioning by Taylor as to the purpose of the UNM program, Ellenberger's response was that it was designed to provide deprived inner-city youth with the skills necessary to improve their ascribed social and economic status. By what justification would so many UNM players be allowed to enter a program when in some cases they were reading and writing at the fourth-grade level? Ellenberger's testimony in part:

ELLENBERGER: Now and then in our recruitment of athletes, in order to get the type of athlete that we need, football, basketball or whatever, at the University of New Mexico, to make the program that good, to make that property fill the seats, to make the program pay the bills of the university, we will go find a downtrodden young man, and some of the best people I know have come from the gutter someplace.

Q: When talking to people at Oxnard, what had [you] meant by asking "Can you get it done?" or words to that effect?

ELLENBERGER: Are they going to take care of Craig, so that he can enter into the University of New Mexico and do the only thing that he ever wanted to do in his life, and that's play basketball and have a chance to be a human being.

Q: What persuaded [you] to go along with the forging of the transcripts and the manufacture of a false Mercer Community College embossed seal?

ELLENBERGER: One of my assistants, or both, or whoever was involved said: Hey, we have got a deal that can fix this thing. We are going to have a seal made. And I can remember that because it ... that ... that thing right there appalled me ... the idea that you could manufacture something like that, to do an act like that, that ... appalled me, and I said, hey, whoa. I said absolutely not. And talking about manufacturing a transcript. Well, the thing went on within the next hour or whatever, and through the insistence and through them brings it down to cold facts that, hey, we can help Andre. We can give him an opportunity.[81]

In objectively analyzing Ellenberger's tortured testimony and his labeling of some recruited players as "downtrodden," it appeared to be a disingenuous attempt to convince a jury that the UNM basketball program was providing the only possible road to leaving an impoverished environment. In reality, once a downtrodden athlete entered the UNM program, he would in all likelihood remain at his ascribed socioeconomic status and maybe regress even lower than before he entered the college.

UNM Regent Calvin Horn had pointed out that for athletes at UNM, whether they wanted to be educated or not, the university offered no mechanisms to ensure that they attained the academic skills that would lead to the possibility of elevating their social status.[82] The university had not implemented any remedial programs for students who entered collegiate life unprepared to complete college-level courses in English, mathematics, or other subjects. In fact, because of the demands of UNM's big-time program, any basketball player who did want to become educated found it impossible because of the time devoted to the sport. The athletes were, for all intents and purposes, powerless in obtaining any semblance of an education, as the university set up easy courses or bought grades to assure continued eligibility.

A basketball scholarship, in theory, is supposed to provide an opportunity to obtain a useful education. Ellenberger's admitted ignorance and lack of responsibility regarding basketball players' academic achievement sent a clear message: the basketball players were there to generate a profit. The development of useful academic skills was too complex to comprehend for players at a young age. By dismissing players as lacking the ability to obtain an education by circumventing eligibility rules with bought and bogus courses, UNM was hiring players simply because of their physical skills. The players were involuntarily relinquishing their opportunity, regardless of whether or not they had a desire to obtain an education. Players' performances were filling The Pit, and NCAA scholarships made them in every sense an employee of the university. The employee-players were generating money, big salaries for the coaches, and revenue to pay for the entire athletic program, while they were asked to accept less than a minimum wage. Added to the educational handicap was the risk of players committing a criminal act if they knowingly rigged games for the gamblers who, according to many observers, passed out money to players.[83]

At UNM, where was the line drawn between accepting money for playing versus accepting money for fixing a final score? In these circumstances, accepting money from the university and booster-gamblers blurred the line between NCAA violations and conspiring to fix games for gamblers. Testimony by Ellenberger that his program needed to cheat to recruit and maintain players' eligibility reflected the mentality that college basketball was a business, and players were more like talented musicians who otherwise might not have chosen to attend college. Ellenberger testified that the basketball program could not operate within the guidelines of the NCAA. If he and his staff were cheating in recruiting and buying bogus eligibility, the recruited players were learning that both sides of the law were working together—if they were illegally recruited and made money for the university, the employer (university) would dismiss the unlawfulness.

Ellenberger's attorney, Leon Taylor, argued that the university had pressured the basketball program to produce a winning team and abandoned the coaches when they were caught cheating. But regardless of where the blame lay, the forging of transcripts or bogus units, according to Taylor, hurt nobody. The only harm or crime was that Ellenberger placed a piece of paper or transcript in the mail. Taylor stated to the jury, "So what if the transcript was changed? There ain't no crime here. Who was hurt in this case? Did he injure anyone? Did he destroy anyone's life?"[84] The prosecutor in the case, U.S. Attorney Don Svet, argued that all the evidence the government expected to show was presented. Svet informed the jury that Ellenberger knew about the forgery but had not attempted to prevent it. He also pointed out that the threshold for conviction in mail fraud was not in successfully executing the mail fraud. Instead, it was whether or not the mail fraud was executed, regardless of its outcome. The prosecutor asked the jurors to direct their attention to the case evidence and not to some outlandish allegations "that everyone in the university is a crook."[85]

The jury's verdict in the federal case was not guilty on all counts. One juror believed the prosecution had not presented sufficient evidence. She stated that her impression was "that Norm didn't know what was going on."[86] Although the Ellenberger-Goldstein tape was played for the jury three times during the trial, she may have not heard or fully understood the conversation. The four counts of wire fraud against Whisenant were dropped following the trial.

The next trial would reveal more criminality by Ellenberger and Goldstein. The state trial began in late June 1981, before Judge Philip Baiamonte in Albuquerque. Ellenberger's attorney again was Leon Taylor. Before the trial, Taylor had successfully convinced the lower court to dismiss the 22 felony charges, based on the manner in which the title of the statutes had been labeled by the New Mexico legislature. The Attorney General appealed the decision before the state's Supreme Court, who remanded the case back to the lower court for trial.[87] In this case, Ellenberger was charged with 22 fourth-degree felony counts involving the filing of false travel vouchers and fraud. Each felony carried a minimum 18-month prison sentence. The prosecution argued that Ellenberger, with the assistance of a girlfriend who worked at a travel agency, defrauded the people of New Mexico of almost $10,000. Vouchers paid by the university, but not used, were returned to the travel agency for refunds. The evidence presented at the trial included Ellenberger billing the university for recruiting and speaking trips that he either did not take or were paid for by an industrial firm. The amount of money, including booked flights that were never taken and paid to Ellenberger, was tallied on a blackboard.[88] In total, 100 UNM and travel agent records were introduced and accepted as evidence.

On the witness stand, Ellenberger indicated that he did not remember when or where he traveled. When asked if President Davis knew about the NCAA violations, he firmly replied, "of course." Assistant Attorney General Stephen Westheimer argued that the numerous NCAA violations presented by the defense were designed to obfuscate the real issue of the crimes of fraud and the filing of false vouchers. The prosecutor also contended that casting aspersions on the reputation of UNM's administrators was not the main issue in the case. Westheimer stated, "This case has little to do with NCAA violations. This is a case where a former state employee was being prosecuted for fraud and filing false travel vouchers."[89]

In this case, Attorney Leon Taylor's strategy was to convince the jury that the UNM president should be on trial, not Ellenberger. This reasoning was based on the theory that the NCAA rules breached by Ellenberger had not been crimes or unlawful. The money that Ellenberger had received for traveling, and not used, was placed in a secret fund to be used at the discretion of the head coach to assist basketball players. In essence, the coach kept none of the money. Taylor also argued that Ellenberger had run a financially successful, winning program that was in accordance with the wishes of UNM President Davis. Stated Taylor, "Davis wanted the Lobo basketball revenues so badly that he was willing to allow Ellenberger to manipulate the travel fund to facilitate under-the-table benefits for Lobo ballplayers in violation of NCAA rules."[90]

The defense's star witness was Lavon McDonald, who testified under oath that Davis had periodically met with him. During these meetings, McDonald had been advised by the president as to which NCAA regulations had been violated in the basketball program. In terms of buying academic credit for athletes, McDonald informed the jury that President Davis was aware of this practice. On July 6, 1981, the jury's verdict found Ellenberger guilty on 21 of the 22 counts of filing false vouchers and fraud. The only charge for which he was found innocent involved Ellenberger cheating assistant coach Charlie Harrison out of $3,000. This was the amount the booster club had given to Harrison to supplement the meager $1,000 salary that the university had allocated for the position.[91]

Two days later, Judge Baiamonte issued the lightest possible sentence to Ellenberger. The judge's feathery tap of Ellenberger's wrist led jury foreman and truck driver Clifford Maricle, when asked about the judge's decision, to state, "I nearly fell out of my chair."[92] The judge deferred Ellenberger's sentence for one year with the stipulation that he would be subjected to unsupervised probation. After one year, all charges would be dropped if he did not violate the terms of his probation. The judge's rationale, when asked about his decision for not punishing Ellenberger:

> The coach was only a cog in the machine of college basketball. Everyone looked the other way as the rules and laws were bent and broken. The real hypocrisy is with the colleges and universities across the country that maintain and establish professional ball clubs while purporting to operate under amateur rules. I'm being asked to sentence a man because he got caught, not because his conduct was unacceptable. The question is how fair is it to incarcerate a man for doing what almost everyone in the community wanted him to do—namely, win basketball games at whatever cost. All the money [taken by Ellenberger] was used by the defendant to keep athletes happy or recruit them in the first place.[93]

The decision by Judge Baiamonte was criticized by New Mexico Attorney General Jeff Bingaman, who stated, "Would the rest of us have been dealt with so lightly if we had committed twenty-one felonies? I felt the judge should have ordered restitution."[94] Utah coach Jerry Pimm believed Ellenberger's conviction would have a long-term positive effect on the coaching profession. "If others are trying to run their programs in a similar way, they'd better take heed," stated Pimm.[95] In Pimm's opinion, Ellenberger had received a coach's version of the "death penalty."

Goldstein was convicted of one count of fraud and one count of filing a false public voucher. He was fined $1,368, ordered to pay $648 restitution to UNM, and placed on probation for 18 months by District Court Judge John Brennan. His sentence had been harsher than Ellenberger's. In 1983, just after the NCAA finals were held at The Pit, Ellenberger was asked by a *New York Times* writer to assess the Lobogate scandal. He commented, "We broke some NCAA rules and that was the extent of it!"[96] Just as President Richard Nixon had never come to understand that Watergate was wrong, Ellenberger still had not grasped the seriousness of his action. He was found guilty of 21 felonies and could have received a sentence of one to five years for each count.

New Mexico head coach Norm Ellenberger, ca. 1978. He oversaw one of the most scandalous basketball programs in the history of the NCAA (courtesy *Albuquerque Journal*).

Judge Baiamonte's observations involving the nature of college basketball reflected the judge's naiveté regarding college sports. Instead of ordering a critical and impartial examination of the UNM basketball program and protecting a vital resource of the state (the university), he placed the blame for the misdeeds on UNM's administration and community—in essence, ignoring the basketball program's negative impact on the entire university and state. The judge's implication was that neither the NCAA nor the institution was capable of preventing athletic corruption in programs that enjoyed the blessing of its state's citizens.

However, not all state judges agreed with Judge Baiamonte's narrowness regarding the nature of big-time college athletics. In January 1982, at the University of Minnesota, a basketball player who had played three years for the Gophers was denied admission into the university program without "due process." The judge's ruling on behalf of the player included his observation that the responsibility of athletes to succeed academically rested squarely on the institution. A court in Minnesota thus established that an institution recruiting athletes solely for the purpose of playing should be held accountable for them receiving an education as a matter of law. Judge Miles W. Lord stated:

> The court is not saying that athletes are incapable of scholarship; however, they are given little incentive to be scholars and few persons care how the student performs academically, including many of the athletes themselves. The exceptionally talented student athlete is led to perceive [that] the basketball, football, and other athletic programs serve as farm teams and proving grounds for professional sports leagues. It may well be true that a good academic program for the athlete is made virtually impossible by the demands of their sport at the college level. If this situation causes harm to the university, it is because they have fostered it, and the institution rather than the individual should suffer the consequences.[97]

Ellenberger's and his coaches' assertions that they were victimized by the university and found it impossible to adhere to NCAA rules would be followed by other coaches who were caught violating NCAA rules and civil laws. In just over eight years following the UNM scandal, a criminal investigation would be conducted involving allegations that North Carolina State basketball players had fixed games during the 1987–1988 season. College basketball once again demonstrated its propensity for ignoring previous gambling scandals.

6

SMU and UNLV Scandals

Boosters Hijacking
College Programs

By the early 1980s, revenue from television, attendance, institutional budgets, post-season appearances, and boosters had become the main sources of funding for college sports. College athletics programs were increasingly relying on boosters to support financial budgets because of increasing deficits, costs and inflation. The number of booster-related questionable activities increased, including excessive allowable payments to athletes and payoffs in the form of jobs, automobiles, and other favors for parents of promising athletes. Recruiting violations involved extravagant entertainment of recruits, payments for travel, and questionable financial arrangements with coaches.

Since the first NCAA penalties were imposed by the organization's Infractions Committee, 1,164 cases were investigated by the committee between 1952 and 1981. Of that number, approximately one-half were booster-related. One of the issues that concerned the NCAA and institutions during that time period was relegating the control of the athletic programs to the boosters. In a number of instances, this loss of control rendered an institution powerless in controlling NCAA violations and other abuses.

Southern Methodist University: A Failure of the NCAA's Death Penalty

SMU began playing football in 1915, hiring Vanderbilt All-American Ray Morrison as their first coach. After winning two games in two years, Morrison was fired by the president, who reportedly told him, "Pressures from downtown make it necessary for me to ask for your resignation."[1] Since its inception, Dallas businessmen had always played a major role in the affairs of the institution. In 1920, the downtown business community had grumbled about the university football program's mediocrity and found an ally when SMU hired its second president, Hiram Bill Boaz. Soon, SMU began to recruit football players in a manner similar to most colleges, as the *Carnegie Report* would cite almost ten years later. Recruiting excesses in football included outright payments from boosters, ignoring admission standards, and operating a semi-professional program.[2]

In the spring of 1922, the Southwestern Conference (SWC) passed a new set of unusually strict regulations. Material persuasion and recruiting a person only for athletic talent were deemed impermissible. SMU recruits who were earlier promised four-year football scholarships because of their football talents would, according to the new standards, be in violation of conference rules. The faculty representatives of the SWC at their annual meeting in December 1922 issued a report that in part stated, "[SMU was] shot through and through with questionable athletics."[3] They recommended the college's suspension from the SWC. The 4–3 vote fell one short of the required two-thirds majority. SMU had saved itself from conference expulsion.

In response to the unfavorable report, the faculty recommended that the institution lose its accreditation with the Southern Association, the organization to which SMU belonged.[4] The SWC investigation was followed by the SMU Board of Trustees, the theoretical governing body of the institution, ordering the Faculty Athletic Committee (FAC) to complete an internal investigation of the football program. The introduction to the report, issued in February 1923, presented a disturbing picture of the role of football at the college:

> Football is becoming a huge and highly specialized business and the amateur element characteristic of college athletics is in danger of disappearing from it. The function of the university is not to provide a spectacle for the entertainment of outside crowds, but to interest as many students as possible in healthful outdoor sports. If football is essential for purposes of entertainment, it should be professionalized outside of the university ... the advertising value of football is undoubted, but it brings to train some harmful effects and it should never be allowed to take precedence over the physical, moral and intellectual needs of the student body.[5]

The committee voted 3–2 to accept the FAC majority report. The minority report of the two dissenting members, coach Ray Morrison and E. H. Jones, professor and chairman of the Mathematics Department, found no abuses in the football program. In declaring two athletes ineligible in accordance with institutional and SWC regulations, the majority report appeared to be striving to maintain a semblance of amateurism, which by the 1920s had become no more than a dream. The faculty overwhelmingly approved the FAC report by a 44–21 vote.[6]

Dallas Judge and one of SMU's founding fathers, Joseph E. Cockrell, presented an 84-page rebuttal to the majority report for distribution to the SMU community. In the report, Cockrell argued that decisions affecting the good name of the university and morality of any individual declared athletically or otherwise ineligible for extracurricular activities should be subject to critical assessment. Also, the process should include external and objective scrutiny. The judge proposed that in certain instances, a prospective student could be admitted to SMU as a "special admit," or, if over 21, "adult admit."[7] The two practices were commonplace in colleges that were sponsoring big-time football programs in the 1920s.

Cockrell devoted a substantial part of the report to Glen Huff and Elvin Smith, the two players declared ineligible by the majority report. The two had served in the military during World War I, exhibited crude behavior on campus, and according to testimony taken by the committee, "were not academically inclined."[8] But they could win football games. In the end, Cockrell's suggestion that SMU's athletic programs should be bound by the strictest guidelines of the Methodist teachings was a worthy vision for athletics at SMU. By 1923, it was too late. The judge's dedication to using sports as a worthy moral teacher was trumped by the financial exigencies that drove football programs in the 1920s.

The battle for the "heart and soul" of the university in 1923 would be repeated a number of times over the next 65 years. What mattered to the business leaders of Dallas, football boosters, and Board of Trustees (BOT) was control of the administration, faculty, and football and basketball programs.[9] In less than one year, the "downtowners" could boast of creating a football program they wanted and had paid for. The program captured its first (SWC) title in 1923 and another one in 1926.[10] In 1928, 700 boosters and the team and coaches traveled by train for five days to West Point, garnering national attention in an intersectional game against Army.

After Morrison was rehired as the freshman coach in 1920, he received a second chance with the varsity in 1922 when the head coach was fired.[11] Morrison's affinity for passing and trick plays almost upset the Cadets, and the Mustangs began to receive national attention from offensive strategists.[12] Featuring an aerial show, SMU began playing before large crowds at Nebraska, Notre Dame, Navy, Syracuse, and UCLA. In the days before wire service polls, winning the Knute Rockne Trophy represented a legitimate basis for claiming the national championship. In 1935, the Mustangs won the SWC title by defeating a Sammy Baugh–led Texas Christian University. Quarterback Bob Finley's fourth quarter, fourth down, 39-yard desperation pass to Bobby Wilson was caught for the winning touchdown in a game broadcast by NBC coast-to-coast.[13] The Mustangs also won a trip to the Rose Bowl, subsequently losing to Stanford, 7–0. Afterward, SMU was awarded the Rockne Trophy. But the program had been created at the expense of academics and almost bankrupted the institution.

In 1926, Ownby Stadium was built on SMU's campus, with $10,000 donated toward its construction by alumnus Jacob Ownby. The venue seated 17,000, and it was assumed winning football teams would easily generate gate receipts to retire the ten-year, $175,000 debt.[14] The mortgage installments were $10,000 a year, including a lump sum balance due after ten years. In 1931, the SMU BOT was informed by its president:

> The impression that college athletics are quite profitable has not been substantiated by our experience at Southern Methodist University. Since 1923, our athletics have produced a debit balance every year with the exception of 1925.[15]

In 1930, Morrison had signed a five-year contract at an annual salary of $12,000. By comparison, the university president was paid $10,000 a year and a full professor $3,500. Two years later as the Depression worsened, a 20 percent across-the-board cut was ordered, followed by a 50 percent, three-month reduction in 1933. Because Morrison was under a long-term contract, neither cut applied to him. After the second round of cuts in 1933, Morrison was earning 60 percent more than the president and approximately five times as much as the highest-paid professor.[16] These numbers were not uncommon in big-time football programs during that time period or today.

SMU's governing structure before 1963 consisted of the BOT, composed of several standing bishops of the South-Central jurisdiction of the Methodist Church and 56 additional members. Forty-eight of the additional members consisted of church leaders selected by church conferences.[17] Whatever external influence resided in the business community, that power was kept within bounds by the authority of the Methodist Church. The adoption of the "Master Plan for Southern Methodist University in 1963" erased those boundaries. In 1967, the non-bishop membership of the board was expanded to 75. These individuals were selected by the BOT and subject to approval of the church.[18] A 21-member Board of Governors (BOG) had been created after 1923. In effect, the BOG administered the affairs of the university through a six-person Executive Committee which became the ruling power of the institution.

The reins of power at SMU were taken out of the hands of the church and transferred to a self-perpetuating body controlled by lay persons. The concept of creating a BOG based on larger representation from the community-at-large made sense from the perspective of diversification. Publicly, few saw the board as radically new. "The Board of Governors will continue to be appointed by the Board of Trustees, report to the trustees, and derive its authority from the Board of Trustees," stated the Master Plan. "This is consistent with the function of the former executive committee; the only change is one in name."[19]

In time, the 21-member BOG grew beyond expectations. For two decades, a few of its wealthiest members assumed control of SMU's athletic program, faculty, and administration, including the president and BOT. This era ended in scandal. As enrollment and academic stature grew, so did a football program that was shut down by the NCAA in 1986 because of repeated infractions.[20] From 1967 to 1987, three men served as chairmen of the BOG: two-term Texas Republican Governor Bill Clements, co-founder of an international drilling and pipeline construction company named SEDCO; Bobby Stewart, chairman of one of the three largest banks in Texas; and Ed Cox, an independent Texas oilman described in *Forbes* as "perceived as being richer than God."[21] Discreetly, the three men ran SMU as their private domain. They were the CEOs of the powerful BOG, the architects of the payoff system in football, and the crisis managers when the NCAA became interested in the program's later success and possible NCAA infractions.[22]

A harbinger of how the BOG would control the leadership, administration, and football program occurred in 1972, when incoming president Paul Hardin fired head coach Hayden Fry. Recording only three winning seasons out of 11, Fry's fate was decided when a faculty athletic committee uncovered evidence of new violations—the second time during Fry's tenure in Dallas.[23] Dave Smith, Hayden Fry's successor in 1973, employed a common practice at SMU and big-time programs—$100 booster handshakes and financial rewards for good plays such as interceptions, fumble recoveries, or completed passes.[24]

The SMU president believed he was obligated by SWC and NCAA bylaws to report Smith's infractions and place the institution at the mercy of the conference and national organization.[25] In a letter to BOG chairman Ed Cox, Hardin outlined a plan for opening up the decision-making at the institution by changing the composition of the BOG. Not unexpectedly, Cox rejected the plan.[26] The sports ethos of the institution and SWC did not fit the president's vision of the role of football at Highland Park. "I'm not properly worshipful of the great god Football," Hardin stated. "We are a community of scholars, not a farm club for professional football and basketball."[27] The crisis was contained within the board in 1972 and 1973. In 1986, it was not.

In 1975, when the SMU job became available, every big-time coach who was approached turned it down. Lou Holtz had accepted the job the previous time it was available, but changed his mind. Johnny Majors and Hank Stram expressed no interest. In a rare move, SMU officials selected a successful Division II coach who was promoted for the job by his two former bosses, Dallas Scouting Director Gil Brandt and Cowboys President Tex Schramm.[28] Ron Meyer, who had converted the University of Nevada, Las Vegas program into a winner, "would have crawled to Dallas on his hands and knees to get the job," stated one individual familiar with the hiring.[29]

SMU had entered the SWC money game late in the 1970s because it had fallen behind other SWC football programs that ignored NCAA rules by paying its players. Meyer would change that beginning in 1976 by out-recruiting SMU's rivals and paying its players. Houston's Kashmere High assistant Richard Frank stated:

> Meyer was flashy, flamboyant, well dressed. He was wearing clothes kids in this neighborhood could relate to—a pretty leather jacket with a turtleneck and a diamond ring or two; they could relate to that. Or a nice, bright, pretty sport coat with an expensive tie and shirt. He didn't come in looking like a hen. He came in looking like a rooster. As the kids would say, he was clean.[30]

Whatever Meyer's ambitions were in ascending the coaching ladder, he was aware that money was needed to exceed the prevailing payoff system existing in the SWC. The new coach crafted a sliding scale payroll that was commonplace in the 1970s in almost all big-time college football and basketball programs. A formula was created that awarded money for extraordinary performances such as the most tackles, interceptions, or touchdowns. "We'll take care of you" was the mantra of the SMU recruiters, as it was among its competitors in the SWC. By the time Meyer accepted the New England Patriots head coaching position in 1981, NCAA's investigators were repeatedly visiting Dallas. In the minds of one Mustangs booster, this was because:

> The NCAA investigators can jump on a plane and be down there (Dallas) in an hour and fifteen minutes. And these guys, these young guys they got workin' for them, all like to go to the joints in Dallas. And they party there. Have a hell of a time. They love it. There's not another big city like it in the world. They go there and chase girls, drink whiskey and have a good time. Why go to College Station [Texas A&M] when you can go there and have a big time. So, it's happy hunting grounds. They just love it. I been out with 'em. The ones that were investigating me, too. I know the girls they were going with.[31]

The boosters' strategy involving the continuing NCAA investigations was an attempt to ignore the payment system that Meyer had implemented after becoming SMU's head coach. After future governor Bill Clements began a three-year term as the BOG chair in 1983, President Donald Shields complained about the payments to him. He was told to "calm down and not be so righteous." Clements told the President in 1985, "stay out of it and go run the university" after Shields again expressed his misgivings about the illegal payments.[32]

By 1986, SMU's program had been in the wrong place at the wrong time as far as the NCAA's ruling powers were concerned. In the booster-run world of the SWC in the 1970s and 1980s, any attempts to match the success of the football programs at the University of Texas and Arkansas reinforced what boosters at the other SWC schools believed and practiced. Paying players was necessary for building and sustaining a successful football program.[33] The Byers-dictated NCAA was not about to snoop into the two programs that perennially played for the conference title, bringing TV money into the conference, institutions, and NCAA coffers.

In 1975, the Supreme Court had upheld a lower court decision in the *University of Georgia v. NCAA* case that football programs were the property of the institutions, which individually could negotiate contracts with the television networks without sharing the profits with the NCAA[34] Critics have alleged that Byers and the NCAA reacted to the court's attack on their perceived absolute power by seeking a convenient victim to send a message— "we will still rule college sports with an iron fist."[35]

By 1986, Division I abuses had become so widespread that if a dart was thrown at a map of big-time college programs, its landing would have marked an athletic program working hard to conceal major abuses. The talk among the college athletic establishment was that the SMU program had risen from the ashes with booster payoffs. The "slush fund" was the source, and the paymasters were Assistant Athletic Director Henry Lee Parker and Athletic Director Bob Hitch. From whom and where the payments came was almost impossible to track, as the money was dispensed in cash, cars, clothes, and direct payments to the athletes.[36] Despite at least five previous NCAA investigations and a slew of penalties, including probation, the NCAA enforcement staff could never find the smoking gun or anyone to admit receiving money from the payroll at the Dallas institution.[37] Remarkably, given the amount of illegal payments the players received during the head coaching stints of Ron Meyer and Bobby Collins, what the NCAA's investigators had uncovered up this point was no more than a misdemeanor by today's standards.

SMU's illegal payment system was publicly exposed by two players who never played a down for SMU. David Stanley was a highly sought-after recruit from Angleton, Texas, and had been admitted to a rehabilitation facility for drug treatment. Pittsburgh, Pennsylvania's Sean Stopperich was offered $5,000 as a recruiting bonus, regular payments, and a job for his father in Dallas.[38] Both individuals were willing to talk plenty to NCAA investigators.

Stanley, in a television interview in the fall of 1986, admitted receiving $52,000 after the university was placed on probation in August 1985 for recruiting violations.[39]

At a spring 1985 meeting at Clements's SEDCO office, a new strategy was devised to placate the NCAA Infractions Committee. SMU would admit to certain violations and blame a few "out of control boosters" as the main culprits, including millionaire Sherwood Blount, as responsible for the latest allegations of paying players.[40] The "Naughty Nine" had to formally disassociate themselves from any contact with the university for varying lengths of time, some for a lifetime.[41] Informally, the few had received a booster version of the "death penalty." In that same year, the NCAA placed SMU on probation for three years and banned the institution from bowl appearances for two years, and prohibited from appearing on live television for one year.[42] Future Texas governor and BOG chair Bill Clements had informed the NCAA Infractions Committee in 1985 that he would control the cheating at SMU. In effect, he attributed the institutional cheating to the nine rogue boosters and informed the NCAA that he would stop the payments. But 21 players were still on the payroll.[43] In the interest of concealing the payments, Clements rolled the dice and approved of Athletic Director Bill Hitch continuing the payments through December 1986. But Stanley was there on Dallas television station WFAA-TV in November 1986, confessing that the payments had not stopped. The television station displayed envelopes with SMU insignia and the initials of assistant athletic director Henry Lee Parker.[44]

In a plea bargain with the NCAA, Hitch informed investigators of the payment scheme. The agreement stipulated that no other individuals would be interviewed. Clements had "crapped out" on his roll of the dice. The football program was shut down in 1986 pursuant to the repeat offender rule recently passed by the NCAA in June 1985.[45] Two major rules violations in five years merited a death penalty for one year, including no recruiting, practices, or games, and no home games the second year. SMU chose not to field a team a year after the penalty year. Hitch, Parker, and Head Coach Bobby Collins were awarded a total of $863,013 in a settlement with the institution.[46]

In the end, few of the SMU boosters were willing to share their wealth for altruistic reasons. Some of them saw the appointment to the BOT or BOG as a way to join an elitist group of individuals with whom they could cut business deals while simultaneously gaining and sustaining notoriety through a university. Some, like Clements, were looking to increase their political capital. Others, like Blount, wanted to put their hooks into the 18- and 19-year-olds as a way to eventually become their agents when they became eligible and negotiate contracts with professional franchises. In fact, Blount and

Texas Christian's head booster would meet yearly and conduct their own draft of the most talented high school football players in the Southwest region to contact as prospective clients.[47]

At SMU, the "money boys" were careful to protect the Texas governor's involvement in the payoff scheme as well as themselves. During Clements' second term, the scandal hung over his administration like a vulture circling an animal about to die. Only after the SMU questions continued to dog Clements' administration did he come clean and apologize for his role in the scandal.[48] The SMU scandal had compromised Clements' credibility with a public that had grown weary of dishonest public officials. On the record, none of the moneyed contributors to the "slush fund" were accused of gambling on SMU or other games.

How about the players? Did the payments support wagering on sports including for or against their own team? That was possible, but the NCAA investigators were not asking. The booster-related events at SMU had demonstrated to the world of commercialized college sports that money could buy a winning team. But never again would the NCAA issue a death penalty to a big-time football or basketball program. The rule is still a NCAA bylaw and has been used to penalize only non-revenue-producing sports. Dropping a nuclear bomb on SMU relegated the Mustangs' athletic program to second-class status among the elites in the two sports. Fining cheaters, prohibiting television appearances, and bans on post-season bowl appearances became the costs of getting caught, as the more recent Sandusky scandal at Penn State has demonstrated.[49]

The saddest sight was the hundred or so big-time football program recruiters who flooded the SMU campus after the NCAA's David Berst announced the program's shutdown. Every available space near the SMU athletics complex was taken up by visiting coaches meeting players as if they were predator animals smelling a piece of fresh meat. Even sadder, the players were enjoying the attention.[50]

University of Nevada, Las Vegas (UNLV)

Jerry Tarkanian's battle with the NCAA during his career with UNLV from 1973 to 1992 was intertwined with the selective enforcement tactics the organization demonstrated during UCLA's ten-year basketball reign. After successful stints at Riverside and Pasadena junior colleges in Southern California, Tarkanian converted Long Beach State into a national power despite its lack of a winning tradition and a "shoestring budget." More importantly, he did so by recruiting African American players other programs would not touch.[51]

Beginning in 1968 at Long Beach and moving to UNLV in 1973, Tarkanian's teams featuring African American players compiled one of the highest winning records in college basketball history. The conventional wisdom that "you start three blacks at home and two on the road" had been blunted in the northern part of the United States as early as 1955. That year, the University of San Francisco (USF) Dons, led by African Americans Bill Russell, K. C. Jones, and Hal Perry, won their first NCAA title.[52] The following year, the Dons captured another NCAA championship. Russell, Jones (ineligible for post-season play) and Perry were regular starters. African American Gene Brown was a key sixth player and replaced Jones during the NCAA playoffs. After the Dons defeated Iowa, 83–71, in the Final Four game, the team completed the season undefeated.[53]

In 1977, 20 years after UNLV became a full-fledged university, and Tarkanian's fourth at the college, the Running Rebels reached the Final Four, losing to Dean Smith's North Carolina Tar Heels, 84–83.[54] Throughout the history of college sports, there had been a number of outstanding black college teams that competed among themselves. However, it was rare that an institution with predominantly African American players would compete with the elite teams of college basketball who dominated the sport. An exception was 1966, when Texas Western (now University of Texas, El Paso) won the NCAA title with five African American starters. Tarkanian was routinely winning high school and junior college titles in California predominantly with rosters of black players, a significant achievement that is overshadowed by Tarkanian's battles with the NCAA.[55]

Tarkanian recruited African Americans because he was seeking the best players to win. While student-teaching and coaching at Fresno's Edison High School in 1956, a school with a predominant minority population, he immediately experienced success with the African American players.[56] At every phase of his Hall of Fame career, basketball analysts attributed his success to his coaching skills and his ability to motivate players of varied ethnicities to play as a team. Racial mores in the 1960s resisted integration, despite the Civil Rights Act of 1964. The door was open, but once African Americans entered the room, they found that the opportunities they sought in social, political, and economic arenas were all but closed to them.[57] Tarkanian was able provide a lifeline to success for African Americans through basketball.

The players he coached did not commit more NCAA violations or run afoul of the law more than any other players in big-time college sports. Just as quickly as UNLV attained success, administrators at the institution were

Coach Jerry Tarkanian (center) in a 1970–71 photograph with Long Beach State players (left to right): Chuck Terry, Ed Ratleff, and George Trapp. The coach's battles
with the NCAA diminished his repeated successes at the junior college and college
levels with predominantly African American players (courtesy Long Beach State
University).

fielding questions from competitors and cynics. How did the program rise from the ashes so quickly? How much money was paid to the players by gambling interests from "Sin City"? How did those players qualify for admission?[58]

Tarkanian had faced these questions before at every step in his career. Other institutions such as Kentucky, UCLA, and Michigan brazenly violated NCAA rules and escaped media scrutiny. The reason? They brought in teledollars to their institutions, conferences, and the NCAA.[59] The image these programs presented to the public was that they were playing athletes who fit white America's long-held and prejudicial definition of how African Americans were supposed to behave in a white-controlled sport. UNLV did not. Articles began to appear in national publications such as *Newsweek*, stating, "Envious rivals grumble that Tarkanian fields a piebald collection of dropouts, gymnasium gypsies and friendless problem children from all over the country. No other coach, they say, could have tried to sneak a crew studded with academic misfits past the administration office."[60] Others labeled him the Father Flanagan of college basketball, referring to the founder of Boys Town, which benefited troubled youth.[61]

In Las Vegas, civic boosterism in the 1960s was associated with the conversion of a two-year college in Southern Nevada into a four-year institution named the University of Nevada, Las Vegas. A booster organization with no formal affiliation to UNLV, the Rebels Club, would finance the athletic program. Its first priority would be to develop a big-time football program. With an already established football program at the state's other flagship university in Reno, the state legislators did not share the same vision as the core boosters of the Rebels Club. Former football player William "Wildcat" Morris, advertising executive Sig Rogich, local investor Brad Welch, Governor Paul Laxalt, his close associate Wayne Pearson, and boxing referee Davey Pearl envisioned a football program attracting out-of-town crowds of 20,000.[62] This was equivalent to a convention crowd of 100,000. Factor in gambling revenue, and the boosters' wallets would bulge five or six fall weekends of the year.[63]

When the Rebels Club approached Academic Vice President Don Baepler with its athletic dreams, the administrator eagerly joined the boosters in believing that winning football and basketball programs were part of every great university. He stated:

> There have been many, many studies done around the country in terms of what a prominent, let's not talk about national championship, but what a prominent football or basketball program means to admissions, the number of people that apply, and particularly the number of out-of-state admissions. And, when you look at state univer-

sities like Michigan, UCLA, North Carolina, it's no accident that they have outstanding football and basketball programs. To be outstanding academically and athletically, I think the two go together. This was part of a plan. This was thought out."[64]

The boosters and vice president had made the UNLV basketball position too attractive to turn down. In essence, they gave Tarkanian everything he wanted, bypassing all normal hiring procedures at the university; "they made it really a big-time job" stated the coach.[65] When the Tarkanians arrived in Las Vegas and appeared at President Roman Zorn's office, inexplicably the president was unavailable because of a scheduling conflict. After a couple of boosters "shared their thoughts" with Zorn, two hours later the president found time to meet the coach. Still, Zorn was upset at the way a small group of boosters had usurped the hiring process: "This group was not chartered by the university. It had no official standing with the university. I did not think the university should relinquish total control of the athletic program to boosters. I wasn't terribly enthused about the way they went about it. I wanted them to look at other people as well as Tarkanian."[66]

In a short time, UNLV did ascend to top ten rankings with a number of players who executed as a team, contrary to the unfounded perception that African Americans could not play disciplined basketball. Other programs that attempted to rise to the top echelons of college basketball by recruiting African Americans, such as Memphis State, University of New Mexico, and Minnesota, would find themselves in the crosshairs of an FBI or NCAA investigation.[67] The NCAA, ever mindful of Tarkanian's continual criticisms of their "selective enforcement process," relentlessly and unsuccessfully attempted to suspend or drive him out of coaching or penalize the programs that he headed at Long Beach State, UNLV and Fresno State.[68] At UNLV, boosters were seeking to benefit financially from the athletic program's success. Donald Baepler's statement that "several studies show how big-time sports and great universities are related" undoubtedly was viewed by academicians at the college with alarm. How could any athletic program entice a future prospective Nobel Prize winner to attend the university that became known as a basketball factory? Despite the economic success of basketball at the Las Vegas institution during Tarkanian's 19 years at the helm, the only remaining remnant of those turbulent times is an imposing physical arena two blocks from The Strip: the 18,500-seat Thomas & Mack Center on UNLV's campus, which opened for the 1983–1984 season.[69] Tarkanian's record included multiple years as the coach of a Top Ten Division I team, yearly NCAA attempts to suspend him, and an NCAA title in 1990. The 1991 team was 30–0 before losing, 79–77, to Duke in a Final Four semifinal game amid rumors that the game was played for gamblers.[70]

Inevitably, the civil war that evolved between the booster-supporters of President Robert Maxson, hired in 1984 to replace the Zorn-Baepler administration, and the Tarkanian boosters erupted into a nasty affair in the spring of 1991. The catalyst was the *Las Vegas Review's* photo of three members of the 1990 NCAA title-winning team appearing in a hot tub with Richie "The Fixer" Perry at his Las Vegas home.[71] The photo had been taken by Perry's ex-wife, Joanne. In 1987, Lamont Sudbury and Perry's then-wife began a romantic relationship after Perry had hired Sudbury to design their driveway. "I had no idea she was married when I met her and had no idea who Richard Perry was," stated Sudbury.[72] Mrs. Perry had asked Sudbury for a photocopy of his completed projects to show other consultants, including landscapers, interior decorators, and masonry contractors. In the process of returning the photos to Sudbury, she mistakenly included the hot tub photo.[73]

In the midst of the UNLV civil war in May 1991, the hot tub photo was given to the *Las Vegas Review-Journal* by Sudbury. The architectural designer believed the local and national media were treating the coach unfairly, and the photo might take their eyes off Tarkanian. In the photo, Perry appeared with three players from the 1990 NCAA-title winning team: Moses Scurry, David Butler, and Anderson Hunt. The photo had to be taken between 1987 and 1990, before the relationship ended between Sudbury and Perry's ex-wife.[74] Scurry and Butler previously had played on an AAU team coached by Perry in New York City. Regardless of the photo's source, it accomplished what the NCAA and Maxson's faction could not, the resignation of Tarkanian. After more investigations, it was discovered that Perry had openly ingratiated himself with the men's and women's basketball programs at UNLV, and was known around the university community as Sam Perry, a commodities broker.[75]

In 1986, Perry financed and delivered a New York high school player to the Rebels' program that even Tarkanian could not rescue. Lloyd Daniels had attended four high schools, suffered from a severe reading disorder, and completed only one high school basketball season in New York City.[76] By all accounts, he was functionally illiterate. Yet, assistant coach Mark Warkentien and his wife adopted Daniels and sent him to Mt. San Jacinto Junior College in Walnut, California, to complete the requisite units to enter UNLV in the spring of 1987. During all of this time, Daniels' cars, motor scooter, living expenses, and other expenses were taken care of by Warkentien, Perry, or Perry's ex-wife.[77] While attending UNLV in February 1987, Daniels was arrested in North Las Vegas for attempting to purchase a controlled substance. His $1,500 bail was posted by Perry, who was called by Warkentien after the arrest. The gambler reportedly became infuriated when Tarkanian announced that "Daniels would never play" for the Rebels.[78] Daniels's costs for drug rehabilitation were paid for by Perry, his attorney David Chesnoff, and Warkentien.

In truth, Perry's closeness to the UNLV athletic department and Tarkanian's denials of having known about the gambler until an April 1989 *Time* article were further embarrassments to the university. The coach's assertion that he only knew Perry as Sam Perry, a commodities broker, seemed less than truthful. Perry's convictions in 1974 and 1982 in connection with bribing harness race jockeys near New York City and the Boston College fixing scandal revealed he'd been the Lucchese crime family's gambling advisor since 1974.[79] Perry was one of 28 individuals indicted for fixing harness racing at Roosevelt and Yonkers Parkways.[80] The indictments included Peter Vario, son of Lucchese's top henchman, Paul Vario. The prosecutors alleged that Perry developed a plan to reduce the odds on specific races by bribing certain drivers to hold back their horses.[81]

Perry's affinity for gambling on sports was based on his ability to catalog and put together voluminous data and then calculate the odds of winning a game or horse race. Among big gamblers, bookies, and according to fellow *wiseguy* (non–Italian member of the mob) Henry Hill:

> Perry could give you the edge. He was a genius. Long before anyone else thought of it, Perry had dozens of people around the country watching college sports for him. He used to find things in small-town college newspapers that never made the wires, and he had people calling him right up to the minute he was ready to bet[82]

Before the 1961 basketball scandal, Jack Molinas was obtaining the same information and selling it to gamblers who were looking to bet on a "sure winner." After Perry relocated to Las Vegas in the spring of 1986, he and his associates, including his brother Alan, a middle school teacher, spotted the lack of supervision in the Las Vegas men's and women's basketball programs.[83] As big-time gamblers, it was their job to find these weaknesses and find players, coaches, and others to bribe or obtain important inside information from. The goal was to bet on "sure winners" and sell the games to other big-time gamblers. Perry's obsession with finding as much information as possible on teams he bet on was made easier by associating with players from the basketball program, and possibly one of Tarkanian's part-time assistants.[84]

In March 1987, a *Newsday* article cited Daniels' incomplete attendance at four high schools and several major NCAA violations in UNLV's men's basketball program. Also, Tarkanian's claims that he did not recruit Daniels were rebutted by telephone records from his home phone to Daniels' home before February 8, 1986. That was the date when the head coach and assistant Mark Warkentien met Perry and Daniels in his office. Despite Perry introducing himself as "Sam" from Las Vegas, he carried rental car keys and wore a shirt with the monogram "RP."[85]

Perry's comment—"I gave them a hundred bucks, so what? Everybody does it. It keeps them out of trouble"—was reported in a 1989 *Time* article.[86] The statement reflected his belief that his presence among college players had not registered with anyone in the UNLV community. Two players (Scurry and Butler) continued to visit Perry's home after Tarkanian had warned his entire roster to stay away from Perry in mid–October 1989, eight months after the *Time* article was published. The article also demonstrated that Nevada's gambling enforcement staff, Las Vegas police, the FBI, and UNLV's athletic administration were not aware of Perry's relationship with specific UNLV players.[87] Even after October 1989, nobody at UNLV pursued the elementary precautions to prevent a scandal by asking the NCAA to investigate Perry as mandated by NCAA Bylaw 10.3.[88] Aware of Tarkanian's low-key approach in administering a program two blocks from the Las Vegas Strip, it's incredible that the small group of 1973 boosters, including Sig Rogich, with his political ties to the Bush administration, did not warn Tarkanian, UNLV, the NCAA, and the FBI about Perry.

On February 20, 1986, 12 days after Daniels and Perry met Tarkanian and Warkentien and continuing through the 1985–1986 and 1986–1987 basketball seasons, Perry and his wife were given complimentary tickets to UNLV games at Thomas & Mack. During this time period, Perry also attended UNLV practices.[89] In Tarkanian's testimony to NCAA investigators in 1991, he claimed he had only seen Daniels twice in his life, but admitted that Perry frequently attended the team's practices at the North Gym.[90] At the end of the 1986–1987 season, Perry requested and was given six Final Four Tickets in the coaches' section from UNLV's ticket allotment.[91] The tickets were authorized by Tarkanian's handwritten signature. The other five tickets may have been given to Perry's gambling associates or sold for premium prices. In 1990 and 1991, Perry was a frequent customer at Richie's Room, a restaurant that employed one of the Rebels' starters, Anderson Hunt. Tarkanian and his son Danny also frequented the restaurant, and a radio talk show originated there featuring Hunt and two other UNLV players, Stacey Augmon and Greg Anthony. Perry was reportedly present during the show.[92]

In 1991, Perry had been videotaped attending at least one home game with attorney David Chesnoff, sitting in complimentary seats assigned to Tarkanian. At the 1991 Final Four in Indianapolis, Perry was photographed by a *Review-Journal* photographer sitting in a floor-level seat alongside David Chesnoff in Tarkanian-assigned seats.[93] Chesnoff's ambitions, booster support, and associations with UNLV players from 1989 to 1991, and his presence in UNLV's locker room, may have been because of his desire to enter the sport agent business. The videotaped appearance was not Perry's most serious alleged association with the UNLV program. Following the two-point loss to Duke in the 1991 Final Four semifinal game, the FBI launched a criminal investigation into Perry's association with UNLV players on the 1990 and

1991 teams. The 1992 inquiry focused on point shaving during the 1990–1991 season, including the two-point loss to Duke.[94]

On January 26, 1992, the following statement appeared in the *Las Vegas Sun*: "It is well known within the gambling world that Perry was booking bets on UNLV basketball, which is a no-no."[95] That was also the time Perry was hanging out with a couple of UNLV players."[96] Perry's passing of money to UNLV's players had been documented. Could he have also bet money on behalf of players? On January 30, 1992, John L. Smith published a column in the *Las Vegas Review-Journal* that referred to the investigation of Perry:

> The IRS, FBI, U.S. Attorney, Metro, Gaming Control Board, Nevada Attorney General, UNLV administrators and news reporters have concentrated on Perry's alarming presence so close to former Rebel recruit Lloyd Daniels and some of Coach Jerry Tarkanian's players. When Michael Barr of the Nevada Organized Crime Strike Force subpoenaed UNLV counsel Brad Booke for all university records regarding Perry and the Rebel program, it was thought to be related only to The Fixer's IRS woes. That logic was flawed; UNLV was unlikely to have much tax information on Perry. Was the federal government hunting for something more? The short answer is yes. The longer answer awaits the findings of a federal investigation and the grand jury inquiry.[97]

After the FBI completed part of its investigation, it issued a report that stated that Tarkanian and UNLV players were cleared of any wrongdoing involving Perry. Technically, that was an accurate statement at that point in the fact-gathering process. But the investigation was not complete. It was widely reported that the FBI was influenced by Sig Rogich and other Washington insiders to release the report.[98] The larger question was: Was Rogich acting to protect the image of UNLV, Tarkanian's and his assistants' knowledge of Perry's true identity, and the players who were associated with the twice-convicted felon? Tarkanian's apparent disbelief when the hot tub photo appeared in the *Las Vegas Review-Journal* did not appear to be genuine.[99]

One of UNLV's part-time coaches, Ron Ganulin, had graduated in the same class at Erasmus Hall High School in Brooklyn as Perry. Playing and coaching around New York City undoubtedly placed him in contact with Perry. While Ganulin coached at UNLV from 1987 to 1991, he was very likely aware of Perry's multiple fixing convictions.[100] The part-time coach certainly knew of Daniels' arrest in the spring of 1997 and had seen Perry at UNLV's practices. NCAA Bylaw 10.3 mandated that Ganulin inform UNLV's athletic department, the NCAA, or FBI of Perry's background. Also, UNLV women's basketball coach Sheila Strike-Bolla, her husband, and the assistant coach had not reported Perry's association with that program. Perry freely associated with the women's basketball program without any concern from UNLV's athletic department.[101]

Other events that took place at UNLV revealed the seriousness of associating with big-time gamblers with possible ties to the Mafia. In 1991, a UNLV committee investigating the basketball program's NCAA violations sought to interview an unnamed former player who reported multiple violations to the institution in 1986. At the interview, the ex-player informed the committee that he feared for his life:

> He said this, okay. I said everything in here is true. Everything here is, everything here is (sobs …) Everything in here is true. I'm just so scared, okay? People tell me I'm going to end up in the desert. I don't want to hear that shit (sobs …) Yes … and people came to me and told me what I'd better say, just deny everything. I'm scared to death, you just don't know, I didn't want to tell you this shit[102]

In 1991, the unnamed player's formal interview in the pending NCAA investigation ended when Danny Tarkanian, now an attorney, and the player exchanged nose-to-nose verbal threats. They were separated by those present. The player had previously testified that Jerry Tarkanian had knowledge of players selling their tickets for cash, which is an NCAA violation. The coach's son was at the hearing, representing an accused staff member.[103]

In 1997, Perry was sentenced to 15 months in prison, fined $30,000, and ordered to pay retroactive taxes totaling $650,000 for unreported gambling income from 1989 to 1991.[104] He was also placed in Nevada's Black Book of persons prohibited from entering casinos and declared "unsavory" and "notorious."[105] Most frightening was the possibility that Daniels and other UNLV players may have played for UNLV while under the financial influence of Perry and, by inference, the Lucchese family. The factors related to Perry's known underground associations and networks in the world of illegal sports gambling supported his involvement in the UNLV basketball program primarily for gambling reasons. Tarkanian's repeated denial of responsibility for program supervision rang hollow with a new generation of administrators, faculty, and boosters. The new breed of faculty hired by UNLV would fight to convert the institution into one known for its academic reputation.

Tarkanian officially resigned on June 7, 1991. Among the many stipulations included in the resignation agreement was that he would coach the Rebels during the 1991–1992 season. The boosters, who had hijacked the UNLV athletic program in 1973 for economic reasons with the complicity of Academic Vice President Donald Baepler, were naive in believing a nationally ranked football and basketball program would bring the university academic notoriety. From all appearances, they genuinely believed an institution's academic reputation would be enhanced by success in the football and basketball programs. Their belief that a basketball program could be immune from the influences of Sin City created an athletic program that was almost destroyed during 19 years of multiple NCAA investigations, penalties, sanctions, probations, and lawsuits filed by Tarkanian against the NCAA. In 1998, the NCAA paid Tarkanian $2.5 million without admitting any guilt in the 19-year war.[106]

In a *Los Angeles Times'* article following the settlement, Tarkanian, then coaching at Fresno State, expressed his belief that the war's origin came when he was at Long Beach State. At that time, the coach was also writing a periodic guest column for the *Long Beach Press Telegram*. In one column, Tarkanian expressed his belief that "the NCAA will go after the small schools but never the big schools.[107]" Citing Western Kentucky as an example, Tarkanian wrote that the institution was placed on probation even though the University of Kentucky's basketball program had committed more NCAA violations. Warren Brown (then the NCAA head) wrote a letter to the Long Beach State athletic director that in part stated, "What does Tark think, Long Beach is a big school?"[108] From that point on, the NCAA hounded Tarkanian for the next 25 years.

The suit against the NCAA was filed in 1992 when Tarkanian completed his last season at UNLV. In preparation for the trial, Tarkanian's attorney, Terry Giles, interviewed former players, officials, and lawyers and believed the weight of the evidence overwhelmingly favored Tarkanian. The NCAA had expressed an interest in a settlement about 30 days before the trial was to begin. As usual, the organization declined to comment on the case except to say they regretted the long battle, had more understanding of Tarkanian's position, and believed their enforcement procedures were enhanced.[109]

The citizens of Nevada as of 1992 had paid $1 million to resolve two decades of disputes. How much did the community of UNLV academicians, students, and, academic supporters pay for working at an institution that became known for its basketball program rather than its achievement and recognition in academic scholarship? A sure bet is that the answer was too much.

7

UCLA and Michigan

Urban Boosterism and Paying Athletes with Laundered Money

By the latter part of the 1950s, bookies were becoming suspicious. "Something is wrong with college basketball," they observed.[1] The NCAA's and colleges' belief that the fixing of games would mysteriously disappear after the 1951 scandal was put to rest on September 24, 1960, with the arrests of longtime fixer Aaron Wagman and student Phil Silber in Gainesville for attempting to bribe Florida fullback Joe MacBeth. During that same weekend in Dearborn, Michigan, Oregon head coach Len Casanova informed the police that one of the team's defensive backs had been offered money to "fall down a few times" while covering University of Michigan's receivers. During the 1959–1960 basketball season, the pair pled no contest for attempting to bribe NYU's Ray Paprocky to manipulate the final score against a Jerry West–led West Virginia basketball team in the NCAA East Regionals. Paprocky had accepted money, but in the heat of a closely contested game, forgot about the agreement as his competitive instincts kicked in. The Violets upset the highly favored Mountaineers and ended up in the Final Four in San Francisco.[2]

The arrests in Florida and Michigan prompted New York County detectives to begin tailing, wiretapping, and collecting evidence detailing widespread game fixing in college basketball, and possibly football. Athletic administrators and coaches began to warn players routinely about reporting and refusing gamblers' offers. After a year and a half of investigations, another gambling scandal in college basketball was laid bare before the American public.[3] College authorities were stunned by the number of players who had chosen to play for gamblers' money. Following the second major blow to college basketball in ten years, attendance in the sport had actually increased. The scandal was quickly forgotten.[4]

In the late 1940s, booster payoffs in football exacerbated the festering suspicions between the northern and southern factions of the Pacific Coast Conference (PCC). In 1924, the PCC suspended USC for one year for violating conference athletic aid standards. Committed to maintaining academic standards and the integrity of athletics, the PCC ordered conference commissioner and former FBI agent Edgar Atherton to conduct a study on student-athlete conduct in 1933.[5] Atherton's report cited payoffs to players, admission of unqualified athletes, abuses of athletic scholarships, and other infractions that were largely ignored by conference members.[6] Similar to previous reform studies of college football and basketball, Atherton's study was relegated to the ash heap. In 1944, attorney Victor O. Schmidt was appointed commissioner and served as the PCC's head until 1959, when the conference was disbanded. The events that led to the breakup included confirmed charges in 1951 that Oregon football coach Jim Aiken had violated conference athletic and subsidy rules, thus forcing his resignation.[7]

Squabbling among conference members came to a head in 1956, when football players at the University of Washington rebelled against and forced the resignation of head coach John Chalberg. Bitter about his forced exit from Seattle, the football coach exposed a not-so-secret illegal payment system. After a PCC investigation, evidence uncovered the existence of a "slush fund" that was managed for years by Roscoe C. "Torchy" Torrance, named the Greater Washington Advertising Fund. The "fund" had lavishly paid Huskies football players for years. Compton Junior College halfback Hugh McElhenny was reportedly paid well to attend school and play for the Huskies. When he signed a professional contract with San Francisco in 1951, sportswriters who covered the PCC quipped that McElhenny "took a pay cut to play professional football."[8]

UCLA

In March 1956, newspapers in Los Angeles published allegations of illegal payments from two booster clubs associated with UCLA: Bruin Bench and Young Men's Club of Westwood. After stonewalling a conference investigation for ten weeks, the institution admitted that "all members of the football coaching staff had for several years known of the unsanctioned payments."[9] Big-time football coaching staffs for years had regularly referred their players to program boosters for money. Not to be outdone, a UCLA alumnus and member of its advisory board exposed conference and NCAA infractions committed by two additional PCC programs. The Southern California Educational Foundation was accused of distributing money to USC players. The athletic program at University of California, Berkeley was cited for setting up a fake job program for athletes known as the San Francisco Gridiron Club. An extension of that program in Southern California was known as the South Seas Fund.[10]

UCLA's unprecedented basketball success from 1964 to 1975 laid the foundation for the sport's entry into the mega-bucks environment of television. Alabama's football and UCLA's basketball programs fueled the outward perception that sports retained a value system on which the college establishment could stand during the 1960s.[11] Sports programs were cited as an antidote to the negative aspects of the ultra-liberalism that was sweeping across most of America during that time period.[12] In reality, big-time football and basketball programs were on the verge of an endless array of gambling payoffs and recruiting and academic scandals beginning in the 1970s. These infractions would not only reoccur, but escalate into more serious law-breaking including drug use, rape, and homicide.[13]

One of the early boosters who bestowed money on UCLA's basketball program was Al Levinson. He owned a major steel company in Compton, near downtown Los Angeles and the hometown of Freddie Goss, a former California Interscholastic Federation (CIF) Player of the Year in 1961. Goss played on UCLA's first undefeated and NCAA title team in 1964–1965. In an interview, Goss remembered: "He [Levinson] gave me ten dollars an hour to study and make straight A's. That was big money in 1960. I remember he had a picture of Marilyn Monroe and a stock ticker in his office. I'd go there and study after school."[14] Levinson had expected that UCLA's new basketball arena would be named after him. When University of California Regent Edwin Pauley contributed one-fifth of the $5 million needed to build the arena, UCLA administrators and alumni decided to name the venue after him. That decision ended Levinson's relationship with Bruins athletics.

Sam Gilbert's role as a UCLA booster was not a secret among college basketball's insiders and the NCAA. His most serious legal issue was his documented connection to organized crime. Charles Young, UCLA's chancellor during the Wooden dynasty, believed that Athletic Director J. D. Morgan genuinely feared Gilbert. Gene Bartow, Wooden's successor, informed and thanked the NCAA in 1993 for not investigating Gilbert in 1976, as he most likely would have ended up in Gilbert's crosshairs.[15] It is likely that powerful people in Southern California or even Gilbert himself may have informed the athletic director and Bartow that he did business on the same side of the law as organized crime. Following Wooden's retirement in 1975, Bartow and his successor, Larry Brown, were invited to a meeting with the self-anointed

UCLA Godfather. According to each coach, they refused Papa Sam's generous assistance.[16]

However, that account does not square with Bartow's later statement to the NCAA. After Gilbert's death in 1987, Morgan's and Bartow's fear of Gilbert appeared to be more reality than perception. According to Seth Davis in *Wooden: A Coach's Life*, Gilbert cultivated the perception that his underground connections could buy his enemies a burial at the bottom of the ocean. Papa Sam made sure anyone who visited his office would not fail to see Mario Puzo's book, *The Godfather*, proudly displayed. Many of his friends sent him a copy of the book when it was published in 1969. Charles Young stated:

> I remember him [Morgan] saying to me in that deep voice of his "Chuck, you don't know about Sam Gilbert. Do you want to end up in a block of concrete at the bottom of the ocean?" J. D.'s view of him was that if you cross Sam, you're likely to be killed, literally. It's the only time I've seen J. D. kind of shaken.[17]

Had Gilbert not died in 1987, a portrait of how he transferred and laundered Miami drug money to Southern California would have been exposed in a Miami trial.[18] According to federal authorities, the elder Gilbert was the "West Coast Head" for a scheme that transferred $12 million from Miami to Los Angeles via the tiny country of Liechtenstein and the British Virgin Islands.[19] Court documents and interviews revealed Gilbert collected a commission on the laundered money and a $2 million fee to finance the construction of the Bicycle Club casino in Bell Gardens, California.[20] In the early 1990 southern Florida trial, documents, memos, cashier's checks, and transcripts of witnesses' testimony illustrated how the elder Gilbert and his Miami associates had organized the illegal operation to build the casino. One of Gilbert's sons, Michael, was indicted and found guilty and served five and a half years in prison for violating specific precepts of the Racketeer Influenced and Corrupt Organizations Act (RICO law). Gilbert had successfully appealed the money-laundering charge. However, he failed to convince the other three appellate judges in 1996 that he was not guilty of the other charges.[21] Gilbert's other son, Robert, was named the first operations director of the casino.

J. Brent Clark had investigated the Bruins' program and Gilbert in one of his first assignments after joining the NCAA's infractions staff. The neophyte investigator completed several inquiries on the UCLA campus, including interviews of key witnesses.[22] His recommendation that the organization investigate the Bruins' basketball program fell on the organization's deaf ears. Clark's superior ignored his report, which included interviews with Gilbert and players Richard Washington and Marques Johnson. The trio had flown to Denver to negotiate professional contracts with the fledgling American Basketball Association (ABA) franchise in 1976 before the two players were eligible to sign a professional contract.[23] "We're not going after [UCLA] right now," stated Bill Hunt, Clark's NCAA superior. Nobody had asked the NCAA how Gilbert had illegally represented Bill Walton. Most of the UCLA players who were interviewed by the NCAA infractions staff believed they were immune from the organization's scrutiny.[24]

In February 1978, Clark testified before a congressional subcommittee after he had quit the NCAA. According to Clark's testimony, the NCAA bribed informants during its investigations, employed "manipulative and corrupt" tactics to obtain information from member schools, tapped phones, and colluded with the organization's investigative staff and committee to hide infractions.[25] Clark further informed the subcommittee that NCAA Executive Director Walter Byers' opinion of a program determined whether or not it was investigated. Although Clark did not reveal names, UCLA and Gilbert were the obvious subjects of his testimony. Four years later in February 1982, in the midst of an investigatory series by *Los Angeles Times* reporters Mike Littwin and Alan Greenberg, Clark stated, "Gilbert was well known to the NCAA for years and years. His name appeared in print many, many times."[26] He suspected NCAA investigators had investigated Gilbert before he did.

After Bill Walton was selected by the Portland Trail Blazers as their number one pick in 1974, he shed his cloak of Wooden-imposed Westwood conservatism. He began to hang out and live with Jack Scott and his wife in Portland. Scott was a former track athlete at Syracuse who found his way to Berkeley, where he obtained a Ph.D. in higher education. Soon, he became one of the anti-establishment's and Black Power's most vocal spokespersons of the 1960s.[27] Also a radical opportunist, Scott and his wife had transported wealthy newspaper heiress and bank robbery fugitive Patty Hearst across the country in a van undetected by law enforcement personnel. Scott's van was widely shown in various media sources transporting Hearst to the East Coast. In Ohio, the Scotts were pulled over by a suspicious state trooper. Scott avoided capture by engaging the individual in a conversation about Ohio State's football game that day. The conversation was enough to convince the Buckeyes fan that Scott was not his man.[28] According to Scott, Walton recounted a number of conflicting stories to him about Gilbert during the 1975–1976 season. Walton had attributed the media's reporting of his pot smoking in the locker room at UCLA to Gilbert. During that season, Scott traveled with Walton and the Trail Blazers and decided to interview Gilbert by phone. According to an account from Scott's book about his travels, knowing Scott had become Walton's confidant, Gilbert advised:

"Be truthful or I'll take considerable efforts and I don't want to tell you what efforts I'll take. Write any fucking thing you want." Then, Gilbert warned, "I don't dig you, Mr. Scott." After Scott reminded Gilbert about threats—including a death threat during the last two years, Scott asked, "Didn't you tell someone who lives with us (presumably Walton) that I was going to find myself at the bottom of the river? I think it was the bottom of the ocean." "It's possible you know," Gilbert responded.[29]

After Scott informed Gilbert he had a signed letter from a former UCLA player (later identified as Walton), which stated that after he signed a professional contract Gilbert would be paid $4,500, Gilbert asked nervously: "Are you going to use that letter? UCLA would have to return four NCAA championships. What I did is a total violation of NCAA rules [signing an athlete to a contract before he's eligible]."[30] A 1974 *Time* magazine feature article on Bill Walton included a half-page on Sam Gilbert. The article had to bring a smile to the faces of college basketball insiders and long-time NCAA critic Jerry Tarkanian. One of most publicized boosters in the history of college sports no longer had to operate behind the Bruins' feigned "Curtain of Secrecy"[31] Publicly, Morgan had created an athletic program with a balanced budget that appeared to be "doing it the right way." Basketball insiders knew better.

In comparison to UCLA, Tarkanian's NCAA and civil violations during his 31 years of NCAA coaching at Long Beach State, UNLV, and Fresno State made Gilbert and the rest of the boosters of the world look like "choir boys."[32] The super-elite model of college sports involving college football and basketball members of the wealthiest and para-professionalized five major conferences can trace its beginnings to UCLA basketball's dynasty years. By the 1960s, it was college football that attracted television money. Before UCLA's success on the court, local television stations controlled whether or not to broadcast the NCAA title basketball game.[33]

The 1968 intersectional game in the Houston Astrodome between the Bruins and Houston was viewed by a national audience of 36 million. This seminal televised event illustrated that college basketball was ready to compete for entertainment and gambling dollars.[34] In May 1972, the NCAA Basketball Tournament Committee announced it was expanding the number of teams in the tournament from 25 to 32 for the 1974–1975 season. Walter Byers and the NCAA were reading the tea leaves because in a few years, a 1984 Supreme Court decision would allow football programs to negotiate their own contracts with the networks. This meant the NCAA would be shut out from sharing television football revenues. It quickly moved to control the basketball tournament's financial profits, ultimately branding the three-week gambling frenzy March Madness.[35] The Tournament Committee moved the semifinals from Thursday to Saturday night and the final game from Saturday to Monday night beginning in 1973.[36] Shutting down UCLA's program would have also killed the profitability of college basketball's television market in Los Angeles, a major media market. UCLA's ten-year run in the NCAA tournament had attracted big advertising dollars to college basketball. The chase for television dollars had begun and "the corrupter was corrupting the corrupted."[37] Boosters at the University of Kentucky had for years unabashedly and openly made Sam Gilbert look like "small potatoes" by comparison.[38] The NCAA and the few money-driven football and basketball programs entered into the Faustian bargains with wide-open eyes.

The NCAA's failure to punish UCLA would set a tone regarding cheating in recruiting, paying players, and academics that reached epidemic levels in the 1980s. The 1987 SMU "death penalty" decimated that college's football and basketball programs and would not be repeated. Assuredly, wealthy booster-attorneys viewed the shutting down of an (arguably) athletic business as a violation of antitrust laws. Financial penalties, vacating of victories, and sidelining coaches caught excessively cheating replaced the death penalty.[39]

Gambling on sports became more profitable for the illegal bookies, and a few college football and basketball players continued to play "with an ear to the betting odds." Betting against their own team not to cover the spread was documented at Northwestern in the 1980s and Boston College in the 1990s.[40] And the creation of the mega-conferences and mega-billion-dollar television contracts placed college football and basketball in the businesses of entertainment, advertising, and marketing.

Administratively, John Wooden may not have been in a position to shut Gilbert down, and he occasionally shared his predicament with Tarkanian, who stated:

> To this day, what blows me away—what still makes me angry—is that Sam Gilbert never tried to hide what he was doing. But, the NCAA was not going to investigate UCLA. They were the marquee team. They had all of their games on television. But, I lived 20 minutes away in Long Beach and I knew what was going on there. The whole country, the NCAA, they all knew what Sam Gilbert was doing at UCLA.[41]

The basketball programs in Division I and the 24/7 advertising dollars that flow into university and NCAA coffers from the three-week gambling March Madness holiday owe a debt of gratitude to John Wooden's extraordinary record, including winning 88 consecutive games and ten NCAA titles, seven of which were successive.[42] One of the greatest coaches in any sport disdained the changes in college basketball that were driven by money. The money needed to buy winning did not begin with the Sam Gilberts of college football and basketball.

Michigan, The Fab Five *and Ed Martin*

In the film "Fab Five," the players are presented as flamboyant, sporting baggy shorts, shaved heads, black shoes, black socks, and a trash-talking hip-hop flavor that created an inevitable controversy among a swath of conservative critics. Some argue they were the greatest recruiting class ever assembled, while cynics point out that their style of play was about entertainment and not pure basketball. All five players were rated among the top 100 high school prospects in 1991.[43]

Chris Webber was ranked number one; Juwan Howard, three; Jalen Rose, six; Jimmy King, nine; and Ray Jackson, 84. All except Jackson were selected to play in the 1991 McDonald's All-Star Game. Poverty and its deleterious effects were not the primary motivators of the five freshmen. Webber, King, and Jackson were products of intact families, while Rose was raised by an unwed mother. His father, Jimmy Walker, had been the NBA's top draft choice in 1967 out of Providence. He never met his father and briefly spoke with him once before Walker's death in 2007. Howard, from Chicago, was raised by a grandmother who died the day he signed to play for the Wolverines. Each of the players was blessed with extraordinary self-confidence, basketball intelligence, and talent.

Their playing style was a combination of sharp passes, unselfishness, and alley-oop passes to open big men near the basket, usually followed by a slam dunk. Their flashiness, including behind-the-back passes, drew criticism from coaches, the media, and basketball purists. Some defined their playing style as showboating and entertaining, which provided their opponents with an incentive to defeat the Wolverines. In the midst of a team slump in early February 1992, Coach Steve Fisher decided to start the five freshmen at Notre Dame. Former Marquette coach and TV analyst Al McGuire's comments about their flamboyant play before a national audience would become synonymous with their successes and failures over the rest of their careers:

> You can tell they're freshmen. They go too much with the French pastry. Too much with the hotdogging…. It's too early for jivin' men, too early for jivin'…. Every play with them gets to be like Hiroshima, Nagasaki, every play has to be a large explosion…. There goes another Harlem Globetrotter pass [behind the back] from Webber. No reason for that. It's French pastry…. Remember, Michigan fans, these are just kids. They'll give you thrills but they're also gonna give you Elvis Presley, Heartbreak Hotel….

The *Fab Five* documentary stated that the recruiting class is remembered more for its contributions to the changing basketball culture than for trophies.

Their impact on creating a brand and style to market and sell products continued into the 21st century. Before the Fab Five, selling college paraphernalia was not unheard-of. But the five freshmen accelerated and opened new visions of that aspect of commercialized college sports.[44] Today, creating a unique brand of products is an objective of every big-time college program. Jalen Rose, an executive producer of the film, characterized the documentary as a "bible" that informed about a legacy that critics would debate is tarnished and unfulfilled.

Especially troubling was Chris Webber's non-appearance in the film and his repeated pre–2002 denials of receiving money from booster Ed Martin. McGuire's observations were prescient, but for different reasons. In November 2002, the two NCAA championship game banners for 1992 and 1993 were removed from Crisler Arena. The bill had come due for the Fab Five's transgressions, including the alleged $280,000 that Martin gave to Webber beginning at the AAU level before high school. Stated Michigan President Mary Sue Coleman at a news conference: "These victories are gone, erased. There is no excuse for what happened. It was wrong, plain and simple. This is a day of great shame for the university."[45]

Michigan's self-imposed sanctions included:

- Vacated the entire 1992–1993 season, and every game from the 1995–1996 through the 1998–1999 seasons, including the 1997 NIT and the 1998 Big Ten tournament titles. Two Final Four games in 1992 were vacated as well as the program's entire NCAA tournament record in 1993, 1996, 1998, and 1999. All the games in which Chris Webber played except two Final Four games were retained. (Forfeiting a game awards a victory to an opponent, while vacating a game does not.)
- Banners commemorating the 1992 and 1993 Final Four appearances, the 1997 NIT title, and the 1998 Big Ten tournament would be removed from the rafters of Crisler Arena.
- Any written material involving victories and plays related to Chris Webber, Robert Traylor, Maurice Taylor, and Louis Bullock would be excised from all programs and written material.
- Repaying the NCAA approximately $450,000, received by the university for postseason NCAA play in 1992, 1993, 1996, 1997, 1998, and 1999.
- Declaring the men's basketball team ineligible to participate in the 2003 NCAA tournament as well as the NIT that year.
  Placing the men's basketball on two years' probation, including the submission of detailed compliance supervised by the university president during that time period.[46]

The Fab Five packed arenas as the freshmen became national celebrities their first year in college. Fab Five T-shirts, Nike black socks and shoes, and maize and blue paraphernalia including jerseys, pennants, caps, posters, and oversized basketball shorts generated sales of at least $10 million in 1992.[47] The athletic department doubled its revenue to $4.2 million from the previous year. By the end of their sophomore year, the media periodically hammered the Fab Five as a number of television and media pundits characterized them as brash villains or worse—thugs.[48]

Because of the Fab Five, the accepted wisdom that multiple freshmen in a lineup would not lead to a successful season was turned on its head. Most great college teams like UCLA had been created from a slow blending of fresh talent with experience in determining the five starters. Juniors Rob Pelinka, James Voskuil, Michael Talley, and Eric Riley were significant contributors, but clearly in supporting roles. Randy Ayers, Ohio State's head coach, commented:

> It takes freshmen a while to grasp the college game. A high school star has an adjustment period learning to accept sacrificing for the good of the team. That almost always takes a year or two, but the Fab Five found their niches immediately. Chris, Jalen, and Juwan were the go-to-guys and the Texas kids were the defenders. And, they played off each other beautifully.[49]

The popularity of the Fab Five overshadowed a feat accomplished by the 1988–1989 team, which won the NCAA title under recently promoted and temporary Coach Steve Fisher. After finishing third in the Big Ten with six losses, the Wolverines received an NCAA tournament bid and were scheduled to play their first game in Atlanta against Xavier. In the interim, Head Coach Bill Freider had accepted the Arizona State basketball position, fully intending to coach the Wolverines in the tournament. When Athletic Director Bo Schembechler was informed by Freider of his decision, he immediately fired him and appointed Fisher. "A Michigan man will coach Michigan," bellowed Schembechler.[50] In an incredible run, the team, including Terry Mills, Rumeal Robinson, Sean Higgins, Glen Rice, and Loy Vought, won six consecutive games and an NCAA title. Of the five starters, only Rice was an All-American. In the Final Four semifinal game against Illinois, which had defeated Michigan by 16 points in a conference game, the Wolverines avenged the loss by defeating the Illini and ending up in the title game against Seton Hall. Schembechler, who was rumored to have been counseled to hire a big-name coach by Indiana's Bob Knight, changed Fisher's employment status from interim to permanent.[51]

By former Michigan President James Duderstadt's account, it was under Athletic Director Don Canham's leadership that the institution's athletic program was transformed into functioning as a business—including marketing, advertising, and promotion. However, the program under Canham began to run deficits as it depended solely on football revenues to support the entire athletic program.[52] Until they won the 1989 NCAA basketball title, no sport at Michigan had won a national title since Al Renfrew's hockey team in 1964. Canham's autocratic leadership was not without problems, including becoming a target of federal investigations involving gender discrimination in intercollegiate athletics under Title IX of the Higher Education Act.[53] The program's administrative unit, separate from the rest of the institution, meant that the Board of Trustees and the President's office lacked any control over athletic department policies, including recruitment, payments to players, and academic cheating.

Canham and the athletic department perennially ignored university regulations and practices involving personnel, financial accountability, and conflicts of interest. During the 1970s and 1980s, almost all commercialized college football and basketball programs were scandalized in some fashion as television dollars became the major source of revenue for athletic programs. Given that most Division I programs had been ignored, it was inevitable that some of the most brazen cheating ever seen in football and basketball programs would reach unprecedented levels. Increasingly, booster contributions were needed to avoid budget deficits. Canham's successor, Bo Schembechler, was not about to tinker with the athletic department's lack of accountability to the President's office. That procedure was not implemented until 1997 at Michigan and other institutions.[54]

Yet the Kentuckys under Eddie Sutton, Alabamas under Bear Bryant, and Notre Dames under Lou Holtz of the world prided themselves on "doing the right thing."[55] Former athletic director Donald Canham confirmed what many insiders suspected when the five freshmen were recruited before 1991. "We had one of the dirtiest programs ever. It's a disgrace. This is just the beginning," stated Canham. "There were more players involved than those in the [2002] indictment and there were more schools than Martin and Michigan."[56] Canham's observations were made in 2002, 14 years after he turned over the reins of the athletic department to Schembechler. It's unlikely the Wolverines' football program under Schembechler and basketball programs under Johnny Orr, Bill Freider, and Steve Fisher were "doing the right thing" in recruiting, player payoffs, and academic cheating. A more likely scenario is that the Big Ten institution basked in its false "doing the right thing" image and had just as many skeletons in its closets as any big-time commercialized football and basketball program.[57]

During Canham's 20-year reign as the athletic program's head, the football program had either shared or outright won the Big Ten title 12 times. Despite perennially filling the "Big House," the athletic program ran deficits, counter to the public perception that football paid all the bills.[58] The Fab Five's commercialized success fit perfectly into the business model of an athletic program that Canham had envisioned as Athletic Director. Former President Duderstadt expressed the Fab Five's impact on the university by stating:

> While television turned the Final Four into the showy spectacle of March Madness, those of us who experienced it as participants developed a more cynical attitude. It represented the extreme of what can happen when one allows the media to transform college athletics into show business. And, while several of our players eventually became big-time winners in the bonanza, in the end, I believe that most of the players, coaches, and university itself were losers.[59]

Michigan's "Fab Five," pictured in 1991, included (left to right): Jalen Rose, Juwan Howard, Jimmy King, Coach Steve Fisher, Chris Webber, and Ray Jackson. Appearing in two Final Four games, the team, because of its association with booster Ed Martin, brought the university more ignominy than success after it was discovered that Martin gave substantial laundered money to at least three of the five players (Bentley Historical Library, University of Michigan).

After Michigan's 1996 to 2002 transgressions were laid bare, NCAA Infractions Committee Chairman Thomas Yeager described the case as "one of the three or four most egregious violations of NCAA bylaws in the history of the association."[60] In the environment of college football and basketball programs in the 1970s and 1980s, Yeager's statement placed the Michigan basketball program in the same category as SMU's football program (death penalty), New Mexico (booster gambling and payoffs to players), and Northwestern (point shaving in basketball, and football players betting against their team).

Less than ten years after all of the Fab Five had played out their eligibility, the public would learn how television money had changed college basketball. In the 1940s and 1950s, basketball programs like LIU, Kentucky, and Iowa could hold tryouts and expect hundreds of prospects to appear as coaches organized scrimmages and selected the best players. Then scholarships and other money deals were informally negotiated between the players, coaches, and program boosters. Whatever NCAA rules existed were loosely enforced or ignored.

In the 1960s and 1970s, ambitious junior college and college coaches began to employ a system that included paid "flesh peddlers" or scouts who would scour the inner cities, looking for players to deliver to out-of-the-way junior college programs in places like Rangely, Colorado, or Coffeyville, Kansas.[61] Or they might supply the majors and small schools like Belmont Abbey in North Carolina, where Al McGuire apprenticed before ending up at Marquette, where he won an NCAA title in 1977.[62] Big-time coaches knew money was needed to recruit top talent and had done so for years with the full knowledge of the NCAA. The big-time programs that were slapped with probation, loss of television revenue, and eligibility for postseason play usually fired the entire staff of the offending program to show the public they were committed to running a clean program. However, they continued to do business as usual.[63]

Except for Bud Middaugh's baseball program infractions that were reported to the NCAA in 1989, programs at Michigan did not catch the attention of the NCAA until 1996.[64] When Steve Fisher abruptly succeeded Bill Frieder on the eve of the 1989 NCAA tournament, he inherited Ed Martin and a program that had probably cheated in football and basketball as much as the USCs, Oklahomas, and Kentuckys of the world.[65] If he had not included Martin in the inner sanctum of Michigan's basketball program, he would have lost a recruiting edge to Iowa's George Raveling or UNLV's Jerry Tarkanian and many other coaches who recruited inner-city players. Martin represented the new breed of booster that head coaches had to be careful not to alienate—especially since he had ingratiated himself into the lives of two of the most prized recruits in the country, Chris Webber and Jalen Rose.[66] "Put yourself in the college coach's place," stated Al Wilkerson, the head coach at Detroit's Romulus High School. "Do you want to piss off a guy who has influence over the kids you need?"[67]

Martin had lived in Detroit since 1951, when he began working at Ford's River Rouge plant as an electrician's apprentice. Eventually, he worked his way into a nomadic position at the plant, moving from the body shop to the assembly line to other parts of the factory. His specialty was putting out fires, making friends, and assisting others in their jobs.[68] During breaks, he would talk sports with the workers. Martin's easygoing personality and access to most of the plant's employees made him a perfect fit for the numbers racket— the plant's other business. Workers placed a couple of dollars on the chance a certain number would be selected. State lottery numbers determined the winners. Runners moved around the plant to collect bets so no time was lost on the Ford clock.[69] Another employee doubled as the house. Martin's access to all parts of the plant allowed him to supplant his electrician's salary with commissions he earned collecting bets. On a good week, the estimated gross take could be as high as $100,000. After he slowly climbed the numbers operation ladder, the entire operation became Martin's in the 1980s, when the head man of the operation retired. Though Martin retired from Ford in 1986, he continued to run the numbers operation, supplementing his retirement income with illegal gambling money.[70]

Before Webber and Rose, Martin cemented his reputation as one of Detroit's urban boosters by funneling basketball players to Southwestern High School as Coach Perry Watson transformed the program into a perennial state power in the mid–1980s. Martin was content to buy the team's meals after games, take some of the players to games, and slip cash to players for the asking.[71] After Southwestern lost in the state finals for the third straight year in 1984, Martin courted Terry Mills' father with $400 in cash, a case of liquor, bottles of perfume, and a free trip to the horse races—just in case Mills, later a standout on the 1989 Michigan NCAA title-winning team, was interested in transferring. He was not, and his father returned the gifts.[72]

From some accounts, the retired electrician's style kicked into high gear when Webber and Rose played together on the same AAU team. "He seemed a little flashy and a little classy," stated the coach's son, Darrell Hervey. "He met us all, but everyone already knew who he was."[73] Soon Webber was receiving a significant amount of Martin's attention, gifts, and money. Throughout 1987, teammates often saw the two meeting privately and riding in Martin's Mercedes. At times, when Webber showed up with a new pair of basketball shoes or an expensive gold necklace, the money to pay for the items came from Martin. For Webber's mother (a teacher) and father (who worked at a factory), these kinds of luxury items were beyond their means.

In the early morning of 1996, a Ford Explorer belonging to Michigan forward Maurice Taylor and paid for by Ed Martin went out of control and overturned while returning from a party in Detroit. The team was scheduled to play Indiana that day. Among the passengers were starters Robert Traylor, who suffered a broken arm, Louis Bullock, Michigan high school standout Mateen Cleaves, who would lead Michigan State to a national title, Willie Mitchell, a Wolverine who later transferred to the University of Alabama, Birmingham, and friend Ron Oliver. Cleaves was on an official recruiting visit.[74] According to some sources, the party at the Westin Hotel included alcohol, drugs, and strippers, although accounts vary.[75] Following two investigations by the university in conjunction with the Big Ten in 1996 and 1997, and a seven-month independent investigation by a law firm, no major NCAA violations were uncovered.

Prior to the investigation, the *Detroit Free Press* and national media sources repeatedly cited and quoted anonymous sources alleging that current and former Wolverines basketball players had continued to receive payments from Martin after he was disassociated from the program in 1997. Evidence the law firm collected included interviews with more than 50 individuals, among them current and former players, families and friends of the involved players, coaches, and university administrators and staff. It also included reviews of hundreds of pages of documents, such as team travel records, telephone bills, and complimentary ticket lists. Also examined were external records, including student-athletes' apartment leases, hotel room rentals, car and truck registrations, and motor vehicle purchases and leases.[76] The investigators were unsuccessful in interviewing Martin and the four players who received money from the "basketball junkie."

One of the law firm's conclusions, that Martin "had developed relationships with standout players for self-interest reasons," was old news to high school, college and AAU coaches. After the second joint investigation was released in March 1997, Martin was officially disassociated from Michigan's athletic program for the second time.[77] For the Martins of the world, this meant they could not operate as openly as before. Michigan President Lee Bollinger and the Board of Trustees were not satisfied, as the basketball program was left "twisting in the wind" and becoming a public relations disaster for the institution. There were still questions about Martin's source of money. The first step was to fire Fisher before the start of practice for the 1997 season.[78] Assistant Brian Ellerbe was hired as an interim coach, and later Duke graduate Tommy Amaker was hired as the permanent head coach. But it was too late.

Most of Martin's illegal activities were uncovered by FBI and Dearborn police investigations and wiretaps of conversations with players and associates in the numbers business. A raid by FBI and IRS agents in April 1999 of the homes of Martin, his son Carlton, and 12 associates uncovered further evidence that Martin had continued to funnel money to players after the university had disassociated him from the program. An FBI memo stated in part:

> Execution of the warrants produced a seizure of approximately $165,000 in United States currency. Three vehicles were also seized, namely, a Mercedes-Benz registered to Eddie Lewis Martin, [redacted] and [redacted]. Additionally, large amounts of gambling records were found, those being located in vehicles, as well as residences. Besides gambling documents, agents also recovered papers in the home of Eddie Lewis Martin. This indicated large cash disbursements from Martin to various basketball players. Preliminary analysis of these papers and bank records previously accumulated indicates expenditures to be large scale and made to the following individuals [several names redacted].[79]

Records seized at Martin's residence substantiated that Robert Traylor and Louis Bullock continued to receive payments after the university first disassociated itself from the booster. This was a person who filed joint income tax returns listing adjusted gross incomes of $22,400 in 1994, $24,220 in 1995, $26,104 in 1996, $20,087 in 1997, and $22,791 in 1998. If the numbers racket posted $100,000 in a good week and Martin's commission was 30 percent, that added approximately $70,000 a week tax-free or $1,560,000 a year to his income.[80] On Martin's retirement income reported to the IRS, that was a lot of money to launder. The Feds and IRS wanted to find out if some of Martin's money was funneled to organized crime. After the legal proceedings had ended, the Michigan case left more questions unanswered than answered.

Martin's illegal income showed he could have easily given millions of dollars in the form of cash, gifts, and other gratuities to the four players and several others over an approximate 20-year period. Was the federal government investigating an organized crime ring that plausibly could have demanded protection money from inner-city illegal numbers games operators? It is also naive to believe that the possibility of Martin betting on Michigan to cover or not cover the spread was not of interest to the FBI.

Conversations between Martin and players in a number of programs besides Michigan were wiretapped. Was the FBI's drawn-out investigation attempting to link Martin and his backers, including organized crime, with game fixing? Especially when a number of the players were indebted to him from several other programs. One of the starters on UNLV's 1990 title-winning team was Detroit's Anderson Hunt from Watson's Southwestern High's program. After compiling a 30–0 record in 1991, the Rebels were upset, 69–67, by Duke in the Final Four semifinal game.[81]

Was Ed Martin also sitting undetected in the same section at the 1990 and 1991 Final Four tournaments? Certainly his connection to UNLV, including Hunt and other Detroit players from previous teams, was common knowledge among college basketball insiders. Was Martin's and Perry's access to players on the Final Four teams monitored by the FBI, other law enforcement personnel, or the NCAA? Those questions were not asked. Also there was Fisher's statement to NCAA investigators that his relationship to Martin was "casual, friendly, but distant."[82] Following the 1996 accident, Fisher continued to plead ignorance concerning his relationship with Martin, despite Martin's presence at Robert Traylor's home on his recruiting visit. Fisher informed the *Detroit Free Press* that he made three calls to Martin between 1991 and 1993, when university records uncovered more than 100 calls during that time period.

Fisher's forging of Perry Watson's initials on an envelope of six complimentary tickets to Martin was brought to the attention of Athletic Director Joe Roberson, who admonished Fisher in a letter:

> I am disappointed that you failed to share with me your findings regarding Martin's efforts, his reputation in the athletic community, his presence in a recruiting visit you made, his relationship with certain basketball student-athletes and his potential influence on them. As we have discussed, it would have been more appropriate for you to have brought Mr. Martin and his activities to my attention at the time you became aware of them rather than for me to only learn of them upon the occasion of our departmental inquiry. I accept your assurances that similar activity by any person(s) in the future will be made known to me immediately.[83]

Fisher's relationship to Martin was serious, dangerous, and disingenuous. At the 1992 Final Four, Martin and Webber's father were given rooms on the same floor as the players. Martin received the same access to players during the 1993 Final Four tournament.[84] A gambler with that kind of access to a team's players assuredly was not missed by the bookies, big-time gamblers, and, later, federal prosecutors. And from whose seats did Martin watch the games? Fisher was not asked that question.

In March 2002, a seven-count federal indictment charged Ed Martin, his wife Hilda, and partner Clarence Malvo with operating an illegal gambling operation, money laundering, and conspiracy to launder money.[85] Some of Martin's associates were included in the charges.[86] Martin had fully expected a repayment of all money given or loaned to players. Later, he pled guilty to one charge of conspiracy to launder money in exchange for agreeing only to talk about his relationships with the Michigan players and the NCAA.[87] Invariably, administrators and coaches at New Mexico, UNLV, Iowa, Syracuse, Michigan State, Missouri, Purdue, and Minnesota breathed a sigh of relief upon hearing of Martin's plea bargain. All of these programs had Detroit Public League players on their rosters at various time periods who may have also received laundered money from Martin.

In September 2002, Chris Webber, his father, Mayce Webber, and his aunt, Charlene Johnson, were indicted on one count of conspiracy to obstruct justice and three counts of false declarations before a Grand Jury in June and August 2000.[88] At the time, Webber, in an attorney-crafted memo, stated: "This case is about a man who befriended kids like myself, preying on our naiveté, our innocence, claimed he loved us and he wanted to support us, but wanting to cash in on that love that we thought was free."[89]

Less than one year later, Webber, then a superstar NBA player with the Sacramento Kings, pled guilty to a lesser charge of criminal contempt, admitting he had lied to the Grand Jury. He also admitted to receiving and paying off $38,200 to Martin in cash, not the $280,000 as Martin had claimed. The death of Martin in February 2003 significantly weakened the case against the Webbers and Johnson.[90] Webber later admitted to lying to a Grand Jury and was fined $100,000 and sentenced to 300 hours of community service. The four charges were reduced to a misdemeanor, and the NBA suspended him for three months.[91] Before his death, Martin also admitted giving former Michigan players Robert Traylor $160,000, Maurice Taylor $105,000, Louis Bullock $71,000, and Albert White $37,000 (White transferred to Missouri after his freshman year). The total amount of Martin's alleged payments to the five players was $737,000. When unreported cash payments to unidentified players, rent for apartments, small cash payouts as admitted to by Jalen Rose in the *Fab Five* documentary, gifts, paid trips for parents and players, and food are added to the above total, the possibility of Martin giving millions to launder illegal gambling profits to college players was staggeringly real.

8

Organized Crime and Sports

"I'll Break Your Legs.
You'll Never Play Again!"

In the late 1940s, Republican politicians and a few journalists looking to embarrass Democratic President Harry Truman had begun to examine organized crime as a nationwide syndicate. For years, the Republicans wanted to investigate the relationship between local criminal activities and Democratic city political machines.[1] Supported for years by Kansas City's Pendergast organization, Truman was further embarrassed when two Democratic leaders were assassinated gangland-style in Kansas City. The incentive to create a congressional committee intensified in 1945, when Truman became president. In May 1950, the Kefauver Committee was created to investigate the existence of a unified national organized crime syndicate and determine if the organization's prime source of revenue was derived from the transmission of horse racing data and operating a lay-off bookmaking business. This practice allowed bookies to balance their bets on horses when too much money came in on one side of a bet.[2]

The committee was also looking for evidence to support what it believed misled the public about the changing nature of sports betting in America in the 1950s. In the 1930s and 1940s, horse racing had been the country's most popular sports gambling activity. Among its many shortcomings, the committee failed to consider the undocumented growth of human sports in the 1940s and 1950s. Gamblers were finding betting on football, basketball, and baseball more satisfying and profitable than horse racing. The increased regulation of horse racing by legislators looking for ways to add revenues to state budgets decreased the amount bet illegally with bookmakers associated with organized crime.[3] The advantages of betting on professional and college sports included selecting from a field of two instead of eight or more, and the ten percent vigorish charged against losing bets. That rate was lower than the 15 to 20 percent charged to losers for playing the horses. Sports bettors also appreciated that once they placed their money on a game or match, the bet was set in stone. Fluctuating odds or point spreads would not affect one's bet. In horse racing, final odds would not be known until post time. Hence, the value of a bet might decease or increase depending on the total money bet on a race.[4]

The Kefauver Committee also failed to understand that the point spread had converted betting into an intellectual challenge that was favored by a younger generation of gamblers and bookies. At the same time that this different way of betting was taking hold, Americans were welcoming television sets into their living rooms and taverns.[5] By 1952, nearly all taverns and one-third of all homes had installed a television set. More than 75 percent of private residences were equipped with sets in 1960. Ironically, the vast audiences of the Kefauver hearings were generated because of television, whose impact was not understood by the committee.[6]

Had they recognized the impact of television, they would have known that the world of horse wire services had been rendered almost obsolete. This new medium was vital in reporting game and individual competitive events in real time to bookies and gamblers. The committee had scheduled hearings on sports corruption while in New York City. Because of time constraints, Kefauver canceled the hearings that would have been held almost simultaneously with the arrests of the players, gamblers, and fixers involved in the 1951 college basketball scandal. The increase in legislation designed to address the increase in illegal bookmaking and wagering on sports did not prevent gamblers from seeking inside information to secure a sure bet. Inside knowledge has always been the *sine qua non* of sports gamblers. David Porter reported that two of the principal characters in the Boston College (BC) scandal of 1978–1979, Henry Hill and James Burke, won big money during the 1970–1971 basketball season. Working in concert with big-time New York City bookmaker Ralph Atlas, the trio allegedly used inside information on college teams obtained from two retired school teachers to crush bookies.

Hill and Burke were longtime organized crime members. According to Douglas Behm, a special prosecutor working with the Organized Crime Strike Force (OCSF) of the Eastern District of New York, the character in the *Goodfellas* movie hardly resembled the real-life Hill. Stated Behm:

> I watched *Goodfellas* and he kind of came off as a lovable schlemiel. Henry was not a loveable schlemiel. Henry was a dangerous guy, and there was an atmosphere of danger around him. I remember when we first met with the FBI agents, one of the first things I told them was, "This guy's got a shtick, and he's good at it, but be careful with this guy."[7]

Hill's and Burke's previous success may have been the impetus for their involvement in the 1978–1979 Boston College (BC) game-fixing scandal. Even though he was a close friend of the notorious Burke, a top associate of the Lucchese family, Hill was not a top-level mobster. Hill drew the immediate attention of another prosecutor, Ed McDonald, a BC graduate, in the course of investigating the Lufthansa heist at New York's JFK airport in December 1978.[8]

The fixers included two BC starters as well as reserve center Rick Kuhn's friends from the suburbs of Pittsburgh, Rocco and Tony Perla. Convicted Pittsburgh drug dealer Paul Mazzei met Hill in prison, and they later hatched the game-fixing plan with Kuhn and the Perla brothers. Besides Kuhn, the involved players included point guard Jim Sweeney and leading scorer Ernie Cobb. Some of the events surrounding the game rigging by the fixers, organized crime members, and three players have been disputed in the documents, media reports, and books about the two trials that followed in October 1981 and March 1984. However, what has not been disputed are the actions of the players in agreeing to consort with at least three associates of a notorious New York crime family. All five defendants in the first trial were found guilty. Rick Kuhn received ten years in prison, the stiffest sentence ever meted out to a college athlete up to that date for conspiring to fix games. Burke received 20 years and was fined $30,000. The judge rationalized Kuhn's sentence by stating, "An argument can be offered that a substantial term of incarceration imposed on the defendant will be recalled by another athlete who may be tempted to compromise his performance."[9] Kuhn's sentence was later reduced to four years and Burke's to 12 years. Mazzei and the Perla brothers received sentences of various lengths that were later reduced. Cobb, in a subsequent trial in 1984, was acquitted. Sweeney was never indicted and testified against his former teammates, Kuhn and Cobb. In the 1984 trial, Peter Vario received jail time and Perry a year's probation and a $5,000 fine. In the end, it was greed that was the undoing of the college players and the outer circles of organized crime.

Hill became known to the Organized Crime Task Force (OCTF) by accident. The OCTF was seeking to apprehend high-ranking Lucchese family members who were hijacking, extorting, and stealing at JFK airport and adversely affecting commerce at one of the nation's biggest airports. Burke had eliminated all but one of the individuals involved in the Lufthansa heist. McDonald saw Hill's testifying to Burke's funding of the alleged six fixed BC games as a way to put Burke behind bars. His bets of $25,000 to $50,000 on a game were pocket change in comparison to the millions he was making from his criminal activities. Considering the amount of money the BC players allegedly received for risking their futures and lives, by all accounts it was bad judgment. The players risked serious physical harm and death to themselves or families. They may not have been aware that their primary financial backer, Burke, and his associates had committed more than 50 murders.

Kuhn was undoubtedly a willing participant in the scheme because of his Pittsburgh connections. Sweeney's and Cobb's attempts to play their best at times, but poorly enough to convince the bettors that they were in "on the deal," does not mitigate the fact they could have prevented the rigging before it started. Sweeney's post-trial rationalization that he was "sucked into the fixing" contradicts his unwise actions during the 1978–1979 season. After seeking the advice of BC football player and roommate Mike Maycock, to whom he admitted his involvement in the fixed games, Sweeney was set to meet with retired FBI agent and BC Athletic Director Bill Flynn and the head coach, Tom Davis. The meeting did not take place, as Sweeney rationalized his change of mind by stating in part: "I didn't have a relationship with those people even though one guy was my coach and the other was the AD. It is just that I didn't have a relationship with them, and didn't feel I had the confidence that I could go there and they would listen."[10]

Sweeney's rationalization points to one of the dangers of college athletes associating with organized crime. In past incidents of game fixing, it has not been uncommon for individuals who find themselves in the crosshairs of mobsters to develop second thoughts about their participation with the underbelly of organized crime and finger these individuals to law enforcement. After BC failed to cover the nine-point spread against Fordham, Sweeney's comment to Rocco Perla further blunts his later testimony under oath that he was an unwilling participant in the fixing scheme. Commenting on missing a late free throw, Sweeney stated to Perla, "I looked up at the rim and saw a pair of cement shoes so I figured I should miss."[11]

An 80 percent free throw shooter, he testified in the 1981 trial that the free throw was missed unintentionally. Also, it was not brought up by any of the defendant's attorneys that in certain games Sweeney, as the point guard— or quarterback of the offense—bypassed Cobb in play selection or did not pass the ball to him. There are two possibilities. First, Sweeney was playing straight and believed his teammate was playing for BC not to cover the spread or lose. Keeping the ball out of Cobb's hands would not allow him to play successfully for the bettors. Or Sweeney was part of the fix and believed Cobb playing his best could disrupt one of the two possible bettor outcomes (i.e., covering the spread or not covering the spread). Both players were deeply suspicious of each other playing for gamblers. We will never know about Sweeney, as he publicly denied the possibility of his involvement in any fix.

Most court observers believed BC graduate McDonald gave Sweeney a pass in exchange for his knowledge of the rigging.[12] Cobb's taking $1,000 after the Harvard game from known gamblers was enough to derail his NBA ambitions. In the formal bylaws of the NBA, any association with gamblers could result in a lifetime ban. In Cobb's case, the professionals showed little interest in drafting him.

College football and basketball abuses, including the possibility of connections to organized crime and illegal gambling, were exposed in an eight-count, 85-page indictment filed by U.S. Attorney Anton Valukas for the Northern District of Illinois in September 1988. New York sports agents Norby Walters and Lloyd Bloom, after an 18-month FBI investigation, were charged with racketeering, mail fraud, and conspiracy to commit extortion, in connection with the signing of 44 athletes to professional contracts before their college eligibility had expired.[13] Federal prosecutors also indicted former Ohio State All-American receiver Cris Carter, then playing for the Philadelphia Eagles, for mail fraud and obstruction of justice. Agent David Lueddeke was charged with perjury and obstruction of justice for falsely testifying before a grand jury and concealing that he had paid Carter $5,000 for signing a contract.[14] For college and professional sports, the indictment demonstrated how the tentacles of organized crime had come within a whisker of controlling college and professional athletes. The indictment stated in part:

> It was further part of the conspiracy that defendants Norby Walters and Lloyd Bloom, together with Michael Franzese, would and did agree to the commission of multiple acts of racketeering on behalf of Norby Walters Associates and World Sports & Entertainment. It was further part of the conspiracy that defendants Norby Walters and Lloyd Bloom would and did use their association with Michael Franzese to obtain and retain clients of Norby Walters Associates and World Sports & Entertainment by extortionate means.... Norby Walters and Lloyd Bloom would and did use their association with Michael Franzese and his reputation in the community as a member of an organized crime family to convey directly and indirectly threats of economic and physical harm to actual and potential clients of Norby Walters Associates and World Sports & Entertainment. It was further part of the conspiracy that in or about 1984 and early 1985, defendant Norby Walters discussed with Michael Franzese expanding the business of Norby Walters Associates to include the representation of college athletes in their professional careers and marketing their abilities. Defendant Norby Walters asked Franzese for $50,000 to help fund the expansion, which money Franzese provided for defendant Norby Walters in cash ... would continue to use Michael Franzese and his reputation as a member of organized crime to obtain and retain clients.[15]

The case drew the attention of the Chicago FBI office and Special Agent George Alexander in March 1987, when sports agent Kathy Clements was beaten mob-style in her office. One of the few women in the cutthroat business of sports agency, she had approached Chicago sports agent and former attorney Steve Zucker in nearby Skokie, Illinois, a year earlier about joining his firm. After joining Zucker, she recruited Washington's Reggie Rogers and Nebraska's Doug DuBose, only to find out they had already signed a contract with Walters and Bloom. Before Clements joined the firm, Tennessee wide receiver Tim McGee had switched to Zucker after signing with Walters and Bloom. McGee was a first-round draft choice, and the Detroit Lions would select Rogers in the first round of the 1987 NFL draft.

Around the same time as the beating, the *Atlanta Constitution* ran a series of articles recounting the activities of Walters and Bloom. For the previous 15 years, Walters had been an agent in the music industry, representing African American entertainers such as Peabo Bryson, Kool and the Gang, Luther Vandross, and Patti LaBelle.[16] The business was noted for using thugs to enforce contracts. Two months earlier in Mobile, Alabama, the site of the Senior Bowl all-star game, Clements met Bloom for the first time. Clements had been sitting at a second-floor bar when Bloom sat next to her on a stool and began to talk about the money McGee owed to World Sports & Entertainment Agency (WS&E). Bloom then stated, "You know, Kathy, where we come from, people who don't pay their bills get their hands broken."[17]

In 1984, Bloom approached Walters by proposing they form an agency representing college athletes in negotiations with professional organizations. The business would target African American football and basketball players projected to be high draft choices and their families. In their first foray in the business at the Senior Bowl in January 1985, Walters and Bloom had little success in signing players because the outstanding ones had already been signed in violation of NCAA rules. Soon Bloom and Walters were beating the agents at their own game and signing players before they were eligible. In an interview with the *Washington Post*, Bloom attributed WS&E's success "to the power of a major music company. And, that music is America."[18]

The pitch was always the same. After Walters or Bloom initially contacted a player, Walters would invite him to his office lined with gold records on the walls, talk about the multimillion-dollar contracts he'd secured for black entertainers, and lay $2,500 on a table in $20 bills—all for the taking if the athlete signed a contract that would be postdated to the time when he became eligible to negotiate with agents.[19] Soon WS&E began forwarding monthly payments for cars, gambling, and multiple trips to various locations and to players' parents and siblings for home repairs, medical bills, and other expenses. Prosecutors calculated that WS&E had distributed at least $800,000 before the first indictment in 1988.

At other times, Bloom and Walters scoured the country, seeking outstanding black athletes projected to go high in the draft. They had traveled an estimated 300,000 miles in two years since entering the business in 1984. Informally, WS&E had signed 58 football and basketball players. Though the indictment named only 44 players, 14 of the football players had compromised their legal standing by engaging in a series of unknowingly illegal acts such as sharing their grand jury testimonies with reporters. In court, their testimonies could be impeached or rendered useless. In the series of articles that appeared in various media sources, Walters unabashedly and publicly contended that the money given to each football and basketball player was a loan that by law had to be repaid.

In one lawsuit filed against Ronnie Harmon, the Buffalo Bills' first-round draft pick in 1986, Walters alleged that the former Iowa running back was given $54,924.42 in cash and gifts, including $32,000 as a down-payment for a lease on a Mercedes. The contract and promissory note were attached as exhibits to the lawsuit, according to one article in the *Atlanta Constitution*.[20] Walters alleged that Harmon had breached a contract signed on March 9, 1985, the spring before his senior year, and was suing the former Iowa running back for $500,000. In the same story, Walters highlighted the hypocrisy of college sports by citing Texas Governor Bill Clements, the head of SMU's Board of Governors, who had approved the secret payoffs to football players at SMU in 1986, leading to a rare NCAA "death penalty" in 1987.[21] Walters vowed to fight the corruption, asserting, "Nobody in this world can intimidate me but God."[22] In this and one subsequent lawsuit filed by Walters to recover his money, the court dismissed the claims.

One of the 13 SMU players receiving secret payments from WS&E was running back Ron Morris, who'd signed a contract with Walters and Bloom in November 1985—late in his junior year. In October 1986, during his senior year, SMU booster Sherman Blount and head coach Ron Meyer had Morris sign a contract as his new agents. Morris now wanted out of the WS&E contract. After a subsequent conversation with Bloom in Dallas and later on the phone from New York, Morris handed the FBI a tape of the conversations. The FBI heard Bloom tell Morris the money he received was from "people in Los Angeles who don't play around, people who don't care what they do to you or your family." In early November 1986, Bloom reminded Morris over the phone that "Walters [will] have someone break your legs.... You'll never play again."[23] Morris was reminded in that same conversation that the "bigger backers in Los Angeles" might blow up his new agents' houses. A tape recorded conversation between Walters and Morris included the agent portraying himself as a "purveyor of cool" and "agent of the stars."[24]

Walters lacked knowledge of sports and background in representing athletes, and his feigned African American style and bravado alarmed the players. All but two of his signees wanted out of the contract they signed with WS&E. Many of the players began to refer to Bloom's Brooklynesque accent as comical, but the threats were taken seriously. In one instance, an SMU player, defensive lineman Jerry Ball, took matters into his own hands when Bloom showed up to convince the All-American to stay with WS&E and repay the $30,000 he was given by Walters. Picking Bloom up at the airport, Ball began to drive toward an unpopulated area outside of Dallas. Pulling off the road, Ball reached under of the seat of his van and pulled out a .357 Magnum. Pointing the gun at Bloom, he warned, "Quit fucking with my brothers." "Come on, Jerry, put the gun away, stop joking around," the agent said. "I ain't joking around," Ball responded. "Everything's cool, nobody's threatened," responded Bloom.[25] The incident was later confirmed by both a reporter and the prosecution. Despite Ball's threat, Bloom continued with the intimidations, and many players genuinely feared for their safety.

After the first indictment, Walters defiantly spoke his mind in a full-page ad in *Billboard* magazine titled "Open Letter to the Industry." In the ad, Walters defended openly paying college athletes:

> As you know, it is not unusual in the entertainment industry that record companies, managers, and booking agencies are frequently called upon to make loans to clients against their future earnings. We had frequently done that for our music clients, and we offered similar accommodations to our new sports clients. We entered into agreements with, and made loans to, many college athletes. In doing so, we believed completely that our conduct did not violate any state or federal law. And when some of those athletes refused to honor their obligations to our firm, our attorneys filed lawsuits against those athletes to protect our contractual rights, which we and our attorneys believed to be lawful, binding, and enforceable.[26]

To prove WS&E used extortionate tactics or caused economic harm to the players, the prosecution would not need to go any further than Temple All-American halfback Paul Palmer. After receiving a $450,000 signing bonus from Kansas City in July 1987, Bloom comingled the bonus with a new business he set up, Lincoln Financial Services, in Los Angeles. Without Palmer's knowledge, $233,000 of the bonus was taken by Bloom. The agent used the money for the following: He purchased a cashier's check for $78,000, payable to Walters as a commission for contract negotiations, and another cashier's check for $30,000, payable to Walters as repayment for a loan. A third cashier's check for $125,000 was payable to Lincolnshire, the credit repair business Bloom had created. Bloom wrote a check payable to himself for approximately $27,000. With that money, he wrote checks for personal expenses such as his American Express account ($1,588), MasterCard ($1,309), Visa ($6,700), accountant ($500), tailor ($138), clothier ($6,959), and karate class fee ($150).

His father was paid $2,500 and his former wife $1,200, and $792 was spent for tableware and home entertainment. Nineteen days later, Bloom spent the Lincolnshire $125,000, purchasing a $200,000 life insurance policy for Palmer with WS&E as the beneficiary.[27] Palmer and John Clay of Missouri were the two players who had not "jumped ship" from WS&E. Stunned by the discovery of Bloom's extravagant spending of his bonus, Palmer recounted to prosecutors that he wanted to purchase a Volkswagen Rabbit for his brother and sister with the signing bonus. When Bloom was asked for advice about a car for his siblings, Bloom responded, "Look at a Yugo or Hyundai, something more economical."[28] Palmer was not aware that Bloom had recently paid $82,247 of his money as down payment for a lease on a new Rolls Royce Corniche convertible for personal use—the world's most expensive car in 1987.

Despite Bloom's filing for bankruptcy, he hired former sports agent Mike Trope as his attorney for the upcoming trial. Trope had revealed how easy it was to bypass NCAA signing rules in *Necessary Roughness*, published in 1987. The book was an account of college sport corruption that Trope had witnessed firsthand, including football programs at Nebraska and Oklahoma and UCLA's basketball program during their NCAA championship run from 1963 to 1975. Trope was admitted to the California Bar the same year the book was published. Despite his unscrupulous reputation as a sports agent, Trope, from 1973 to 1985, represented more NFL first-round draft picks than any other agent, including six Heisman Trophy winners, and negotiated more than 200 contracts.[29] Trope's involvement in Bloom's case was a godsend for the loose cannon, who had threatened several players with implicit references to organized crime.

Clearly, the two agents were using and spreading organized crime influence in the sports world. As a rookie attorney, Trope, in representing Bloom during the investigative stages of the WS&E signings, had completed his homework. Realizing that Bloom's life was in the hands of Walters because of Walters' long association with John and Michael Franzese and other organized crime figures, he knew there was no way Bloom could give up Walters to the prosecution.[30] "It wasn't about the schools getting defrauded," stated Trope. "It was about Norby and the mob. They didn't say the name, but they [the prosecution] made it clear that they thought Norby was hooked up big-time to the mob."[31] Trope proceeded to seek the best lawyer for Bloom in Chicago and recommended he hire Dan Webb, rated as one of the top ten trial lawyers in the United States. Trope also joined Bloom's legal defense team.[32]

As the prosecution prepared for the trial, other premature signings by basketball players would emerge. To put out fires and recruit clients, African

Americans Terry Bolar and former Detroit Lions star Ron Jessie were hired by WS&E. Bloom had signed each ex-player for $3,000. At Alabama, Derrick McKey had signed with WS&E. McKey was the Southeastern Conference Player of the Year in 1987 as a junior, with one year left of eligibility. An FBI investigation in Tuscaloosa uncovered that McKey and starting guard Terry Caner had been recruited by Terry Bolar.[33] For using two ineligible players, the NCAA docked Alabama $253,447. The university wanted Walters to pay that amount and was planning to file a lawsuit against him. Mike Trope had already cut a deal for Bloom to testify against Walters. The university had calculated that McKey was worth $250,000 for the championship he helped deliver his junior season and $250,000 in lost revenue for a possible championship the next season.[34] Ultimately the university settled with Walters for $200,000, in the wake of being criticized by the NCAA for pursuing the lawsuits.

As the federal investigation progressed toward a trial that involved the universities and players, the widespread corruption that existed in college football and basketball in the 1980s was so deep and pervasive that the prosecutors did not dare expose it to a jury. In an incident at Clemson, South Carolina, not reported by the media, an Atlanta salesman heard loud voices from a hotel room adjacent to the one he occupied in June 1986. Gary Defauw, a high-tech electronics salesman, recognized the names of Clemson football stars Terrence Flagler and Terrance Roulhac and realized they were listening to Walters loudly selling something that was obviously wrong. After overhearing the players agreeing to sign contracts and a subsequent celebration, Defauw was convinced he'd overheard information that should be reported, at least, to Clemson head coach Danny Ford or the school's athletic director. Stepping outside his door into the hallway, he was confronted by Walters and Bloom and unwittingly said, "I heard everything." He was invited to an unwanted meeting in a closed part of the hotel's coffee shop. There Walters warned Defauw, "If you say anything to anybody about this, you're...."[35]

After more threats, DeFauw contacted the Clemson police, and the three individuals were hustled into a room at the police station by a detective with a tape recorder. Soon a sergeant appeared and suggested the three "hash this out between each other." Incredibly, after repeated requests to speak with coach Danny Ford or the Clemson athletic director, Defauw was asked to sign a paper by the police stating that he would not pursue any further action against Walters, Bloom, or the two Clemson players and would leave town as soon as possible.[36] Defauw was dumbfounded. When he returned to Atlanta, his lawyer advised him to contact the local newspaper. The suggestion was rejected by the salesman.

When the *Atlanta Constitution* broke the news about WS&E in a series of articles in the spring of 1997, Defauw was tempted to share his story—but still remained silent. Without any knowledge they were ineligible, Flagler and Roulhac played the entire 1986 season. Assuredly, the Clemson head coach, AD, and local police were aware of their ineligibility. During the subsequent investigation in Chicago, Defauw shared his notes and tape with the FBI in Atlanta. How many other ineligible players had played entire seasons, after signing with agents, is unknown. The larger question is: How many coaches and universities had chosen not to report ineligible players who had signed with agents?

Before the trial, prosecutors Anton Valukas and Howard Pearl had viewed enough evidence to charge the involved players with defrauding the universities and committing tax evasion. By all accounts, they were aware that accepting the money violated NCAA rules. The gifts that Walters gave to players suddenly made them flush with money. They were certainly aware that drawing attention to themselves, especially among their teammates, coaches, and compliance directors, would invite questions. When asked by coaches if they were involved with gamblers, invariably they responded in the negative. Coaches were not about to risk exposing their programs to an investigation by reporting their suspicions to the FBI. The players justified their receipt of the money by citing that they and their families were "flat broke."[37]

However, the records, if they are to be believed, tell a different story. Most of the money was spent by the involved players, and only one refused Walters's and Bloom's money. Their hands were always out, and it appears very few if any were expecting to repay the debt. It appeared the involved players, coaches and other athletic officials, if given the opportunity, ignored the NCAA rules. The individuals in athletic programs responsible for monitoring adherence to NCAA and institutional rules "knew the game was to see [new cars and clothes] but not act." Stated Tennessee wide receiver Tim McGee, "I took the money because my mother had bills. If the coaches knew about it, no way would they report it."[38]

After interviewing the players, the prosecutors and FBI Agent Alexander came to realize that the SMU payoffs were not the exception.[39] At first the prosecutors wanted to charge the players with fraud for accepting scholarships and income tax evasion for not reporting the money received from Walters. In the players' minds, they were only violating NCAA rules that were routinely abused by most big-time colleges. However, if that strategy was pursued, the jury might take its eyes off the ball and allow the main culprits, Walters and Bloom, to walk. Thus the prosecution established a Pre-Trial

Diversion Program for the involved players. If they chose to cooperate, testify, perform community service, and repay the schools the money a scholarship was worth for the year they played ineligibly, they would not be charged with (and possibly convicted of) a felony.

After interviewing several players, the prosecution realized not all of them could be presented as naive victims of Walters's and Bloom's defiant plundering of top athletic talent. In court, some would assuredly paint a picture of the colleges operating as plantations where physicality was all that mattered in their quest for lucrative television contracts. First-round Detroit draftee Reggie Rogers, by the spring of 1997, was an emotional mess. A year earlier his brother Don, who'd played one year in the NFL and was selected to the Pro Bowl, died of a cocaine overdose at his bachelor party in Sacramento. Rogers had also signed with another agent, was unable to converse lucidly, and possessed a limited attention span.[40] By the end of the prosecution's pre-trial interview, it was evident that Rogers could not read. But, he was eligible to compete for the University of Washington in football and basketball…. After several DUIs, including one in which three people were killed, and several run-ins with the police, Rogers died of a heart attack in Seattle in October 2013 at the age of 49.[41]

The WS&E's contracts were not carefully read by the players and were the worst the NFL Players Association had ever seen. Several parts of the contracts were seriously flawed, and it was a toss-up as to which one was the most one-sided. Clauses that jumped out included:

> An agreement "that Walters could endorse Player's name upon and cash check and retain therefrom all sums owing to WS&E."[42]
>
> The statement "that Walters would be paid his percentage based upon the total value of the contract and payable within three days."[43]
>
> Total value included the total of all salaries, signing, and other bonuses, and all other cash or cash equivalent compensation to which player could receive under such contract or series of contracts.[44]

The government's key witness at the Walters-Bloom trial was Michael Franzese, a former capo in the Colombo crime family. A prodigious moneymaker for the crime syndicate, Franzese and his partner, Lawrence Iorizzo, illegally controlled a significant portion of the gasoline business in New York City and northern New Jersey. During the Walters-Bloom investigation, he was serving a ten-year sentence in Long Beach, California, at the Federal Correction Institution at Terminal Island. The federal government had been after the "Mafia Prince" because he and his partner, Iorizzo, had failed to pay state and federal excise taxes. This allowed his company to undercut its competitors by selling gasoline at cut-rate prices. From 1981 to 1985, it was estimated that the company defrauded the federal and state governments of $1 billion by using a chain of dummy companies.[45] The tax debt was passed along until it ended up with a company about to collapse. The Colombo family's muscle, influence, and power assisted in running the company. The feds estimated that the mob earned $300 million in one transaction. Reportedly, Franzese personally earned $50 million from the operation.

The Mafioso also set up a movie production company in Miami and produced four "B" grade movies, including *Savage Streets*. Incredibly, the Miami city fathers toasted Franzese, even though the gasoline profits were laundered through the production company. After Iorizzo was arrested in Panama, he flipped on Franzese, leading to his 28-count indictment by a Brooklyn grand jury in 1985.[46] By March 1986, Franzese's lawyers worked out a plea agreement that included ten years in prison and restitution of $15 million. A federal judge, hoping the government might retrieve the rest of the embezzled money, issued an order allowing the mobster, under the supervision of federal marshals, to continue in the film business. When Franzese passed bad checks to the marshals, he was remanded back to prison to serve the ten-year sentence.

Michael Franzese, pictured here in both portrait and profile, a capo in the Columbo crime family, who funded part of music agent Norby Walters's foray into prematurely signing college football and basketball players (photograph 2009 by Jens Astrup, https://commons.wikimedia.org).

In August 1987, the Chicago prosecutors were presented a big gift when former U.S. Senate investigator Bruce Selcraig's interview with Michael Franzese was included in an article written by Craig Neff and published by *Sports Illustrated (SI)*. Unlike Iorizzo, who joined the federal Witness Protection Program, Franzese loved the publicity, including his picture in *SI*. The *Atlanta Constitution's* series on WS&E quoted players who reported that Bloom and Walters on several occasions indicated that their operation was backed by "people who broke legs."[47] Selcraig had interviewed Walters' brother Walter, who rebutted any assertion that his brother was not connected to the five New York Mafia families through the nightclub they formerly owned in New York. In fact, the club lost its liquor license when mobsters Oresto Joseph Bruni and Rosario "Sonny" Parisi were shot to death in the club in March 1966. The two Mafiosos were associates of crime boss Carmine Lombardozzi, who was escorted by Norby Walters through a passageway to an adjacent nightclub before the police arrived. The nightspot also had a "highly adverse police and license history for assaults and prostitution activities."[48] Stated Walter about the clientele who visited the club: "All five [New York Mafia] families were well represented. We were friends with all of them. They were good customers.... He [Norby] could bull---- with anybody. He could talk with a Mafia captain. He could talk with a hooker off the street. He knew how to handle anybody."[49] Hoping to link the Clements beating to Walters, FBI agent Alexander and the two Chicago prosecutors believed that Franzese's testimony might put away the music agent and Bloom for a long time.

The next step was to bring the jailed Mafia kingpin to Chicago and investigate the Colombo family's connection to WS&E. What the prosecutors learned from Franzese left no doubt that at least one crime syndicate was planning to use college and professional athletes as a source of ensuring it won big money betting on football and basketball. In 12 hours of interviews with one of the few Mafia members who quit the mob and were not buried in New York's East River, the brilliant moneymaker and wannabe movie producer gave the government a compelling account of Walters' Mafia connections. After Walters entered the music business, exclusively booking African American entertainers, he found it necessary to use "muscle" to convince agents of performers to sign with his agency. He used connections with the Colombo family, primarily through Sonny Franzese, Michael's father.

Walters entered into a 50–50 agreement with the organization when agents needed to be prodded into signing with him. Using his connection to the Colombos, Walters became one of the most prolific booking agents in the United States. If a performer's agent was sitting on a fence, Walters, according to Michael Franzese, would say, "Hey, I'm with Michael and Sonny, and my act belongs in here, and I want it all."[50] The agent to the stars had not lived up to his part of the financial bargain even as he earned millions. When Sonny Franzese was released from jail, he realized Walters had stiffed him and he wanted him whacked for not honoring his agreement. Despite a meeting with Michael Franzese warning Walters about his playing games with the mob, he continued to scam the mob and would have been killed without the younger Franzese's intervention. Envisioning using some of Walters's entertainers in his movie business, he spared his life. After the Walters-Bloom WS&E threats surfaced in 1987, the Atlanta reporter writing the story reported receiving several phone calls alleging that in the music industry, "Norby Walters' reputation is that he walks with a violin case."[51] The most compelling information during the interview was Franzese's recollection about his $50,000 investment in WS&E and his knowledge of the Clements beating. Regarding the Colombo family's foray into the sports world, in the mobster's words:

> There's no question in my mind that had Norby been successful, and both my associates and I realized we had some control over a number of major league [NFL and NBA] ballplayers, that at some time we'd try and use this to our advantage. Even if it was distasteful to me and I'm not saying it was totally distasteful—I'm quite sure other family members and superiors in the family would have approached me without a doubt. I mean the mob loves to gamble. The mob is built upon … almost everybody is a gambler. It's a major enterprise. I saw that as a tremendous possibility. Just establishing a line, throwing the bets the right way, making the bets tilt the right way. That would have been a tremendous advantage.[52]

When mobsters bet big money on games, such as $20 million, someone playing for gamblers is always a possibility. If the athlete is in debt or filmed in a compromising situation, extortion is also a possibility. Although Walters had sold himself as a successful businessman to the athletes, in reality, the Colombo family controlled him. His financial debt to the family did not allow him to freely represent athletes without some kickback or payoff to the mob. It was not implausible to infer that college or professional athletes who ended up controlled by Walters and mobsters had used poor judgment. They would in all likelihood have continued to make poor choices, including rigging games to ensure big paydays for mobsters. The number of athletes who made big money but ended up broke was not lost on Franzese. As far as he was concerned, "If Norby was doing it [signing athletes to contracts]; it was like me doing it. So I told him, 'Pursue it.'"[53]

In Franzese's opinion, once the scheme was in operation, other Colombo family or La Cosa Nostra crime families would have come to the table, asking to share in the fixed games. The notorious mobster denied sanctioning any of WS&E threats and believed what he had heard, that Bloom's style was bad business. "But, let me tell you the guy was stupid," stated Franzese.[54] The closest the prosecutors would come to connecting Walters to the Clements attack was Franzese receiving a request from the booking agent for "assistance with some broad in Chicago." Jerry Zimmerman was one of Franzese's associates and a former film director. Franzese asked him to contact his father's chauffeur, Frankie Campione, in New York to assist Walters. Campione was never identified as the Clements assailant and was later sentenced to three years in prison in January 2010 for a shakedown of a gambling club in Long Island.[55]

By now the prosecutors were convinced that Franzese would be a significant witness at the trial, as his knowledge of WS&E and its strategies in exploiting the players corroborated the evidence already collected. Franzese's denial of having discussed using the players in a fixing scheme with WS&E made sense despite his investment of $50,000 about the time the business was started. Heavy surveillance and wiretaps shut him down as far as entering into another illegal venture, and he was facing a 28-count indictment. The prosecutor's strategy at the trial needed to be a delicate balance between demonstrating to the jury that Walters and Bloom had violated federal statutes, including mail fraud, and not to place commercialized college football and basketball on trial. In fact, trial judge George Marovich advised the defense attorneys at the beginning of the proceedings that the trial was not going to be a "morality play" about college sports.[56]

The trial began in the spring and ended in the summer of 1989. At times it was an indictment of college sports. It was impossible to portray any of the players who testified in any way other than unscrupulous, with hands out to the highest bidder and part of a deeply flawed college system. All nine on the witness stand acknowledged that they played while academically ineligible, assisted the programs in earning millions, and were clueless about how to earn an undergraduate degree.[57] They were all well-versed in working the system, knowing college officials would ignore any NCAA or civil violations unless caught. A widespread rumor was that Ron Harmon had played for gamblers by fumbling four times and muffing a sure touchdown pass in Iowa's 20–16 loss to UCLA in the 1986 Rose Bowl. Following the game, heated words were exchanged between Harmon and his teammates who were fully aware that the halfback had received money from WS&E. Lawmakers in Iowa were on the verge of probing Harmon's performance against UCLA. They were cut off by the Justice Department, which wanted to prosecute and uncover Walters' and Bloom's connection to the Colombos. The fixing rumors persisted, as Harmon had conned WS&E out of more than $50,000. However, it should be noted that Harmon played 12 years in the NFL and compiled a 3.4 rushing average, numbers that suggest he did not play for gamblers.

Bloom's defense attorney, Dan Webb, persuasively argued that the NCAA was a private club whose rules were not law. In fact, a powerful argument was presented by Walters' attorney, Robert Gold, that WS&E had been legally advised that signing amateur players prematurely was not a violation of civil law.[58] Some of the players who suddenly were driving new cars were asked by their coaches if they were involved with gamblers— a perfunctory question that could only be answered honestly by a wiretap.

None of the coaches or compliance administrators had requested that the FBI wiretap any of the players who appeared with a brand new car. Of course, booster-provided new cars were a common practice in colleges. Michael Franzese's testimony was a significant turning point for the prosecution's win. His suave demeanor, intelligence, and deep knowledge of the possibilities of organized crime's infiltration into college and professional sports were daunting and persuasive.[59] He was a real-life version of

The 1986 Iowa All-American halfback Ron Harmon, who owed mob-funded Norby Walters's talent agency $54,000. It was widely suspected that Harmon's subpar performance in the 1986 Rose Bowl was because of the unpaid debt (courtesy of University of Iowa Archives and Special Collections).

"The Godfather," Michael Corleone, according to some observers. The presence of Michigan's Bo Schembechler and Notre Dame's Father Theodore Hesburgh on the witness stand hardly blunted the dismal portrait of college sports during the 1980s.

The closing arguments by Howard Pearl, one of the prosecuting attorneys, was noteworthy for integrating commercialized college sports' hypocrisy, how Walters and Bloom attempted to exploit the colleges' greed, and how the involved athletes were less than heroes. The violation of the mail fraud statute, argued Pearl, had occurred by placing statements in the mail certifying the athletes were NCAA eligible and sent to the various conferences.

Many legal theorists for the trial questioned the justice department's expenditure of extensive funds on the basis of this statute, reinforcing the belief that their target was the mob supporting WS&E. Legal points argued by the defense included distinctions between violating NCAA rules and violating public statutes. The defense attorneys further asserted that intending to deceive was dissimilar from actual fraud and that out of 58 athletes from 32 colleges who allegedly defrauded colleges, only nine schools and nine athletes were accusing WS&E of some type of fraud.[60]

These were the main issues the jury would need to consider in their deliberations regarding the guilt or innocence of Walters and Bloom. The prosecution could not submit records of WS&E giving money to athletes, its relations with organized crime, or receiving advice from the legal firm Shea & Gould that the signing of players prematurely was legal. Hence, the jury would have to rely substantially on the extensive court testimony in rendering a verdict. On April 14, 1989, the jury found Walters and Bloom guilty of defrauding Michigan and Purdue, conspiracy, and extortion.[61] The jury did not find that Iowa's and Michigan State's football and basketball programs had been defrauded by the agents.

In a post-trial interview, the jury forewoman didn't miss the opportunity to comment on the state of college athletics by saying, "We did want to send a message to the schools that they need to look at themselves, just as Norby Walters and Lloyd Bloom needed to do."[62] At the sentencing hearing in June 1989, Judge George M. Marovich commented on the state of college sports by stating: "If Walters and Bloom are guilty of mail fraud, racketeering, and conspiracy, so too may be alumni and other boosters who pass money or cars under the table and conspire with the athlete to lie about it, so too may be the coach or administrator who acts in like fashion."[63]

In June 1989, Walters was sentenced to five years in a federal prison and forfeiture of his assets collected in the enterprise, which by that time were down to $200,000. Bloom received three years in a federal prison and was ordered to make restitution of $145,000 to Paul Palmer. Chris Carter sobbed and begged for mercy at his sentencing. He was sentenced under strict federal guidelines and received five years' probation, was fined $15,000, and had to perform 1,500 hours of community service. Conservatively, losing one year of eligibility cost him at least $100,000 when he was eligible to sign a professional contract. Agent David Lueddeke received 26 months of jail time for two counts of perjury and one count of obstruction of justice. He was the only defendant who served time in jail. Over a year later in September 1990, the jury decision was overturned by the U.S. District Seventh Circuit Court of Appeals, which cited two errors by the presiding Judge Marovich.[64] The court also ruled that Bloom's and Walters's prosecutions in the lower court could proceed, but Walters and Bloom had to receive separate trials. Walters would begin negotiations to reach a plea bargain to avoid jail time, and Bloom was headed for a new trial.

In August 1993, Bloom was found murdered on Pacific Coast Highway in Malibu, California—not surprising to his close associates. The killing was believed to be mob-related and was never solved.

The manner in which the athletes accepted money from Walters and other agents hardly mattered to the public, mass media, and college establishment. It was reasonable to believe that some athletes may have used the money to gamble and risked potentially prosperous careers. Athletes have always been aware of their power in terms of controlling games' outcomes and the jobs of coaches. Within earshot of a trainer, Kansas City's Paul Palmer told a teammate in 1988 that he held the coach's security in his hands. How? "By putting the ball on the ground," he stated.[65] Head coach Frank Gantz soon after suspended Palmer indefinitely for undisclosed reasons. Palmer later played for Dallas, St. Louis, and Cincinnati, which released him in 1991.

Few people believe that the higher echelons of organized crime don't share in the profits from illegal sports gambling. Professional athletes' salaries and gambling enforcement by the leagues in almost every sport in the United States have significantly decreased the temptation, risk, and possibility of athletes, coaches, and game officials accepting offers to play for gamblers. By 2016, college sports had become a multi-billion-dollar football and basketball business. Scandals in gambling, booster payoffs, academic fraud, and recruiting have been routinely documented in commercialized college sports since their inception. College athletes still only share a small percentage of billion dollar television contracts, and few measures exist to prevent its revenue producers from playing for gamblers.

Epilogue

College football was conceived with the avowed goal of enhancing the reputation of the universities. Terms involved such as "courageous," "undaunted," "intelligent," and "uncanny" were used to describe the ideal football player during the late-19th century. These terms were also used because they were synonymous with the creation of a typical college student and amateur athlete. Today, commercialized and professionalized college football has shed its cloak of amateurism with games scheduled seven days a week as the sport has morphed into an entertainment product for the university and the media. College presidents find themselves in a quandary as they attempt to explain the role of sport on their campuses as football and other entertainment sports exists on a campus for reasons that have little relationship to amateur sport.

College basketball has been no stranger to gambling scandals. Fortunately, college basketball spectators and fans have been more interested in following the sport than in reading about the sport's gambling exploits. In the 1960s, the sport's attendance experienced a growth surge highlighted by the UCLA-Houston televised game on January 20, 1968, in the Houston Astrodome witnessed by nearly 53,000 spectators. UCLA's record on the court between 1964 and 1975 and the program's success in capturing a sizable television audience in the Los Angeles region demonstrated how television could become an economic force in college basketball.

Bringing the game to the fan, as did ABC and other networks by adding several cameras on the field, allowed televised audiences to experience the same environment as audiences at the venue. This was a revolutionary event in television coverage, and its acceptance by spectators marked a change from viewing competitive events in the old dry and staid manner to a new style that would entertain viewers and predated sport's appearance around the clock (ESPN) on television. Roone Arledge's innovation of bringing the microphone and camera to the spectators was prescient in another way. It introduced many young people to sports on television and converted these individuals into sports fans who could spend their lifetime following their favorite athlete or team.

Brutality lost its appeal to football spectators because it failed to appeal to the reason the individual was at the event in the first place—to see his or her favorite player in person and on television. Once that was taken away because of an injury, spectators lost interest in the contest. Injured players lessened their monetary value to a team's bottom line because they were unable to contribute to a team's success.

The Butts-Bryant football conversations during the 1962 football season were in all likelihood not for the purpose of exchanging pleasantries. During that same season, Butts had offered to share UG's offensive and defensive schemes with at least three other Southeastern Conference teams. More than likely, SEC Commissioner Bernie Moore was aware of Butts' offers to share vital game strategy with UG's opponents, but chose to remain silent on the matter and avoid risking a scandal. Paul "Bear" Bryant's court testimony, which was thinly connected to game strategy was, according to most court observers, the reason the jury found in favor of Butts.

The New Mexico scandal of 1979 illustrated how a college administration was willing to close its eyes to the transgressions committed by its basketball program. The infractions including the skirting of academic requirements were deep and widespread and led the NCAA to conclude that the scandal had been one of the worst it had ever investigated. The institution's attempt to build a program in basketball exacerbated and highlighted the school's less than stellar academic standing. The state's citizens viewed the university as a glorified high school because of the negative publicity generated by the basketball program.

The SMU scandal reflected the NCAA's frustration in not catching violations during SMU's most successful years in football. The first slew of penalties came down banning the institution from bowl games for two seasons and cutting 45 scholarships over a two-year period (at the time the penalties were considered some of the harshest in the NCAA). The institution was also ordered to stop its payments to players immediately. Instead boosters implemented a phase-out program whereby all players who were promised money until their eligibility expired continued to receive payments. Two players who never played a down for SMU were the "smoking guns" who were willing to talk plenty to NCAA investigators after the institution assured the organization it had stopped paying players. The NCAA penalized the university with the "death penalty" by shutting down its football program for one year in 1987. The university chose to close its program for two years because they did not have enough players to field a football team in 1988.

Despite the NCAA's fanatical pursuit of Jerry Tarkanian, the organization in 1992 settled the court battle with Tarkanian after two decades of attempting to sideline the coach. Tarkanian's association with convicted gambler Richard Perry proved to be his downfall, which forced his resignation from UNLV. Perry had been convicted in previous gambling scandals in 1974 and 1982 before arriving in Las Vegas. The 1982 conviction was for Perry's role in the 1978–1979 Boston College Scandal. While in Las Vegas, Perry had become an informal advisor to some of the UNLV's players. Even though Perry's background required that he register as a convicted gambler, his presence near UNLV's players was not viewed as out of the unusual by UNLV's officials. When Perry's association with UNLV's players became known, the faction that was backing president Robert Maxson in the booster warfare between the pro– and anti–Tarkanian forces seized the opportunity to remove Tarkanian as UNLV's head basketball coach.

To most followers of UCLA's basketball program, the name Sam Gilbert was associated with being a "sugar daddy" who took care of players' needs in full violation of NCAA rules. Gilbert cherished his role as the "money person" for UCLA's basketball program. Sam Gilbert's passing in 1987 could not prevent his son Michael from being indicted for violating specific aspects of the RICO Law and serving five and a half years in federal prison. The elder Gilbert, according to court documents, and his Miami associates had organized an illegal money laundering operation to build a gambling casino in Bell Gardens, California.

In East Lansing, Michigan, Ed Martin, a "basketball junkie," befriended Michigan's basketball players by passing money to them. Martin's source for the money was from a numbers operation he operated at the River Rouge Ford plant near Detroit. Needing a write-off to shield his illegal multi-million dollar income, Martin found it convenient to launder this money to players. Martin died after he was indicted, rendering it virtually impossible to find out how much money he had illegally passed to Michigan's and other program's basketball players. Estimates are that Martin shared close to one million dollars with the players.

In June 1989, sports agent Norby Walters was sentenced to five years in a federal prison and forfeiture of his assets, which then numbered $200 000. Lloyd Bloom, Walter's partner, received a three-year federal prison sentence and was ordered to pay $145,000 in restitution to Paul Palmer (the amount he stole from the player as his agent). In September 1990, Walters and Bloom were ordered to be retried (in separate cases) by an appellate court which found two trial errors were committed by the presiding judge. Walters immediately planned to plea bargain, but he was murdered gangland-style in Southern California. His homicide was never solved.

Chapter Notes

Chapter 1

1. Alan Sack, *Counterfeit Amateurs: An Athlete's Journey Through the Sixties to the Age of Academic Capitalism* (University Park: Pennsylvania State University, 2008), 75–76.
2. Paul Gallico, *Farewell to Sport* (New York: Knopf, 1938), 215–221.
3. Frank DeFord, quoted in Jerome Carter, "Winning or Learning? Athletics and Academics in America," *Kaplan Special Report* (May 1986), K—K-9.
4. *Ibid.*, K2.
5. Eliot Asinof, *Eight Men Out: The Black Sox and the 1919 World Series* (New York: Holt, Rinehart and Winston, 1963), 11.
6. *Ibid.*
7. David G. Schwarz, *Roll the Bones: The History of Gambling* (New York: Gotham Books, 2006), 338.
8. John R. Betts, *America's Sporting Heritage: 1850–1950* (Reading, PA: Addison Wesley Publishing Company, 1974), 211.
9. Walter Camp, *Walter Camp's Book of College Sports* (New York: The Century Co., 1893), 9.
10. Frederick Rudolph, *The American College and University: A History* (New York: Random House, 1990), 377.
11. Arthur Twining Hadley, "Wealth and Democracy in American Colleges," *Harper's* CXlll (1906), 262.
12. *Ibid.*, 375.
13. Mark F. Bernstein, *Football: The Ivy League Origins of an American Obsession* (Philadelphia: University of Pennsylvania Press, 2001), 19.
14. *Ibid.*
15. Harriet Ward Beecher, *Gamblers and Gambling* (Philadelphia: Henry Altemus, 1896), 16–17.
16. Rudolph, *The American College and University*, 373–374.
17. *Ibid.*, 374–375.

18. Amos Alonzo Stagg, *Touchdown* (New York: Longmans Green, 1927), 20.
19. Henry Davidson Sheldon, *The History and Pedagogy of American Student Societies* (New York: D. Appleton, 1901), 251–252.
20. Rudolph, *The American College and University*, 380.
21. *Ibid.*
22. Gerald F. Robinson, "The Strenuous Life: the Cult of Manliness in the Era of Theodore Roosevelt" (Ph.D. diss., Michigan State University, 1977).
23. John J. Miller, *The Big Scrum: How Teddy Roosevelt Saved Football* (New York: HarperCollins, 2011), 161–162.
24. "The New Football," *Nation*, November 29, 1894, 399–400.
25. Charles Henry Rammelkamp, *Illinois College: A Centennial History, 1829–1929* (New Haven: Yale University Press, 1928), 281.
26. William Warren Ferrier, *Origin and Development of the University of California* (Berkeley: Sather Gate Book Shop, 1930), 624; James Albert Woodburn, *History of Indiana University: 1820–1902* (Bloomington: Indiana University Press, 1940), 448.
27. Rudolph, *The American College and University*, 382–384.
28. *Ibid.*
29. *Ibid.*
30. Sanford Gove, "Athletics at Williams," *Outing* XVll (1890), 245–249.
31. Samuel Eliot Morison, *Three Centuries of Harvard, 1636–1936* (Cambridge: Harvard University Press, 1936), 406.
32. John Nauright, "Writing and Reading American Football: Culture, Identities and Sport Studies," *Sporting Traditions* 13, no. 1 (November 1996), 109–127.
33. David Riesman and Reuel Denney, "Football in America: a Study in Cultural Diffusion," *American Quarterly* lll (1951), 231.

34. *Ibid.*

35. Ferrier, *Origin and Development of the University of California*, 624.

36. Howard J. Savage, Harold. W. Bentley, et al., *American College Athletics* (New York: Carnegie Foundation for the Advancement of Teaching, 1929), 29–32.

37. Morris Allison Bealle, *The History of Football At Harvard, 1874–1948* (Washington: Columbia, 1948), 17.

38. *Ibid.*, 380–404.

39. Rudolph, *The American College and University*, 392.

40. Kent Sagendorph, *Michigan: The Story of a University* (New York: E. P. Dutton, 1948), 150.

41. "Last Hurrah in Allegheny, the 3A's Exit in a Blaze of Glory," in *Pro Football: From AAA to '03*, Bob Carroll and Bob Brunwart (Guilford, NY: Professional Football Researchers Association Publications, 1991).

42. *Ibid.*

43. Richard Sasuly, *Bookies and Bettors: Two Hundred Years of Gambling* (New York: Holt, Rinehart and Winston, 1982), 70–75; Raymond Schmidt, *Shaping College Football: The Transformation of an American Sport, 1919–1930* (Syracuse: Syracuse University Press, 2007), 26–38.

44. Sasuly, 70–75.

45. Arthur S. Link, "Entry into World War I," in *Progress, War, and Reaction: 1900–1933*, B. Ross, Alden T. Vaughn, et al. (New York: Thomas Y. Crowell, 1970), 139–140.

46. Quoted in Schmidt, *Shaping College Football*, 40.

47. Arthur S. Link, "The 1920s: Decade of Decline or Destiny?" in *Interpretations of American History: Pattern and Perspectives, Volume 2, Since 1865*, Gerald N. Grob and George Athan Billias (New York: Free Press, 1967), 249–278.

48. Schmidt, *Shaping College Football*, 27–28.

49. Link, "The 1920s," 250–253.

50. *Ibid.*

51. John Kieran, "When the Twain Meet," *New York Times*, September 29, 1929, 224.

52. Schmidt, *Shaping College Football*, 31–33; Michael Oriard, *King Football: Sport and Spectacle in the Golden Age of Radio and Newsreels, Movies and Magazines, the Weekly and the Daily Press* (Chapel Hill: University of North Carolina Press, 2001), 75.

53. Valerie H. Ziegler, "C6-H0: the Centre Harvard Game of 1921," *Grace Doherty Library*, http://library.centre.edu/sc/special/C6h0/ziegler.html (accessed September 23, 2014); "Centre Conquers Harvard, 6–0," *New York Times*, October 30, 1921, 1.

54. Quoted in Ziegler, "C6–H0."

55. Schmidt, *Shaping College Football*, 58–59.

56. Curley Grieve, "Sports Parade," *San Francisco Examiner*, November 15, 1932.

57. "The Pig-Skin Game: Football's Newest By-Product," *Saturday Evening Post*, February 8, 1936, 14.

58. John Waterson, *College Football: History-Spectacle-Controversy* (Baltimore: Johns Hopkins University Press), 177.

59. Richard O. Davies and Richard G. Abram, *Betting the Line: Sports Wagering in American Life* (Columbus: Ohio State University Press, 2001), 41–43.

60. *Reach Guide, 1921*; Robert Patterson, *Cages to Jump Shots: Pro Basketball's Early Years* (Lincoln: University of Nebraska Press, 1990), 72.

61. *Ibid.*

62. Neil D. Isaacs, *All the Moves: A History of College Basketball* (Philadelphia: J. P. Lippincott, 1975), 102; Peter C. Bjarkman, *Hoopla: A Century of College Basketball* (Indianapolis: Masters Press, 1996), 39–58.

63. Bjarkman, *Hoopla*, 51.

64. Richard R. Lingeman, *Don't You Know There's a War On? the American Home Front 1941–1945* (New York: Paperback Library, 2003), 390–391.

65. *Ibid.*

66. *Ibid.*

67. *Ibid.*

68. William Howard Moore, *The Kefauver Committee and the Politics of Crime* (Columbia: University of Missouri Press, 1974), 25–33.

69. "Army-Notre Dame Game Will be Last for an Indefinite Period," *New York Times*, December 31, 1946, 57; "College Football Games Rated by Tipsters for Benefit of Gamblers, Prosecutor Says," *New York Times*, December 18, 1946, 34; "Pro Careers end for 2 Giants Backs," *New York Times*, April 4, 1947, 27.

70. Ben Gould, *Brooklyn Eagle*, May 28, 1950, 1.

71. *Ibid.*

72. Stanley Cohen, *The Game They Played* (New York: Da Capo Press, 2000), 93; Charles Rosen, *Scandal of '51: How the Gamblers Almost Killed College Basketball* (New York: Seven Stories Press, 1999), 65.

73. Sasuly, *Bookies and Bettors*, 172.

74. *Ibid.*

75. Bjarkman, *Hoopla*, 59–79.

76. Moore, Kefauver Committee, Jorge Gregorio Simonovich, "Basketball Fixer," in *The Business of Crime*, Robert Rice (Westport, CT: Greenwood Press, 1956), 251–261.

77. Albert J. Figone, *Cheating the Spread:*

Gamblers, Point Shavers, and Game Fixers in College Football and Basketball (Urbana: University of Illinois Press, 2012), 24–40.

78. *Ibid.*

79. Cohen, *The Game They Played*, 85.

80. Leonard Koppett, *24 Seconds to Shoot: The Birth and Improbable Rise of the NBA* (Kingston, NY: Total Sports Illustrated Classics, 1999).

81. Sperber, *Onward to Victory*, 285–299.

Chapter 2

1. Murray A. Sperber, *Onward to Victory: The Crises That Shaped College Sports.* (New York: Henry Holt, 1998).

2. Hall, *Crossroads: American Popular Culture*, 37–50.

3. *Ibid.*

4. *Ibid.*

5. *Ibid.*

6. "Five Minutes Away from Never," *ESPN. com.* http://espn.go.com/abcsports/wwos/ rarledge.html (accessed August 11, 2014).

7. William O. Johnston, *Super Spectator and the Electric Lilliputians* (Boston: Little, Brown, 1971), 151.

8. Greg Easterbrook, *The King of Sports: Football's Impact on America* (New York: Thomas Dunne Books, 2013), 77–108.

9. Phil Patton, *Razzle Dazzle: The Curious Marriage of Television and Football* (New York: Dial Press, 1984), 62–72.

10. Powers, *Supertube*, 121.

11. *Ibid.*

12. *Ibid.*

13. Patton, *Razzle Dazzle*, 62–72.

14. *Ibid.*

15. Roone Arledge, *Roone: A Memoir* (New York: HarperCollins, 2010), 30–31.

16. *Ibid.*

17. *Ibid.*

18. *Ibid.*, 39.

19. Richard O. Davies and Richard G. Abram, *Betting the Line: Sports Wagering in American Life* (Columbus: Ohio State University Press, 2001), 86–88.

20. "Welcome to BetMagnet: Sports Betting Record Keeping on the Internet," *Bet Magnet.* www.betmagnet.com/en/ (accessed August 18, 2014).

21. Powers, *Supertube*, 233.

22. Patton, *Razzle Dazzle*, 113–119.

23. *Ibid.*, 236–242.

24. *Ibid.*

25. *Ibid.*

26. *Ibid.*

27. *Ibid.*

28. *Ibid.*

29. *Ibid.*

30. *Ibid.*

31. Gary T. Brown, "NCAA answers calls to reform: the 'Sanity Code' leads association down path to enforcement program," *The NCAA News*, November 22, 1999, http://fs.ncaa.org/ Docs/NCAANewsArchive/1999/19991122/ active/3624n24.html.

32. *Ibid.*

33. *Ibid.*

34. *Ibid.*

35. *Ibid.*

36. John Thelin, *Games Colleges Play: Scandal and Reform in Intercollegiate Athletics* (Baltimore: Johns Hopkins Press, 1994) 121–124.

37. Brian L. Porto, *The Supreme Court and the NCAA: The Case for Less Commercialism and More Due Process in College Sports* (Ann Arbor: University of Michigan Press, 2012), 49–54.

38. *Ibid.*

39. Keith Dunnivant, *The Fifty-Year Seduction: How Television Manipulated College Football, from the Birth of the Modern NCAA to the Creation of the BCS* (New York: Thomas Dunne Books, 2004), 180.

40. *Ibid.*

41. *Ibid.*

42. *Ibid.*

43. Kristi Dosh, *Saturday's Millionaires: How Winning Football Builds Winning Colleges* (Nashville: Turner Publishing, 2013), 50–76. Dosh, a sports business reporter for ESPN and past practicing attorney, presented an economic perspective on how elite colleges denigrated their academic missions to realign themselves geographically into five major conferences to capture the most lucrative TV markets.

44. *Ibid.*, 50–76.

45. *Ibid.*

46. *Ibid.*

47. Walter Byers with Charles Hammer, *Unsportsmanlike Conduct: Exploiting College Athletes* (Ann Arbor: University of Michigan Press, 1995); Josh Luchs with James Dale, *Illegal Procedure: A Sports Agent Comes Clean on the Dirty Business of College Football* (New York: Bloomsbury, 2012);54ttttttttttttttttr\?" Don Yeager, *Tarnished Heisman: Did Reggie Bush Turn His Final Season Into a Six-Figure Job?* (New York: Pocket Books, 2008).

48. John Matthew Smith, *The Sons of Westwood: John Wooden, UCLA, and the Dynasty That Changed College Basketball* (Champaign: University of Illinois Press, 2013). Smith's book

is generally complimentary about the dominance of UCLA's basketball program from 1963 to 1975. However, the content includes convincing evidence that rules violations in the program, including illegal payments from Sam Gilbert and other boosters, were common knowledge among college basketball coaches and the NCAA, which refused to investigate the program ostensibly because of its falsely crafted amateur image and revenue production.

49. *Schooled: The Price of College Sports*, dir. by Ross Finkel (2013; EPIX). http://press.epixhd.com/programming/schooled-the-price-of-college-sports/ (accessed September 27, 2014).

50. Kevin Ota, "ESPN Digital Media Sets Sports Category Traffic Record in September," *ESPN Front Row* (accessed September 27, 2014).

51. Ramogi Huma and Ellen J. Staurowsky, "The $6 Billion Heist: Robbing College Athletes Under the Guise of Amateurism." This report was collaboratively produced by the National College Players Association and Drexel University Sport Management Department, 2012. http://www.ncpanow.org (accessed September 27, 2014).

52. Dunnivant, *The Fifty-Year Seduction*, 2004.

53. Ray Glider, *How the SEC Became Goliath: The Making of College Football's Most Dominant Conference* (New York: Howard Books, 2012), 179–193.

54. David M. Carter, *Money Games: Profiting from the Convergence of Sports and Entertainment* (Stanford, CA: Stanford University Press, 2011), 155–171.

55. Gilliam Spear, "Think Sports' Gambling Isn't Big Money? Wanna Bet?" *NBC News*, July 15, 2013. http://www.nbcnews.com/news/other/think-sports-gambling-isnt-big-money-wanna-bet-f6C10634316 (accessed September 27, 2014).

56. Brad Wolverton, "NCAA Proposal Would Give Powers to Biggest Leagues," *Chronicle of Higher Education*, January 10, 2014; Kristi Dosh, "College TV rights deals undergo makeovers," *ESPN.com*, May 10, 2012. http://espn.go.com/blog/playbook/dollars/post/_/id/705/college-tv-rights-deals-undergo-makeovers. (accessed December 16, 2016).

Chapter 3

1. Stanley Cohen, *The Game They Played* (New York: Farrar, Straus and Giroux, 1977). Cohen's book was the first book published on the 1951 scandals. a New York City native, Cohen recounts his personal experiences and recollections as a college basketball player in New York City during the late 1940s and early 1950s, when the scandals unfolded. the narrative is reasonably accurate but suffers from a lack of documented sources.

2. Albert J. Figone, *Cheating the Spread: Gamblers, Point Shavers, and Game Fixers in College Football and Basketball* (Champaign: University of Illinois Press, 2012), 40.

3. Mike Puma, "Bear Bryant 'Simply the Best There Ever Was,'" ESPN Classic. http://espn.go.com/classic/biography/s/Bryant_Bear.html (accessed September 28, 2014).

4. Paul "Bear" Bryant with John Underwood, *Bear: The Hard Life & Good Times of Alabama's Coach Bryant* (Chicago: Triumph Books, 2007), 39.

5. *Ibid.*

6. *Ibid.*

7. Michael Oriard, *Bowled Over: Big-Time College Football from the Sixties to the BCS Era* (Chapel Hill: University of North Carolina Press, 2009), 37.

8. Frank DeFord, "Bull Sullivan: the Meanest Coach Ever," *Sports Illustrated*, April 30, 1984, 25.

9. Keith Dunnivant, *The Missing Ring: How Bear Bryant and the 1966 Alabama Crimson Tide Were Denied College Football's Most Elusive Prize* (New York: Thomas Dunne, 2007).

10. Shannon Ragland, *The Thin Thirty: The Untold Story of Brutality, Scandal and Redemption for Charlie Bradshaw's 1962 Kentucky Football Team* (Louisville: The Set Shot Press, 2007), 16–17. Ragland, a former lawyer, presents a compelling account of the brutality that was known in the 1950s and 1960s as Coach "Bull" Sullivan's and Paul "Bear" Bryant's formula for winning and was branded "smash-mouth" or "Total Football." Unlike other accounts of Bryant's career, which downplay the emotional and physical brutality of his methods, this book celebrates the players who stayed in the Bryant program (*The Thin Thirty*) and the ones who left, enjoyed football success in other programs, and built successful personal and professional lives. Bryant's methods were extreme, but Total Football as a football mentality was common among many coaches during this time period. This type of football coaching was favored by Cold War militarists who viewed the counterculture liberals as a threat to this country's security.

11. *Ibid.*, 98.

12. *Ibid.*, 108. Bradshaw was declared ineligible three games into the 1949 season because of an SEC rule involving World War II veterans

who lost playing time serving in the military. Freshmen who played before July 1, 1947, were granted four years of eligibility. Players not participating before that time were allowed three years of competition. in Bradshaw's case, he had not played in 1942 before joining the military.

13. *Ibid.*

14. Quoted in Ragland, *The Thin Thirty*, 140.

15. *Ibid.*, 137–138.

16. Dr. Michael Minix, telephone interview with author, July 20, 2014.

17. Michael Oriard, *King Football: Sport & Spectacle in the Golden Age of Radio & Newsreels, Movies & Magazines, the Weekly & the Daily Press* (Chapel Hill: University of Carolina Press, 2001), 37–39.

18. Ragland, *The Thin Thirty*, 143.

19. *Ibid.*

20. Russell Rice, *The Wildcats: A Story of Kentucky Football* (Huntsville, AL: Strode Publishers, 1976).

21. Ragland, *The Thin Thirty*, 149. in the *SI* article, Ford recounted how as a first-year coach at Alabama, he struck an angry player, who retaliated. in the coaches' meeting the next day, Bryant stated that "he'd never tell a coach what to do, but if an angry player was struck by a coach and responded in kind, he would not discipline the player." That explanation seems to be less than truthful. Why then would any coach risk a serious injury by unnecessarily brutalizing a person who very well might permanently injure him? Later, during the 1962 season, when fewer than 22 players appeared at UK's practice, coaches had to fill in for players. in one incident, freshman coach Bill Jasper was filling in for the defensive team and two players intentionally hit him above the waist and one below it, causing a serious knee injury. Jasper was on crutches for the rest of 1962. Bradshaw was unable to protect his coaches, as some of his staff's brutality did not stop. Homer Rice informed a sportswriter that he told Bradshaw "if the brutality continued, he'd quit."

22. John Thelin, *Game Colleges Play: Scandal and Reform in Intercollegiate Athletics* (Baltimore: Johns Hopkins, 1994), 121–124. Kentucky coaches Bryant and Rupp were known for their blatant cheating. There were no restrictions on recruiting, the number of players in programs, and athletic scholarships. If rules existed, most programs did not enforce them. One player estimated he practiced 11 months a year in Bryant's program. More than 100 players attended UK's August football camp before classes started. Rupp's success in basketball was attributed to his team's conditioning, teamwork, and defensive play. Most SEC and other coaches were aware of UK's blatant cheating and were not surprised when the basketball program was reported in 1951 to have been routinely rigging games since the mid-1940s. the Kentucky and out-of-state gamblers, bookies, and writers were also aware of the gambling problems at UK, but shielded the public from them.

23. *Ibid.* a number of the state's internal and external studies in part concluded that UK was under-utilizing a valuable resource of the state (academics and education) because of the public's resource commitment to football and basketball.

24. Carl Modecki, "37 Quit Football Team," *Kentucky Kernel*, April 1962.

25. Morton Sharnik and Robert Creamer, "The Rage to Win," *Sports Illustrated*, October 8, 1962, 17.

26. Figone, *Cheating the Spread*, 40.

27. Sharnik and Creamer, "The Rage to Win," 1962.

28. *Ibid.*

29. *Ibid.*

30. *Ibid.*

31. *Ibid.*

32. Ragland, *The Thin Thirty*, 160. Bradshaw's church statement was reported to Shannon Ragland by quarterback Shelby Lee, who attended the same church as Bradshaw. in "win at all costs," commercialized football, it was not uncommon for Total Football apostles to believe that God and football reconciled the brutality that common sense dictated was a violation of civil rights laws and was morally wrong. Even prison guards then and now cannot inflict excessive punishment on prisoners.

33. Sarnik and Creamer, *The Rage to Win.*

34. Ed Asford, "UK Victim of Hatchet Job," *Lexington Herald*, October 9, 1962.

35. *Ibid.*

36. Earl Ruby, "Vaught Needles Bradshaw," *Louisville Courier-Journal*, September 4, 1962.

37. Byers with Hammer, *Unsportsmanlike Conduct*, 59.

38. *Ibid.*

39. Dr. Minix, e-mail correspondence with author, July 27, 2014.

40. DeFord, "Bull Sullivan."

41. *Ibid.*

42. Larry Boeck, "Shively Defends Scholarship Purge," *Louisville Courier-Journal*, September 4, 1962.

43. Russell Rice, "Avoid Embarrassing the Boys," *Lexington Leader*, September 21, 1962.

44. Russell Rice, "Helmers Reconsiders," *Lexington Leader*, September 4, 1962.

45. *Ibid.*

46. Larry Boeck, "Thin Thirty Named," *Louisville Courier-Journal*, September 22, 1962.

47. Ed Ashford, "Bear Bryant Purge," *Lexington Herald*, September 13, 1962.

48. Ed Ashford, "UK Can Win with 30," *Lexington Herald*, September 14, 1962.

49. "History of American Football," 2008. http://www.thepeoplehistory.com/football history.html. (accessed September 28, 2014).

50. Billy Thompson, "Thompson Vouches for the Practices," *Lexington Leader*, September 5, 1962.

51. Billy Thompson, "Thompson's Ode to the Team," *Lexington Leader*, September 22, 1962.

52. Larry Boeck, "Gumbert Cites the Films," *Louisville Courier-Journal*, September 21, 1962.

53. *Ibid.*

54. *Ibid.*

55. Ragland, *The Thin Thirty.*

56. Furman Bisher, "College Football is Going Berserk: a Game Ruled by Brute Force Needs a Housecleaning," *Saturday Evening Post*, October 20, 1962, 10.

57. *Ibid.*

58. *Ibid.*

59. *Ibid.*

60. *Ibid.*

61. *Ibid.*

62. Mark F. Bernstein, *Football: The Ivy League Origins of an American Obsession* (Philadelphia: University of Pennsylvania Press, 2001). as Harvard's president from 1869 to 1909, Eliot lauded athletics at his inauguration. by 1887, however, he had reached the conclusion that football was beyond saving. That year, the *Chicago Tribune* reported that 18 players had been killed and seriously injured. in the *Boston Medical and Surgical Journal*, Harvard's Dr. Edward Nichols reported that Crimson football players had collectively missed 175 days of class due to injury and 1,057 days of incapacitation (from some form of injury).

63. Earl Cox, *St. Matthews Voice Tribune*, August 28, 2007.

64. Richard O. Davies and Richard G. Abram, *Betting the Line: Sports Wagering in American Life* (Columbus: Ohio State University Press, 2001), 43–60. Betting on a predetermined outcome in wrestling bordered on illegality. in fact, in 1920, bettors became enraged when a fix was exposed. Most likely they were on the losing side of the bet. However, professional wrestling did not disappear, and regional audiences replaced national promotions. by the 1950s, televised wrestling became a staple because of Jim Barnett's idea of studio wrestling. Matches could be held under bright lights with one camera in one location. Bookies and promoters could sell wrestling as entertainment, promoting the notion that pre-determined outcomes were not known to bookies and gamblers; therefore, they could bet on the "garbage sport." However, Nevada did not allow wagering on wrestling in 1963. Illegal bookies have always booked wrestling bets.

65. Ragland, *The Thin Thirty*, 178.

66. Alex Kreit, "Professional Wrestling and its Fans: a Sociological Study of the Sport of Pro-Wrestling," Sollie's Wrestling DVDs, 1998. http://www.solie.org/articles/pwandfans.html (accessed September 28, 2014).

67. *Ibid.*

68. Ragland, *The Thin Thirty*, 176–177. Ragland's extensive research involving the Lakewood residence uncovered that in 1962, several players' wives drove out to Barnett's residence looking for their husbands and to catch a glimpse of Hudson. of the 60 interviewed by Ragland, one-third had been to the house. Almost all the rest had heard the rumors but had not been to the house. Minix, in a personal phone interview with this author on July 7, 2014, revealed that he loved to study as a pre-med major, did not know about Lakeside Drive, and was not socially involved with his teammates. Ragland's interviews confirmed that three of the best players on the 1962 team were the most frequent visitors to the residence, received the most gifts, and encouraged their teammates to attend the parties. the three players were not identified, and it was not known if they engaged in sex at the residence. Quarterback Jerry Woolum had been a three-year starter, and his subpar play in the Xavier game points to him possibly playing for gamblers.

69. *Ibid.*, 173–182.

70. *Ibid.*

71. Figone, *Cheating the Spread*, 92.

72. Weldon Grimsley, "Keystone Cops and Woolum Called Play," *Paducah Sun-Democrat*, November 20, 1962, in the huddle, UK's left tackle argued with Woolum about calling the pitch option because it had not been executed smoothly in practice. Woolum's response, according to Ragland, was, "Bradshaw would kill [me] if [I] did not call the play." the quarterback did wear a written band on his wrist that listed which plays to call given the down, distance, field position, time, etc. It's possible, but highly unlikely considering that UK was 18 inches from a touchdown, that the unorthodox play called was one of Woolum's options, or that Bradshaw or Homer Rice had called the play. UK lost the game, 14–9.

73. *Ibid.*
74. *Ibid.*, 228.
75. *Ibid.*, 253.
76. *Ibid.*, 271.
77. Dr. Minix, telephone interview with author, July 7, 2014.
78. Ragland, *The Thin Thirty*, 273.
79. Editorial, "What of Quieter Victories," *Kentucky Kernel*, September 29, 1964.
80. Sid Webb, "Is It Worth It? Yes Sir!" Editorial Cartoon, *Kentucky Kernel*, September 29, 1964.
81. *Ibid.*
82. Figone, *Cheating the Spread*, 40.
83. *Ibid.*, 284.

Chapter 4

1. Quoted in Ed Ashford, "Editorial," *Lexington Herald*, September 16, 1952.
2. Quoted in Byers, *Unsportsmanlike Conduct*, 59.
3. *Ibid.*, 60–61.
4. Paul W. Bryant and John Underwood, *Bear: The Hard Life and Good Times of Alabama's Coach Bryant* (New York: Little, Brown, 1975), 28. Underwood's account of Bryant's life and career reads like an autobiography. for this author, it's the most accurate and compelling story of Bryant's iconic career. It also presents the most contradictions about the events surrounding the Butts-Bryant telephone conversations in September 1962, 29
5. *Ibid.*
6. Quoted in *Ibid.*
7. David Sumner, "Libelous—But True: Another Look at Butts v. Curtis Publishing," Paper presented at the Association for Education in Journalism and Mass Communication Conference Annual Conference, Montreal, Quebec, August 8, 2014.
8. Quoted in *Ibid.*
9. "Background on Request for Retirement by Coach Wallace Butts," January 27, 1963, 3, O. C. Aderhold Collection 1920–1975, Box 97–100:2, Hargrett Rare Book & Manuscript Library, University of Georgia (hereafter referred to as HMLUG).
10. Figone, *Cheating the Spread*, 75.
11. Quoted in *Ibid.*, 76.
12. James Kirby, *Fumble: Bear Bryant, Wally Butts and the Great College Football Scandal* (New York: Dell, 1986), 15–45.
13. Quoted in Sumner, "Libelous—But True."
14. Quoted in Kirby, *Fumble*, 44.
15. Figone, *Cheating the Spread*, 74–75.
16. Frank Graham, "The Story of a College Football Fix," *Saturday Evening Post*, March 23, 1963.
17. Curtis Publishing v Butts. (n.d.), Curtis Publishing Co v Butts on Prezi. http://prezi.com/jeajlghweqta/curtis-publishing-v-Butts (Accessed June 5, 2016); Kirby, *Fumble*, 56.
18. *Ibid.*, 68.
19. Albert J. Figone Phone Conversation with Former University of Georgia–Athletic Department Publicist Shelley Smith, June 1, 2012; Georgia Tech-Alabama game 1962.
20. Kirby, *Fumble*, 68–69.
21. Director, FBI to SACS New Orleans, Jacksonville, Miami, "Possible Information Relating to Betting Activities of Alabama University Football Coach Paul 'Bear' Bryant" (April 9, 1963); FBI memo obtained through FOI request, August 9, 2014.
22. SAC, Denver, to Director, FBI (March 19, 1964). FBI memo obtained through FOI request, July 29, 2013.
23. Figone, *Cheating the Spread*, 78–79.
24. Business Directory.com. http://www.businessdictionary/com/definition/proof-beyond-a-reasonable-doubt.html (accessed December 20, 2014). in the legal environment, reasonable doubt is applied in criminal cases by judges and juries when deciding the guilt or innocence of a defendant. Although its definition varies, one can use a "rule of thumb" of not requiring absolute certainty; if the evidence is overwhelmingly on the side of the prosecutor, a reasonable person would find the defendant guilty. in assessing all of the evidence related to Butts-Bryant conversations, this author believed "beyond a reasonable doubt" that both individuals were exchanging vital game strategies to ensure that Alabama would defeat Georgia by more than the 14- to 17-point spread.
25. Quoted in Figone, *Cheating the Spread*, 78.
26. Kirby, *Fumble*, 100–109.
27. *Ibid.*
28. Frank Litsky, "Leonard Tose, 88, Is Dead; Owned Philadelphia Eagles," *New York Times*, April 16, 2003. http://www.nytimes.com/2003/04/16/sports/leonard-tose-88-is-dead-owned-philadelphia-eagles.html (accessed September 28, 2014).
29. Richard Hoffers, *Rambling and Gambling Across Our Landscape of Luck: Jackpot Nation.* (New York: Harper, 2007), 90.
30. Kirby, *Fumble*, 113.
31. Director, FBI to SACs, Atlanta, Birmingham (June 6, 1963). FBI memo obtained through FOI request, August 29, 2013.

32. Kirby, *Fumble*, 47–48.

33. "Background on Request for Retirement," 1 (HMLUG).

34. Director, FBI to SACs Atlanta, Birmingham, March 8, 1963. FBI memo obtained through FOI Request, September 27, 2013.

35. Quoted in Frank Graham, *A Farewell to Heroes* (New York: Viking Press, 1981), 297.

36. Written statements from LeRoy Pearce to James H. Terrell, Assistant Attorney General; Wyatt Posey to Terrell, John Tillitski to Terrell, John W. Gregory to Terrell, Bobby Proctor to Terrell, and Frank E. Inman to Terrell (March 26, 1963). Attorney General Eugene Cook's Butts-Bryant Report, Part One (1963), O. C. Aderhold Collection 1920–1975, Box 97–100:2; in David Sumner, "Libelous—But True: Another Look at *Butts V. Curtis*."

37. Wallace Butts, Plaintiff v. Curtis Publishing Company Defendant, Civ. A, no. 8311 225 F. Supp. 916-Dist Court, ND Georgia, January 14, 1964.

38. Curtis Publishing Company Appellant, v Wallace Butts, Appellee. Wallace Butts, Appellant v. Curtis Publishing Company, Appellee, 351 F.2d 702 (5th Cir.1965), July 16, 1965, Rehiring Denied October 1, 1965, http://justia,com/cases/federal/appellate-courts/F2/351/702/27/278587/ Accessed June 16, 2016; Kirby, *Fumble*, 189.

39. Quoted in Harland, Supreme Court NO. 37, Supreme Court of the United States, 388 U.S., 87 S. Ct. 1975, argued February 23, 1967, decided June 12, 1967. http://www.bc.edu/bc_org/avp/cas/comm/free_speech_/curtis.html. Accessed, June 16, 2016.

40. Kirby, *Fumble;* 189, Figone, *Cheating the Spread*, 84; "Sumner, Libelous—But True."

41. Randy Roberts and Ed Krzemienski, *Rising Tide: Bear Bryant, Joe Namath & Dixie's Last Quarter* (Boston: Twelve: Hatchett Book, 2013), 196.

42. Quoted in Jeff Nilsson, "Million Dollar Fumble," *Saturday Evening Post*, November–December 2013.

43. Quoted in Kirby, *Fumble*, 160–163.

44. *Ibid.*, 198–199.

45. Keith Dunnivant, *The Missing Ring: How Bear Bryant and the 1966 Alabama Crimson Tide Were Denied College Football's Most Elusive Prize* (New York: St. Martin's Press), 11–12.

46. Kirby, *Fumble*, 198.

47. *New York Times Co. v. Sullivan*. 376 U.S. 967 84. Ct. 1130 12L. Ed. 2d 83 1964 U.S. the constitutional guarantees require a federal rule that prohibits a public official from recovering damages for a defamatory falsehood relating to official conduct unless the plaintiff proves that the statement was made with actual malice—that is, with knowledge that is was false or with reckless disregard of whether it was false or not.

Chapter 5

1. John R. Thelin, *Games Colleges Play: Scandal and Reform in Intercollegiate Athletics* (Baltimore: Johns Hopkins University Press, 1996), 1–11, 155–168.

2. *Ibid.*

3. Quoted in Walter Byers with Charles Hammer, *Unsportsmanlike Conduct: Exploiting College Athletes* (Ann Arbor: University of Michigan Press, 1995) 48–51.

4. Richard A. Davies, *Sports in American Life: A History* (Malden, MA: Blackwell Publishing, 2007).

5. Albert J. Figone, *Cheating the Spread: Gamblers, Point Shavers, and Game Fixers in College Football and Basketball* (Urbana: University of Illinois Press, 2014), 87–95.

6. *Ibid.*, 97.

7. V. B. Price, "Administration of William E. Davis," in William E. Davis, *Miracle on the Mesa: A History of the University of New Mexico, 1889–2004* (Albuquerque: University of New Mexico Press, 2006), 250–294.

8. John Papanek "Now New Mexico Feels the Heat," *Sports Illustrated*, December 19, 1979, 58.

9. "NCAA Slaps New Mexico Team with Three-Year Punishment," *Kentucky New Era*, December 4, 1980, 24.

10. Papanek, "Now New Mexico Feels the Heat," 58.

11. *Ibid.*

12. Calvin Horn, *University in Turmoil and Transition: Crises Decades At the University of New Mexico* (Albuquerque: Rocky Mountain, 1981), 305.

13. *Ibid.*

14. *Ibid.*

15. *Ibid.*, 309.

16. William C. Dowling, *Confessions of a Spoilsport: My Life and Hard Times Fighting Sports Corruption At an Old Eastern University* (University Park: Pennsylvania University Press, 2007), 13–29.

17. Papanek, "Now New Mexico Feels," 58.

18. *Ibid.*

19. Price, *Administration of William E. Davis*, 255.

20. *Ibid.*

21. Papanek, "Now New Mexico Feels," 58.

22. *Ibid.*

23. *Ibid.*

24. Dowling, *Confessions of a Spoilsport*, 13–29.

25. *Ibid.*

26. *Ibid.*

27. Papanek, "Now New Mexico Feels," 58.

28. *Ibid.*

29. *Ibid.*

30. *Ibid.*

31. Dowling, *Confessions of a Spoilsport*, 13–29.

32. *Ibid.*

33. Quoted in Dowling, *Confessions of a Spoilsport*, 13–29.

34. *Ibid.*

35. Quoted in *Ibid.*

36. Quoted in *Albuquerque Journal*, December 23, 1979, 1; Gail Rosenbloom, "Lobos Forfeit Victory, 5 Players Ineligible," *New Mexico Daily Lobo*, December 7, 1979, 1.

37. Dave Whitford, *A Payroll to Meet: A Story of Greed, Corruption, and Football At SMU* (Lincoln: University of Nebraska Press, 2013), 13.

38. Horn, *University in Turmoil*, 305.

39. *Ibid.*

40. "Sport: Double Trouble," *Time*, December 17, 1979.

41. *Ibid.*

42. Robert H. Boyle, "A Scandal That Just Gets Worse," *Sports Illustrated*, June 1980, 76.

43. *Ibid.*

44. Horn, *University in Turmoil*, 250.

45. *Ibid.*

46. *Ibid.*

47. *Ibid.*

48. Quoted in Dowling, *Confessions of a Spoilsport*, 19–33.

49. Quoted in *Ibid.*

50. *Ibid.*

51. *Ibid.*

52. Boyle, "A Scandal That Just Gets Worse," 77.

53. Quoted in *Ibid.*

54. *Ibid.*

55. Quoted in *Ibid.*

56. *Ibid.*

57. *Ibid.*

58. Horn, *University in Turmoil*, 251.

59. Quoted in Boyle, "A Scandal That Just Gets Worse," 78.

60. *Ibid.*

61. Quoted in *Ibid.*

62. Quoted in Horn, *University in Turmoil*, 298.

63. "New Mexico Investigates Point Shaving, Gambling," *New York Times*, January 30, 1980, A22.

64. *Ibid.*

65. *Ibid.*

66. Quoted in Boyle, "A Scandal the Just Gets Worse," 78.

67. *Ibid.*

68. Quoted in Boyle, "A Scandal That Just Gets Worse," 77.

69. Quoted in *Ibid.*

70. Horn, *University in Turmoil*, 298.

71. "UNM 125: Athletic Housecleaning Continues: Daily Revelations Rock Department," *New Mexico Daily Lobo*, January 14, 1980.

72. Horn, *University in Turmoil*, 298.

73. Price, *Administration of William E. Davis*, 255.

74. *Ibid.*

75. *Ibid.*

76. Horn, *University in Turmoil*, 267.

77. *Ibid.*, 269.

78. "Witness says Transcript Altered," *News Services*, June 17, 1980.

79. *Ibid.*

80. Horn, *University in Turmoil*, 257.

81. Quoted in Dowling, *Confessions of a Spoilsport*, 18.

82. Horn, *University in Turmoil*, 257.

83. Boyle, "A Scandal That Just Gets Worse," 77.

84. Quoted in Horn, *University in Turmoil*, 289.

85. Quoted in *Ibid.*

86. Quoted in *Ibid.*

87. *State of New Mexico V. Norman Ellenberger*, 983, 1980, Court of Appeals of New Mexico, 109.

88. John Papanek, "A Mockery of Justice," *Sports Illustrated*, July 20, 1981, 48.

89. Quoted in *Ibid.*

90. *Ibid.*

91. "Ellenberger Found Guilty," *New York Times*, July 8, 1981, A19; "Ellenberger Guilty, Avoids Prison" *Facts on File World Digest*, September 4, 1981.

92. Quoted in Papanek, "A Mockery of Justice," 49.

93. Quoted in Horn, *University in Turmoil*, 315.

94. *Ibid.*

95. Malcolm Moran, "Coaches Split Over Ellenberger Case," *New York Times*, July 16, 1981, B9.

96. Dave Anderson, "Sports of the Times: in the Pit, Lobogate Lives," *New York Times*, April 3, 1983, C87.

97. *Mark D. Hall V. University of Minnesota*, 530 Fed. Supp., Case 104, 1982, U.S, District Court, District of Minnesota, 104–111.

Chapter 6

1. Quoted in David Whitford, *A Payroll to Meet: A Story of Greed, Corruption, and Football At SMU* (Lincoln: University of Nebraska Press, 2013), 13.

2. *Ibid.*

3. Quoted in *Ibid.*, 70.

4. *Faculty Affairs Committee Report*, 1923, SMU Football Archives (hereafter named SMUFA).

5. Quoted in *Ibid.*

6. *Ibid.*

7. "Joseph E. Cockrell, Letter to the Friends and Enemies of Southern Methodist University, Within and Without," Dallas, TX, February 12, 1923. in this independent assessment of the FAC football report, Cockrell, a judge and founding father of SMU, excoriated the FAC primarily for its "strict interpretation" of newly enacted Southwestern Conference bylaws that declared two football players ineligible for further competition at the institution. the majority report was also sent to the Southern Accreditation Association, which voted not to accredit the institution.

8. *Ibid.*

9. Whitford, *A Payroll to Meet*, 14.

10. *Ibid.*

11. *Ibid.*

12. *Ibid.*, 14–15.

13. *Ibid.*, 15.

14. *Ibid.*, 73.

15. Quoted in *The Bishops' Committee Report on SMU*: "Report to the Board of Trustees of Southern Methodist University from the Special Committee of Bishops of the South Central Jurisdiction of the United Methodist Church," June 19, 1987, Southern Methodist University Archives (hereafter named SMUA, 12–14).

16. *Ibid.*, 1–89.

17. *Ibid.*

18. *Ibid.*

19. Quoted on *Ibid.*, 26.

20. *Ibid.*

21. Quoted in *Ibid.*, 45.

22. *Ibid.*

23. *Ibid.*

24. *Ibid.*

25. *Ibid.*

26. *Ibid.*

27. Quoted in *Ibid.*, 54.

28. Karen Blumenthal, "Overzealous Boosters Threaten the Integrity of College Sports," *Wall Street Journal*, December 27, 1985, 1.

29. Quoted in *Ibid.*

30. Quoted in *Ibid.*

31. Quoted in J. Brady McCollough, "A Death in Texas," *Kansas City Star*, August 26, 2007. http://www.ncaatop25.com/smu.htm (accessed September 29, 2014).

32. David Barron, "Remembering Bill Clements and the SMU Death Penalty," *Sports Update*, May 2011. http://blog.chron.com/sports update/2011/05/remembering-bill-clements-and-the-smu-death-penalty/ (accessed August 8, 2016).

33. Selena Roberts, "Big Boosters Calling the Shots on Campus," *New York Times*, January 2, 2005, SP1.

34. Brian Porto, *The Supreme Court and the NCAA: The Case for Less Commercialization and More Due Process in College Sports* (Ann Arbor: University Michigan Press, 2012), 39–48.

35. Quoted in Chris Dufresne, "Life After Death: SMU Has Never Bounced Back from NCAA's Penalty to Football Program Nearly two Decades ago," December 28, 2005. http://articles.latimes.com/2005/dec/28/sports/sp-smu28 (accessed September 29, 2014).

36. Barron, "Remembering Bill Clements."

37. *Ibid.*

38. *Ibid.*

39. Thomas C. Hayes, "S.M.U. Football May Face 2-Year Ban," *New York Times*, November 15, 1986. http://www.nytimes.com /1986/11/15/sports/smu-football-may-face-2-year-ban.html (accessed January 20, 2015).

40. Nicholas Lehmann, "Sherwood Blount's First Million," *Texas Monthly*, October 1979, 27.

41. *The Bishops' Committee Report*, 78.

42. Blumenthal, "Overzealous Boosters Threaten."

43. Whitford, *A Payroll to Meet*, 22.

44. Blumenthal, "Overzealous Boosters Threaten."

45. *Ibid.*

46. *The Bishops' Committee Report*, 78.

47. Lehmann, "Sherwood Blount's First Million."

48. Barron, "Remembering Bill Clements."

49. Nick Schwartz, "ESPN's Keith Olbermann Eviscerates Penn State," *For the Win*, January 17, 2015. http://ftw.usatoday.com/2015/01/keith-olberman-penn-state-paterno-win (accessed January 20, 2015).

50. J. Brady McCullough, "A Death in Texas."

51. Jerry Tarkanian and Terry Pluto, *Tark: College Basketball's Winningest Coach* (New York: McGraw-Hill, 1988), 35–59.

52. James W. Johnson, *The Dandy Dons: Bill Russell, K. C. Jones, Phil Woolpert, and One of College Basketball's Most Innovative Teams* (Lincoln, NE: Bison Books 2009), 1–25.

53. *Ibid.*

54. Jerry Tarkanian with Dan Wetzel, *Runnin' Rebel: Shark Tales of "Extra Benefits," Frank Sinatra, and Winning It All* (Champaign, IL: Sports Publishing, 2005), 13–19.

55. *Ibid.*; Andrew McGregor, "Jerry Tarkanian and Sport as Boosterism," *Sport in American History*, February 12, 2015. https://ussporthistory.com/2015/02/12/jerry-tarkanian-and-sport-as-boosterism/ (accessed May 26, 2016).

56. Tarkanian with Wetzel, *Runnin' Rebel*, 15

57. *Ibid.*

58. Tarkanian and Pluto, *Tark*, 320.

59. "College Athletics for Sale," in Ron Powers, *Supertube: The Rise of Television Sports* (New York: Coward-McCann, 1984), 221–231.

60. Quoted in Don Yaeger, *Shark Attack: Jerry Tarkanian and His Battle with the NCAA and UNLV* (New York: HarperCollins, 1992), 78.

61. *Ibid.*

62. A. D. Hopkins, "Jerry Tarkanian," *Las Vegas Review Journal*, September 12, 1999. http://www.reviewjournal.com/news/jerry-tarkanian (accessed September 29, 2014); Yaeger, *Shark Attack*, 63–74.

63. McGregor, "Jerry Tarkanian and Sport."

64. Quoted in *Report of the Board of Regents of the University of Nevada*, May 22, 1993, Tarkanian File, University of Nevada Archives (hereafter named UNLVA). the Board of Regents report was a detailed and chronological description of all the events that had taken place during Tarkanian's 19 years as the basketball coach at UNLV.

65. Quoted in *Ibid.*

66. Quoted in *Ibid.*

67. *Ibid.*

68. Michael James, "Because of Jerry Tarkanian and UNLV What Happened in Vegas Didn't Stay in Vegas," *The Tribe Sports*, February 11, 2015. http://www.thetribesports.com/thanks-to-tark-what-happened-in-vegas-stayed-in-vegas/ (accessed May 26, 2016).

69. Byron Craft, "The Men Who Made Las Vegas: Tark the Shark," *Strip Las Vegas*, no date. http://www.striplv.com/site/mag/issue65/stories/Vegas-JerryTarkanian-TarkTheShark.html (accessed September 29, 2014).

70. William C. Rhoden, "College Basketball; U.N.L.V. Under Federal Inquiry, Paper Says," *New York Times*, February 14, 1992. http://www.nytimes.com/1992/02/14/sports/college-basketball-unlv-under-federal-inquiry-paper-says.html?module=Search&mabReward=relbias%3Ar (accessed September 29, 2014). During the 1990–1991 season, UNLV was 30–0 before losing to Duke in the Final Four semifi-

nal. According to federal law enforcement authorities, the inquiry's primary focus was on Richard "The Fixer" Perry, a twice-convicted felon (for fixing Superfecta horse races and basketball games during the 1978–1979 season involving Boston College). Perry was seen at UNLV basketball games and was known to associate with some of the team's basketball players. Despite Tarkanian's vigorous denials of specific players playing for Perry and his associates in one of the most important games of the season, this would not have been the first time a major college's players had rigged a game for gamblers in a postseason NCAA tournament. the 1949 Kentucky team, including All-Americans Ralph Beard and Alex Groza and teammate Dale Barnstable, played for gamblers during that season and were upset by an underdog Loyola team in the first NIT game. All three players confessed to rigging that game.

71. A. D. Hopkins, "Source of Photos Surfaces," *Las Vegas Review-Journal*, July 22, 1992, 1A.

72. Quoted in *Ibid.*, 10A.

73. *Ibid.*

74. *Ibid.*

75. Scott Burnstein, "Tark the Shark's Run at UNLV Tanked Because of Team's Mob Ties," *The Gangster Report*, N.D. http://gangsterreport.com/tark-sharks-run—unlv-tanked—teams-mob-ties (accessed May 26, 2016).

76. *Report of the Board of Regents*, 25.

77. *Ibid.*

78. Quoted in Yaeger, *Shark Attack*, 220.

79. Burnstein, "Tark the Shark's Run At UNLV."

80. Ted Gup and Brian Doyle, "Education: Playing to Win in Vegas," *Time*, April 3, 1989, 30.

81. Burnstein, "Tark the Shark's Run At UNLV."

82. Quoted in Nicholas Pileggi, *Wiseguy* (New York: Simon & Schuster, reissued, 2011), 58.

83. Gup and Doyle, "Playing to Win in Vegas."

84. *Report of the Board of Regents*. 26; Danny Robbins and Gene Wojciechowski, "Report: Point Shaving Inquiry at UNLV: College Basketball: Newspaper says Federal Authorities Examining Relationship between Players and Convicted Sports Figure," February 14, 1992. http//articles.latimes.com/1992–02–14/sports/sp-2218_1_unlv-president-robert-maxon (accessed May 26, 2016).

85. *Ibid.*

86. Shelley Smith, "The Shark Attacked: Jerry Tarkanian, Succumbing to the Las Vegas Heat, says he'll Call it Quits Next Season," *SI.com*, June 17, 1991. http://www.si.com/vault/1991/06/17/124400/the-shark-attacked-jerry-

tarkanian-succumbing-to-the-las-vegas-heat-says-hell-call-it-quits-after-next-season (accessed January 26, 2015).

87. *Ibid.*

88. *Report of the Board of Regents*, 30–39.

89. *Ibid.*

90. *Ibid.*

91. *Ibid.*

92. *Ibid.*

93. *Ibid.*, 46.

94. Danny Robbins and Gene Wojciechowski, "Report: Point Shaving Inquiry at UNLV."

95. Quoted in *The Report of the Board of Regents*, 40.

96. *Report of the Board of Regents*, 57.

97. *Ibid.*

98. *Ibid.*

99. "Jerry Tarkanian said he is so upset at the attacks on his...," *Baltimore Sun*, June 2, 1991. http://articles.baltimoresun.com/1991–06-02/sports/1991153121_1_perry-rono-tarkanian (accessed September 29, 2014).

100. Danny Robbins, "Did UNLV Break Rules in Recruiting of Love?: College Basketball: Rebels allegedly accepted the help of Utah businessman and part-time coach to secure reserve center, in violation of NCAA rules?" April 23, 1991. http://articles.latimes.com/1991–04-23/sports/sp-670_1_junior-college-basketball/5 (accessed May 26, 2016).

101. "Gambling on College Sports: What's the Big Deal?" *NCAA.org*. http://www.ncaa.org/about/resources/media-center/gambling-college-sports (accessed September 29, 2014). Technically, NCAA Bylaw 10.3 covers all types of sport gambling and the penalties for the violation of each. the FBI has consistently warned college athletes about the ease of becoming heavily influenced by or associated with gamblers of any age.

102. Quoted in *Report of the Board of Regents*, 67.

103. *Ibid.*

104. "Perry Sentenced on Tax Evasion Charges," *New York Times*, September 8, 1997. http://www.nytimes.com/1997/08/09/sports/perry-sentenced-on-tax-evasion-charges.html (accessed September 29, 2014).

105. Ed Vogel, "Black Book Adds Perry 'the Fixer,'" *Las Vegas Review-Journal*, October 29, 1992; William C. Rhoden, "As Glitz Wore Out, the Coach Wore Thin," *New York Times*, July 2, 1991, B1.

106. Larry Stewart, "Tarkanian, NCAA Settle for $2.5 million," *Los Angeles Times*, April 2, 1998. http://articles.latimes.com/1998/apr/02.sports/sp-35333.

107. Quoted in *Ibid.*

108. Quoted in *Ibid.*

109. *Ibid.*

Chapter 7

1. Joe Goldstein, "Explosion Two: the Molinas Period," *ESPN Classics*, November 19, 2003. http://espn.go.com/classic/s/basketball_scandals_molinas.html (accessed September 29, 2014).

2. *Ibid.*

3. Albert J. Figone, *Cheating the Spread: Gamblers, Point Shavers, and Game Fixers in College Football and Basketball* (Urbana: University of Illinois Press, 2012): 102–103. The 1961 college gambling scandal illustrated what most gambling insiders, basketball beat writers, and a few "street smart coaches" knew ten years earlier. Many of the fixers and players who escaped unscathed in 1951 continued to manipulate final basketball scores throughout the 1950s. Until the arrests of fixer-gamblers Wagman, Silber, Rosenthal and Budin in September 1960, the worst-kept secret among the gambling cognoscenti was that college football and basketball players were routinely contacted and offered money to rig games. It's naïve to believe the two arrests that prompted the subsequent wiretaps and investigations by New York County detectives uncovered widespread fixing only in college basketball. It's plausible that game rigging may have taken place in college football in the 1950s and early 1960s.

4. John R Thelin, *Games Colleges Play: Scandal and Reform in Intercollegiate Athletics* (Baltimore: Johns Hopkins Press, 1994) 54–55.

5. *Ibid.*

6. *Ibid.*

7. John Gerald Tobin, "The Pacific Coast Conference Football Scandal and the Los Angeles Press," (Master's Thesis, University of California, Los Angeles, 1959).

8. Quoted in Dan Raley, "The Untold Story of Hugh McElhenny, the King of Montlake," *Seattle Post-Intelligencer*, September 1, 2004 http://www.seattlepi.com/sports/article/The-untold-story-of-Hugh-McElhenny-the-King-of-1153112.php (accessed January 20, 2014).

9. Quoted in Tobin, "The Pacific Coast Conference," 56.

10. *Ibid.*

11. Allan Matusow: *Unraveling of America: A History of Liberalism in the 1960s* (Athens: University of Georgia Press, Revised ed., 2009), 100–135.

12. *Ibid.*

13. Thelin, *Games Colleges Play*, 67.

14. Quoted in John Matthew Smith, *The Sons of Westwood: John Wooden, UCLA, and the Dynasty That Changed College Basketball* (Urbana: University of Illinois Press, 2013), 258–260.

15. Danny Robbins, "Bartow Was in Fear of UCLA Booster: Former Bruin coach believed an NCAA investigation of Sam Gilbert would have endangered his life," *Los Angeles Times*, August 4, 1993, http://articles.latimes.com/1993-08-04/sports/sp-20220_1_sam-gilbert (accessed September 29, 2014).

16. *Ibid.*

17. Quoted in Seth Davis, *Wooden: A Coach's Life* (New York: Henry Holt, 2014), 374.

18. *Ibid.*

19. Glenn F. Bunting and Tina Griego, "Miami Trial Gives Startling Portrait of Sam Gilbert," *Los Angeles Times*, April 23, 1990. http://articles.latimes.com/1990-04-23/news/mn-107-1_sam-Gilbert (accessed June 7, 2016).

20. "Testimony of Eduardo Gonzales before the United States Senate Committee on Governmental Affairs—The Asset Forfeiture Program—A Case Study," *Forfeiture Endangers American Rights*, 2004. http://fear.org/gonzalez.html (accessed September 4, 2014).

21. United States of America, Plaintiff, v. Benjamin Barry Kramer, et. al. Defendants, No. 87–879-cr. 957 F. Supp. 223. United States District Court of Florida, S.D. Florida, March 20, 1997. United States of America v. Michael Gilbert 244 3rd 888 (11 Cir. 2001). the two trials provide a comprehensive description of Sam Gilbert's, Michael Gilbert's, and Robert Gilbert's roles in the international money laundering scheme.

22. *Ibid.*, 259.

23. John Matthew Smith, *The Sons of Westwood: John Wooden, UCLA, and the Dynasty That Changed College Basketball* (Urbana: University of Illinois Press, 2013), 258–260.

24. *Ibid.*

25. *Ibid.*

26. *Ibid.*, 259.

27. Richard Goldstein, "Jack Scott, a Prominent Critic of Sport's Excesses, Dies at 57," *New York Times*, February 8, 2000. http://www.nytimes.com/2000/02/08/sports/jack-scott-a-prominent-critic-of-sport-s-excesses-dies-at-57.html (accessed September 29, 2014).

28. *Ibid.*

29. Quoted in Jack Scott, *Bill Walton: On the Road with the Portland Trail Blazers* (New York: Quadrangle/New York Times, 1976), 213–214.

30. Quoted in *Ibid.*

31. "Sport: Walton: Basketball's Vegetarian Tiger," *Time*, February 25, 1974.

32. Quoted in Figone, *Cheating the Spread*, 47.

33. John Matthew Smith, *The Sons of Westwood: John Wooden, UCLA, and the Dynasty That Changed College Basketball* (Urbana: University of Illinois Press, 2013): 119–127.

34. *Ibid.*

35. NCAA v Board of Regents of the University of the University of Oklahoma, 468 U.S.85 (1984). the Court held that the NCAA regulation of live telecasts of college football games was an unreasonable restraint of trade in violation of the Sherman Antitrust Act. the justices reasoned that college football should enjoy a free market in which colleges could negotiate directly with television networks to determine if, when, and how often their teams would appear on television and how much they would earn per appearance. in essence, the Court's decision favored sports over education. the incongruous union between big-time sports' and post-secondary education's legal implications would, in the future, render football and basketball programs even more beholden to booster and television money.

36. Smith, *The Sons of Westwood*, 218–219.

37. Yaeger, *Shark Attack*, 79–83.

38. Betty Boles Ellison, *Kentucky's Domain of Power, Greed and Corruption* (San Jose, CA: Writers Club Press, 2001), 225–252.

39. Pete Axthelm, et al., "The Shame of College Sports," *Newsweek*, September 22, 1980, 54.

40. Figone, *Cheating the Spread*, 137–150.

41. *Bergen County Record*, "Adrian Wojnarowski: UCLA's Tainted Dynasty," *Carnage and Culture*, April 3, 2006 (accessed September 29, 2014), http://carnageandculture.blogspot.com/2006/04/adrian-wojnarowski-uclas-tainted.html.

42. Davis, *Wooden*, 367.

43. *Ibid.*

44. Ramzy Nasrallah, "Five Guys," *Eleven Warriors*, March 10, 2011. http://www.elevenwarriors.com/2011/03/five-guys (accessed February 23, 2014).

45. Quoted in Andrew Bagnato, "Michigan Tainted by 'Great Shame,'" *Chicago Tribune*, November 8, 2002. http://articles.chicagotribune.com/2002-11-08/sports/0211080229_1_fab-five-era-michigan-self-imposed-sanctions (accessed February 23, 2014).

46. *Ibid.*

47. Hubert Mizell, "Fab Five Glory Has Turned into Gloomy Story at Michigan," *St. Petersburg Times*, November 17, 2002 (accessed September 30, 2014), http://www.sptimes.com/2002/11/17/Columns/Fab_Five_glory_has_tu.shtml.

48. Dr. Tommy Whittler, "NCAA Hypocrisy—

Black Scholars get Blocked, but Black Athletes get Recruited," *Black Blue Dog*. http://blackbluedog. com/2013/06/news/dr-tommy-whittler-ncaa-hypocrisy-black-scholars-get-blocked-but-black-athletes-get-recruited/ (accessed March 10, 2014).

49. Quoted in *Ibid*.

50. Jason Kohler, "1989 and beyond: How Michigan's national championship was its best moment and biggest curse," *The Michigan Daily*, March 17, 2009. http://www.michigandaily.com/content/2009-03-18/Michigan-basketball-1989 (accessed September 30, 2014).

51. *Ibid*.

52. James J. Duderstadt, *Intercollegiate Athletics and the American University: A University President's Perspective* (Ann Arbor: University of Michigan Press, 2003), 20–21.

53. *Ibid*.

54. Richard J. Hunter Jr., and Ann M. Mayo, "Issues in Antitrust, the NCAA, and Sports Management," 10 Marq.Sports L. J. 69 (1999) http://scholarship.law.marquette.edu/sportslaw/vol10/issue1/5 (accessed June 8, 2016).

55. John R. Gerdy, *Air Ball: American Education's Failed Experiment with Elite Athletics* (Jackson: University Press of Mississippi, 2006).

56. Quoted in George Dohrmann, "A Tangled Webber," April 1, 2002, *Sports Illustrated*. http://connection.ebscohost.com/c/articles/6398802/tangled-webber (accessed March 10, 2014).

57. *Ibid*.

58. Ben Mangrum, "Is College Football Profitable for Universities?" *Ethos: A Digital Review of Arts, Humanities, and Public Ethics*, March 27, 2014. http://www.ethosreview.org/intellectual-spaces/is-college-football-profitable/ (accessed March 12, 2014).

59. Quoted in Duderstadt, *Intercollegiate Athletics*, 180.

60. *Ibid*.

61. Jim Benagh, *Making It to #1: How College Football and Basketball Teams Get There* (New York: Dodd Mead, 1976), 88–100.

62. *Ibid*.

63. *Ibid*.

64. "University of Michigan Infractions Report," *NCAA Infractions Committee*, March 25, 1991.

65. "University of Michigan Redacted Report of Self-Investigation of Alleged NCAA Rules Violations in the University's Men's Basketball Program," Freedom of Information Act Office, University of Michigan, October 9, 1997. Michigan President Lee C. Bollinger requested that an outside law firm conduct an independent investigation after the U.S. Justice Department's prolonged investigation of Ed Martin's association with the university's basketball program beginning in the early 1990s. the NCAA, lacking subpoena powers, had not reported any major violations and only charged the university with three secondary violations involving Martin's association with the basketball program, despite the statement of one NCAA executive who labeled the program one of the "four or five dirtiest ever in the history of college basketball." the report is noteworthy for associating Martin with a number of events, alleged payments, relationships with players and their relatives, transporting players' relatives to away games, receiving "comped" seats from Steve Fisher, and recruitees' visits paid by Martin. After the report was given to the university, Fisher was fired, and the university disassociated itself from Martin a second time.

66. Chad Millman, "Fab Friend," *ESPN: The Magazine*, June 18, 2002. http://espn.go.com/magazine/vol5no13michigan.html (accessed March 20, 2014).

67. Quoted in *Ibid*.

68. *Ibid*.

69. *Ibid*.

70. *Ibid*.

71. *Ibid*.

72. *Ibid*. Ed Martin's numbers operation at the Ford plant was investigated by Dearborn police and plant security officials in 1997. His reputation as a "money man" among high school and college players was common knowledge in Detroit's basketball circles beginning in the mid-1980s. the FBI did not pursue Martin after learning about his illegal activities until April 1999, because they were collecting evidence that led to the conviction of crime boss Jack Tocco in 1998.

73. Millman, "Fab Friend."

74. Jim Cnockaert, "Accident effects still felt six years later: Roberson: It changed the athletic department," *Ann Arbor News*, March 22, 2002. http://web.archive.org/web/20020827003820/http://mlive.com/wolverines/aanews/basketball/index.ssf?/stories/wolverines/20020322accident_effects.html (accessed March 22, 2014).

75. *Ibid*.

76. Bruce Madej, "U-M Announces Findings of Men's Basketball Investigation," October 9, 1997. http://www.mgoblue.com/genrel/100997aaa.html (accessed March 30, 2014).

77. Big Ten Conference and University of Michigan, "Joint Enquiry Report to the NCAA in Response to Allegations Involving the Men's Basketball Program," March 4, 1997, Athletic Department, Box 7B, University of Michigan Archives.

78. Associated Press, "Fisher Fired, basketball

program needs higher standards, Goss says." *Ann Arbor News*, October 11, 1997. http://web.archive.org/web/20070927194302/http://www.mlive.com/wolverines/aanews/basketball/index.ssf?/stories/wolverines/19971011fisher_fired.frm (accessed September 30, 2014).

79. FBI Memo, "Results of execution of search warrants at 12 locations at 12 locations in Detroit metropolitan area," May 4, 1999, FBI memo obtained through FOI Request, June 9, 2014.

80. Millman, "Fab Friend."

81. *Ibid.*

82. "How Steve Fisher Survived Michigan's Saga Unscathed," *Lost Letterman*, January 24, 2011. http://www.lostlettermen.com/article/feature-how-steve-fisher-survived-michigans-saga-unscathed (accessed September 1, 2014).

83. Quoted in *ibid.* Edward Martin's numbers operations at the Ford Plant in Dearborn, Michigan, and possibly other parts of the Detroit area were in all likelihood not operating independently from organized crime.

84. Big Ten Conference and University of Michigan, "Joint Enquiry Report."

85. United States District Court, Eastern District of Michigan, Southern District, the United States of America, Plaintiff, vs. D-1 Eddie L. Martin, Hilda Martin, and Clarence Malvo, Defendants, March 22, 2002.

86. Nick Baumgardner, "Ed Martin scandal disassociation ends for Chris Webber; a look back at the timeline," *MLive*, May 8, 2013. http://www.mlive.com/wolverines/index.ssf/2013/05/ed_martin_scandal_disassociati.html (accessed September 4, 2014).

87. Geralda Miller, *Associated Press*, "Martin pleads guilty to federal conspiracy charge," *Ann Arbor News*, May 28, 2002. http://archive.today/5BNHZ (accessed September 30, 2014).

88. United States of America, Eastern District Court of Michigan, Southern Division, the United States of America, Plaintiff, vs. Mayce Christopher Webber, III, a/k/a Chris Webber, a/k/a C Webb, Mayce Webber, Jr., a/k/a Deacon Webber, and Charlene Johnson, Defendants, September 9, 2002. *FindLaw*, Pro Basketball: "Webber Indicted on Charge of Lying," *New York Times*, September 10, 2002, 1. http://www.nytimes.com/2002/09/10/sports/pro-basketball-webber-indicted-on-charge-of-lying.html (accessed September 8, 2014).

89. "Pro Basketball: Webber Will Fight Charges He Lied to Federal Grand Jury," *New York Times*, September 11, 2002. http://www.nytimes.com/2002/09/11/sports/pro-basketball-webber-will-fight-charges-he-lied-to-federal-grand-jury.html (accessed September 30, 2014).

90. "Death Blow to Webber Case," *Gaming News*, February 17, 2003. http://www.casinocitytimes.com/news/article/death-blow-to-webber-case-130367 (accessed September 30, 2014).

91. Caitlin Nish, "Basketball; Webber Avoids Jail, Pleading Guilty on a Contempt Charge," *New York Times*, July 15, 2003. http://www.nytimes.com/2003/07/15/sports/basketball-webber-avoids-jail-pleading-guilty-on-a-contempt-charge.html?module=Search&mabReward=relbias%3Ar (accessed September 25, 2014).

Chapter 8

1. Richard O. Davies and Richard G. Abram, *Betting the Line: Sports Wagering in American Life* (Columbus: Ohio State University Press, 2001), 79–80.

2. *Ibid.*

3. *Ibid.*

4. Richard Sasuly, *Bookies and Bettors: Two Hundred Years of Gambling* (New York: Holt, Rinehart and Winston, 1982), 91–105.

5. Charles Fontenay, *Estes Kefauver: A Biography* (Knoxville, TN: University of Tennessee Press, 1991), 45–89.

6. *Ibid.*

7. David Porter, *Fixed: How Goodfellas Bought Boston College Basketball* (Boulder, CO: Taylor Trade Publishing, 1990), 44.

8. Henry Hill and Douglas S. Looney, "How I Put the Fix In," *Sports Illustrated*, December 29, 1981, 12; Douglas S. Looney, "The Cast of Characters in the BC Caper," *Sports Illustrated*, February 16, 1981, 14.

9. Albert J. Figone, *Cheating the Spread: Gamblers, Point Shavers, and Game Fixers in College Football and Basketball* (Champaign: University of Illinois Press, 2012), 123.

10. Porter, *Fixed: How Goodfellas Bought Boston College Basketball*, 76–90.

11. *Ibid.*, 89.

12. Larry Elkin, "Witness says Cobb agreed to fix game," *Daily Collegian*, March 20, 1984, 12; "Figure in point shaving case held," *The NCAA News*, April 29, 1984, 8.

13. Bruce Selcraig, "Agents of Violence," *Sports Illustrated*, April 6, 1987, 25.

14. *Ibid.*, *U.S. v. Walters*, 711, F.Supp, 1435, 1989.

15. Chris Mortensen, *Playing for Keeps: How One Man Kept the Mob from Sinking Its Hooks Into Pro Football* (New York: Simon & Schuster, 1991), 214. in seeking to prosecute Walters and Bloom, the U.S. government presented a novel interpretation of the mail fraud statute. the Jus-

tice Department attorneys in Chicago argued that the agents' scheme in signing college athletes in violation of NCAA rules constituted an attempt to defraud universities of their property interests in athletic scholarships. the mails were used in advancing the plan when the players lied on their eligibility forms that were subsequently mailed to regional athletic conferences pursuant to NCAA rules. Prior to this case, never had a university's interest in athletic scholarships been argued to constitute property under the mail fraud precept. the lengthy trial included testimony from a small number of academic figures, university and athletic administrators, coaches, and players. It exposed a number of heretofore unknown disturbing elements in commercialized football and basketball. a number of legal scholars disputed the federal government's interpretation of the mail fraud statute on the basis that the law's intent was not to prosecute "bad" sport agents representing athletes from colleges that were routinely violating NCAA rules. Instead, argued the critics, without addressing the underlying problems of commercialized football and basketball and questionable behaviors of the NCAA—the colleges, coaches, and players—targeting only sport agents who violate criminal statutes is misguided.

16. *Ibid.*, 23.

17. *Ibid.*, 20.

18. Bill Brubaker, "A Quiet Affair: How Sports Agents Bloom, Walters Worked in Secrecy," *Los Angeles Times*, July 19, 1987. http://articles.latimes.com/1987-07-19/sports/sp-4975_1_sports-agents/4 (accessed September 30, 2014).

19. Mortensen, *Playing for Keeps*, 22.

20. *Ibid.*

21. Bishops' Report, "Report to the Board of Trustees of Southern Methodist University from the Special Committee of Bishops of the South-Central Jurisdiction of the United Methodist Church," June 19, 1987, Southern Methodist University Archives (hereafter referred to as SMUA).

22. Mortensen, *Playing for Keeps*, 23.

23. *Ibid.*, 34.

24. *Ibid.*

25. *Ibid.*, 125.

26. *Ibid.*, 220–221.

27. *Ibid.*, 204–205.

28. *Ibid.*, 205.

29. Mike Trope, *Necessary Roughness: The Other Game of Football Exposed by Its Most Controversial Superagent* (Raleigh, NC: Contemporary Books, 1987)129–147; William O. Johnson & Ron Reid, "Some Offers They Couldn't Refuse," *Sports Illustrated*, May 21, 1979, 28. Trope entered the agent business as an undergraduate history major at USC and immediately enjoyed success in the business by signing future NFL stars, including Lawrence Taylor, Eric Dickerson, and Tony Dorsett. in 1979, Trope attempted to bypass NCAA rules in dealing with agents by offering athletes an "offer sheet." This made an offer revocable at the will of an athlete. Trope did not sign or accept a player's offer sheet until one month after the expiration of eligibility. the NCAA challenged Trope's interpretation of the NCAA rules. Athletes who have exhausted their eligibility may sign with an agent while enrolled in school.

30. Mortensen, *Playing for Keeps*, 216–217.

31. *Ibid.*, 159.

32. Michael Franzese, "Prince of the Mafia," May 8, 2010. http://www.lifestory.org/component/myblog/prince-of-the-mofia.html (accessed September 30, 2014).

33. Trope, *Necessary Roughness*, 129.

34. *Ibid.*

35. Mortensen, *Playing for Keeps*, 109.

36. *Ibid.*

37. *U.S. v Walters*, 711, F.Supp.

38. Mortensen, *Playing for Keeps*, 60.

39. Bishops' Report, SMUA.

40. Steve Rudman, "EX UW Star Reggie Rogers: a Rolling Tragedy," October 25, 2013. http://sportspressnw.com/2167164/2013/ex-uw-star-reggie-rogers-a-rolling-tragedy (accessed September 30, 2014).

41. Jennifer Sullivan, "Former UW football player star Reggie Rogers found dead," *Seattle Times*, October 25, 2013 (accessed September 30, 2014).

42. Craig Neff, "Agents of Turmoil," *Sports Illustrated*, August 3, 1987, 37.

43. Mortensen, *Playing for Keeps*, 63.

44. *Ibid.*, 6.

45. M. Anthony Lednovich, "Gas-Tax Fraud Tied to Mob Families," *Sun Sentinel*, March 26, 1985. http://articles.sun-sentinel.com/1985-03-26/news/8501110652_1_gas-tax-michael-franzese-colombo-crime-family (accessed September 30, 2014).

46. Edward Barnes and William Shebar, "Crime: Quitting the Mafia: the Mob's Young Genius Says He Want Out," *Life*, December 1987, 109–112.

47. Selcraig, "The Deal Went Sour," *Sports Illustrated*, September 5, 1987, 28.

48. *Ibid.*

49. *Ibid.*

50. Mortensen, *Playing for Keeps*, 163.

51. Neff, "Agents of Turmoil."

52. *Ibid.*
53. *Ibid.*
54. *Ibid.*
55. Pete Kotz, "Mafioso Frank Campione Blasts His Son from Prison for talking to the FBI," *True Crime Report*, January 13, 2010. http://www.truecrimereport.com/2010/01/mafioso_frank_campione_blasts.php (accessed September 30, 2014).
56. *U.S. v. Walters*, 711 F.Supp.
57. *Ibid.*
58. *Ibid.*
59. *Ibid.*
60. *Ibid.*
61. *Ibid.*
62. Steve Fiffer, "College Sports; Agents' Trial: Why Bother?" *New York Times*, April 16, 1989. http://www.nytimes.com/1989/04/16/sports/college-sports-agents-trial-why-bother.html (accessed January 30, 2015).
63. *Ibid.* Unlike alumni, boosters are not affiliated with any part of a college except the athletic program. They have been a major source of NCAA rules infractions. Boosters have been cited for using inside information to gamble, giving athletes cash, cars, "no show" jobs, and gifts including women, parties, dinners, money, and arranging jobs for parents. in many cases, boosters have assumed the dual roles of booster-agent.
64. William Grady, "Convictions of Walters, Bloom Overturned," *Chicago Tribune*, September 18, 1980. http://articles.chicagotribune.com/1990–09-18/sports/9003180738_1_appeals-court-walters-and-bloom-sports-agents-norby-walters (accessed September 30, 2014).
65. "Palmer is Suspended and Sent Home by K.C.," Philly.com, November 28, 1988. http://articles.philly.com/1988–11-28/sports/26247115_1_chiefs-coach-frank-gansz-herman-heard-paul-palmer (accessed September 30, 2014).

Bibliography

Articles and Books

Abrams, Roger I. *The Dark Side of the Diamond: Gambling Violence, Drugs, and Alcoholism in the National Pastime*. Burlington, MA: Rounder Books, 2007.

_____. *Sports Justice: The Law & the Business of Sports*. Lebanon, NH: University Press of New England, 2010.

Adler, Patricia A., and Peter Adler. *Backboards & Blackboards: College Athletes and Role Engulfment*. New York: Columbia University Press, 1991.

Alfieri, Gus. Lapchick: *The Life of a Legendary Player and Coach in the Glory Days of Basketball*. Guilford, CT: Lyons Press, 2006.

"Amid New NCAA Football Scandals, 'The Root of the Problem Is Money.'" *PBS NewsHour,* September 2, 2011. http://www.pbs.org.newshour/bb/sports/july-dec11/football2_09–02.html (accessed April 24, 2012).

Arledge: Roone. *Roone: Memoir*. New York: HarperCollins, 2003.

Armstrong, Ken & Nick Perry. *Scoreboard Baby: A Story of College Football, Crime, and Complicity*. Lincoln: University of Nebraska Press, 2010.

Asinof, Eliot. *Eight Men Out: The Black Sox and the 1919 World Series*. New York: Henry Holt, 1963, Reprinted in 1987.

Avanzado, Melvin. "Entertainment & Media Litigation: Former UCLA Basketball Player Reeves Nelsen Sues Sports Illustrated for Defamation." *Entertainment Litigation Blog*. March 25, 2012. http://www.entertainmentlitigationblog.com/2012/05/entertainment_media_litigation_7.html (accessed May 11, 2014).

Axthelm, Pete. *The City Game: From the Garden to the Playgrounds*. Lincoln: University of Nebraska Press, 1970.

Bacon, John U. "Reflections from the Dome." *Detroit News,* No Date. (Available at: http://www.irishlegends.com/pages/reflections/reflections12.html (accessed August 23, 2010).

_____. *Three and Out: Rich Rodriguez and the Michigan Wolverines in the Crucible of College Football*. New York: Farrar, Straus and Giroux, 2011.

Baker, Aaron, and Todd Boyd, eds. *Sports, Media, and the Politics of Identity*. Bloomington: Indiana University Press, 1997.

Banker, Lem, and Frederick C. Klein. *Lem Banker's Book of Sports Betting*. New York: Plume, 1986.

Barrett, Paul M. "Four Blunt Points About UNC, College Sports, and Academic Corruption." *Businessweek,* January 20, 2014. http://www.businessweek.com/articles/2014–01–20/four-blunt-points-about-unc-college-sports-and-academic-corruption (accessed October 2, 2014).

Bennett, Brian. "NCAA board votes to allow autonomy for five power conferences." *ESPN.com*, Aug. 7, 2014. http://espn.gocom/college-sports-story/_/id/11321551/ncaa-board-votes-allow-autonomy-five-power-conferences (accessed October 21, 2014).

Bergan, Ronald. *Sports in the Movies*. New York: Proteus, 1982.

Bissinger, H. G. *Friday Night Lights: A Town, a Team, and a Dream*. New York: HarperCollins, 1991.

Bjarkman, Peter C. *Hoops: The Biographical Dictionary of Basketball*. Chicago: Masters Press, 2000.

_____. *A Century of College Basketball*. Indianapolis, IN: Masters Press, 1996.

Boorstin, Daniel J. *The Americans: The Democratic Experience*. New York: Random House, 1973.

_____. *The Americans: The National Experience*. New York: Random House, 1965.

_____. *Hidden History: Exploring Our Secret Past*. New York: Vintage, 1989.

_____. *The Image: A Guide to Pseudo-Events in America*. New York: Atheneum, 1987.

Boyd, Todd. *Young, Black, Rich & Famous: The Rise of the NBA, the Hip Hop Invasion, and the Transformation of American Culture*. New York: Doubleday, 2003.

Brinkley, Alan. *The Unfinished Nation: A Concise History of the American People, Vol. 2 from 1865*. New York: McGraw-Hill, 2008.

Brondfield, Jerry. *Rockne: Notre Dame Idol, Coaching Genius, Celebrity—A Legend Revisited*. New York: Random House, 1976.

Brown, David L. *Gambling: Athlete Career Killer. All Bets Are Off*. Niles, OH: Parkway, 2010.

Bryant, Paul, and John Underwood. *Bear: The Hard Life & Good Times of Alabama's Coach Bryant*. Chicago: Triumph, 2007.

Burnham, John C. *Bad Habits: Drinking Smoking, Taking Drugs, Gambling, Sexual Misbehavior, and Swearing in American History*. New York University Press, 1993.

Byers, Walter, and Charles Hammer. *Unsportsmanlike Conduct: Exploiting College Athletes*. Ann Arbor: University of Michigan Press, 1995.

Cady, Edwin Harrison. *The Big Game: College Sports and American Life*. Knoxville: University of Tennessee Press, 1978.

Carroll, Bob, and Bob Braunwart. *Pro Football, from AAA to '03: The Origin and Development of Professional Football in Western Pennsylvania, 1890–1903*. N. Huntington, PA: Professional Football Researchers Association (PFRA), 1991.

Carroll, John M. *Red Grange and the Rise of Modern Football*. Urbana: University of Illinois Press, 1999.

Christgau, John. *The Gambler & the Bug Boy: Los Angeles & the Untold Story of a Horse Racing Fix*. Lincoln: University of Nebraska Press, 2007.

_____. *The Origins of the Jump Shot: Eight Men Who Shook the World of Basketball*. Lincoln: University of Nebraska Press, 1999.

Chu, Don. *The Character of American Higher Education and Intercollegiate Sport*. Albany: State University of New York Press, 1989.

Clotfelter, Charles T. *Big-Time Sports in American Universities*. Cambridge: Cambridge University Press, 2011.

Coakley, Jay J. *Sport in Society: Issues and Controversies*. 10th ed. St. Louis: Mosby, 2010.

Cohen, Stanley. *The Game They Played*. New York: Farrar, Straus and Giroux, 1977.

Collins, Randall. *The Credentialed Society: A Historical Anthology of Education and Stratification*. New York: Academic Press, 1979.

Constable, Nick. *This Is Gambling*. London: Sanctuary Publishing Limited, 2003.

Cox, Landis. "Targeting Sports Agents with the Mail Fraud Statute: United States V Norby Walters & Lloyd Bloom." *Duke Law Journal* 41, 1157–1210, 1992.

Daly, Dan. *The National Forgotten League: Entertaining Stories and Observations from Pro Football's First Fifty Years*. Lincoln: University of Nebraska Press, 2012.

Davies, Richard O., and Richard G. Abram. "The Age of Jimmy the Greek: Sports Wagering in Modern America." *Nevada Historical Society Quarterly* 42 (1) Spring 1999, 21–44.

_____. *Betting the Line: Sports Wagering in American Life*. Columbus: Ohio State University Press, 2001.

Davis, Seth. *Wooden: A Coach's Life*. New York: Henry Holt, 2014.

Davis, William E. *Miracle on the Mesa: A History of the University of New Mexico, 1889–2003*. Albuquerque: University of New Mexico Press, 2006.

Deardorff, Donald L. *Sports: A References Guide and Critical Commentary, 1980–1999*. Westport, CT: Greenwood, 2000.

Degler, Carl N. *Out of Our Past: The Forces That Shaped Modern America*, 3d ed. New York: Harper & Row, 1984.

Denlinger, Ken. *For the Glory: College Football Dreams and Realities Inside Paterno's Program*. New York: St. Martin's Griffin, 1994.

DeVico, Peter J. *The Mafia Made Easy: The Anatomy and Culture of La Cosa Nostra*. Mustang, OK: Tate, 2007.

DiLorenzo, Thomas J. *Organized Crime: The Untarnished Truth About Government*. Auburn, AL: Ludwig von Mises Institute, 2012.

Dohrman, George. "Under-the-radar 'freelancers' a main source of college corruption." *SI.com* September 16, 2010. http://www.si.com/more-sports/2010/09/16/college-agents (accessed September 9, 2014).

Donohue, Steve. *Spiral Revolutions: College Football's Conference Warfare*. North Charleston, SC: CreateSpace, 2012.

Dosh, Kristi. "College TV Rights Deal Undergo Makeover." *ESPN.com*. May 10, 2012. http://espn.go.com/blog/playbook/dollars/post/_/id/705/ (accessed March 23, 2004).

_____. *Saturday's Millionaires: How Winning Football Builds Winning Colleges*. Nashville, TN: Turner, 2013.

Dowling, William. *Confessions of a Spoilsport: My Life and Hard Times Fighting Sports Corruption At an Old Eastern University*. University Park: Pennsylvania State University, 2007.

Duderstadt. James J. *Intercollegiate Athletics and the American University: A University President's Perspective.* Ann Arbor: University of Michigan Press, 2003.

Dunnivant, Keith. *Coach: The Life of Paul "Bear" Bryant.* New York: Simon & Schuster, 1996.

_____. *The Fifty-Year Seduction: How Television Manipulated College Football.* New York: St. Martin's, 2004.

Durso, Joseph. *The Days of Mr. McGraw.* Englewood Cliffs, NJ: Prentice-Hall, 1969.

_____. *Madison Square Garden: Years of History.* New York: Simon & Schuster, 1979.

_____. *The Sports Factory: An Investigation Into College Sports.* New York: Quadrangle/New York Times Book Co., 1975.

Dyerson, Mark. "Reading Football History: New Vistas in the Landscape of American Sport." *Journal of Sport History* 29, no. 2 (Summer 2002), 203–220.

Easterbrook, Greg. *The King of Sports: Football's Impact on America.* New York: Thomas Dunne, 2013.

Edwards, Harry, *Sociology of Sport.* Homewood, IL: Dorsey, 1973.

Eichelberger, Curtis, and Charles R. Babcock. "Football-Ticket Tax Break Helps Colleges Get Millions." *Bloomberg.com,* October 24, 2012. http://www.bloomberg.com/news/2012-10-25/got-college-football-tickets-take-a-tax-break (accessed September 3, 2014).

Eisen, George, and David K. Wiggins, eds. *Ethnicity and Sport in North American History and Culture.* Westport, CT: Praeger, 1994.

Eitzen, D. Stanley. *Fair and Foul: Beyond the Myths and Paradoxes of Sport,* 3d ed. New York: Rowman & Littlefield, 2006.

Eskenazi, Gerald. "North Carolina State Facing Questions About Point Shaving." *New York Times,* March 1, 1990. http://www.nytimes.com/1990/03/01/sports/north-carolina-state-facing-questions-about-point-shaving.html (accessed September 21, 2014).

Feinstein, John. *The Last Amateurs: Playing Glory and Honor in Division 1 College Basketball.* Boston: Little, Brown, 2000.

Feldman, Bruce. "Exclusive: Ex-Employee Details How Hurricanes Program Unraveled in Scandal." *CBSSports.com,* September 21, 2012. http://www.cbssports.com/collegefootball/story/20310408/exclusive-employee-details-how-hurricanes-program-unraveled-in-scandal (accessed October 20, 2014).

Ferrier, William Warren. *Origin and Development of the University of California.* Berkeley, CA: Sather Gate Book Shop, 1930.

Findlay, John M. *People of Chance: Gambling in American Society from Jamestown to Las Vegas.* New York: Oxford University Press, 1986.

Fish. Mike. "Gambling Is Big Mania on Campus: Betting Is a Growing Sport Among Students and Athletes, Especially in the Southeast." *Atlanta Journal and Constitution,* February 1, 1998, D1.

_____. "Most Powerful Boosters." *ESPN.* January 12, 2006. http://sports.espn.go.com/ncf/news/story?id=2285986 (accessed August 12, 2013).

Fisher, Aaron, Michael Gillum, M.A., and Dawn Daniels, with Stephanie Gertler. *Silent No More: Victim 1's Fight for Justice Against Jerry Sandusky.* New York: Ballantine, 2012.

Fleder, Rob. *The College Football Book.* New York: Sports Illustrated, 2008.

Fort, Emeline. *Sporting Scandals, Vol. 2: College Sports Scandals. Including the Resume Fabrication of George O'Leary, the Murder of Pat Denehy, the Duke….* City Unknown: Six Degrees Books. www.sixdegreesbooks.com (accessed June 20, 2012).

Fort, Rodney D. *Sports Economics.* Upper Saddle River, NJ: Prentice-Hall, 2003.

Fox, Stephen. *Big Leagues: Professional Football, Basketball, & Baseball in National Memory.* Lincoln: University of Nebraska Press, 1994.

Funk, Gary D. *Major Violation: The Unbalanced Priorities in Athletics and Academics.* Champaign, IL: Human Kinetics, 1991.

Gallico, Paul: *Farewell to Sport.* New York: International Polygonics, 1966.

"Gambling and Collegiate Athletics." *Free Online Library,* January 1, 2009. http://www.thefreelibrary.com/Gambling+and+collegiate+athletics.-a0249053648 (accessed May 10, 2013).

Gerdy, John. *Air Ball: American Education's Failed Experiment with Elite Athletics.* Jackson: University Press of Mississippi, 2006.

Gildea, Dennis. *Hoop Crazy: The Lives of Clair Bee and Chip Hilton.* Fayetteville: University of Arkansas Press, 2013.

Ginsberg, Daniel E., *The Fix Is In: A History of Baseball Gambling Scandals and Game Fixing Scandals.* Jefferson, NC: McFarland, 1995.

Glenny, Misha. *McMafia: A Journey Through the Global Criminal Underworld.* New York: Alfred Knopf, 2008.

Goodman, Mark C. "The Federal Mail Fraud Statute: the Government's Colt 45 Renders Norby Walters and Lloyd Bloom Agents of Misfortune." *10 Loy. LA. Ent. L. Rev. 315,* 1989. http://digitalcommons.lmu.edu/elr/vol/10/iss/1/9 (accessed October 25, 2014).

Gorn, Elliott J, and Warren Goldstein. *A Brief History of American Sports.* New York: Hill and Wang, 1993.

Goudsouzian, Adam. *King of the Court: Bill Russell and the Basketball Revolution.* Berkeley: University of California Press, 2010.

Grassi, Diane M. "Rip Off: College Students Forced to Subsidize Big-Time College Athletics." *Renewamerica.com,* December 24, 2013. www.collegeathleticsclips.com/index. php/home/guestcommentaries/8556-rip-off-college-students-forced-to-subsidize-big-time-college-athletics-?tmpl=coupon (accessed June 9, 2014).

Griffin, Sean Patrick. *Gaming the Game: The Story Behind the NBA Betting Scandal and the Gambler Who Made It Happen.* Fort Lee, NJ: Barricade Books, 2011.

Grob, Gerald N., and George Athan Billias. *Interpretations of American History: Volume Two Since 1865, Patterns and Perspectives.* New York: Free Press, 1967.

Guttman, Allen. *A Whole New Ball Game: An Interpretation of American Sports.* Chapel Hill: University of North Carolina Press, 1988.

Habiger, Scott. "Roger Goodell and Mark Emmert: Goodfellas," October 31, 2014. *Last Word on Sports.* http://lastwordonsports.com/2014/10/31/roger-goodell-and-mark-emmert-goodfellas/ (accessed May 28, 2014).

Harris, David. *The League: The Rise and Decline of the NFL.* Toronto: Bantam, 1986.

Harvey, Sean D. *One Moment Changes Everything: The All-American Tragedy of Don Rogers.* Champaign, IL: Sports Publishing, 2007.

Hayes, Thomas C. "S.M.U. Football May Face 2-Year Ban." *New York Times,* November 15, 1986. http://www.Nytimes.Com/1986/11/15/Sports/Smu-Football-May-Face-2-Year-Ban-Html (accessed June 26, 2013).

Hickson, Mark III, and Julian B. Roebuck. *Deviance and Crime in Colleges and Universities: What Goes on in the Halls of Ivy.* Springfield, IL: Charles C. Thomas, 2009.

Hill, Declan. *The Fix: Soccer and Organized Crime.* Toronto: McClelland & Stewart, 2008.

Hinton, Matt. "Agents, Rogue Coach, Academic Fraud, North Carolina Accused of Perfect Storm of NCAA Death." *Dr. Saturday,* No Date. Http://Sports.Yahoo.Com.Ncaa/Football/Blog/Dr_Saturday/Post/Agents-Rogue-Coaches-Academic-Fraud-North-Carolina-Accused-Of-Perfect-Storm-Of-Ncaa-Death? Urn. (accessed September 7, 2014).

Hochman, Stan. "Even College Sports Has Too Much Money Involved." *News Inter@Ctive,* 1998. http://dailytitanfullerton.edu/issues/spring_98/dti_03_11/evencollege.htmi (accessed January 23, 2014).

Hoffer, Richard. *Jackpot Nation: Rambling and Gambling Casinos Across Our Landscape of Luck.* New York: Harper, 2008.

Hoie, Bob. "1919 Baseball Salaries and the Mythically Underpaid Chicago White Sox. *Baseball* 6, no. 1 (Spring 2012). https://www.Questia. Com/Read/1p3–2707713311/1919-Baseball-Salaries-And-The-Mythically-Underpaid (accessed March 20, 2015).

Horn, Calvin. *The University in Turmoil and Transition: Crisis Decades At the University of New Mexico.* Albuquerque: Rocky Mountain, 1981.

Hruby, Patrick. "Does Tennis Have a Match Fixing Problem?" *SportsonEarth,* http://www.sportsonearth.com/articles/51670382/ (accessed February 9, 2013).

_____. "The NCAA'S Theater of the Absurd." *SportsonEarth.com,* December 16, 2013. http://www.sportsonearth.com/article/64719536/the-ncaas-theater-of-the-absurd#!bvyDhH (accessed January 19, 2014).

Huma, R., and E. J. Staurowsky. "The $6 Billion Heist: Robbing College Athletes Under the Guise of Amateurism." *National College Players Association and Department of Sport Management, Drexel University,* 2012. http://www.ncpanow.org (accessed December 25, 2014).

Hunt, Darren. "UTEP'S Moore, Ragland Still Suspended; FBI Won't Confirm, Deny Investigation into Team." *News-Home,* January 6, 2014. http://www.lvia.com/news/uteps-moore-ragland-still-suspended-fbi-wont-confirm-deny-investigation-into-basketball-team/ 23802610 (accessed July 28, 2014).

Ingrassia, Brian M. *The Rise of the Gridiron University: Higher Education's Uneasy Alliance with Big-Time Football.* Lawrence: University Press of Kansas, 2012.

Isaacs, Neil D. *The Great Molinas.* Bethesda, MD: Wid Publishing, 1992.

Jay, Katherine. *More Than Just a Game: Sports in American Life Since 1945.* New York: Columbia University Press, 2004.

Jeffries, James, as told to Charles Oliver. *The Book on Bookies: An Inside Look At a Successful Sports Gambling Operation.* Boulder, CO: Paladin Press, 2000.

Jenkins, Dan. "The Fighting Illini." *SI Vault,* March 3, 1967. http://sportsillustrated.cnn.com//vault/article/magazine/MAG1079593/2/index.htm (accessed January 24, 2013).

_____. *You Call It Sports, but I Say It's a Jungle Out There.* New York: Simon & Schuster, 1990.

Kalb, Elliott. *The 25 Greatest Sports Conspiracies Theories of All Time: Ranking Sports' Most Notorious Fixes, Cover-Ups, and Scandals.* New York: Skyhorse, 2007.

Kane, Don. "Austin's UNC Transcript Raises Question: the Former Tar Heel Began Academic Career with High-Level Course in African-American Studies," *NewsObserver. com,* August 21, 2011. (Available at: http://www/ newsobserver.com/2011/08/21/1425946/uncs-austin-got-unusual-start.html (accessed August 10, 2011).

Katz, Stephen. *Gambling Facts and Fictions: The Ant-Gambling Handbook to Get Yourself to Stop Gambling, Quit Gambling or Never Start Gambling.* Indianapolis: AuthorHouse, 2004.

Keith. Harold, *47 Straight: The Wilkinson Era At Oklahoma.* Norman: University of Oklahoma Press, 2003.

Kemper, Kurt Edward. *College Football and American Culture in the Cold War.* Urbana: University of Illinois Press, 2009.

Kirk, Dana, with Mark Davis. *Simply Amazing: The Dana Kirk Story.* No publisher, 1988 (copyrighted by Dana Kirk).

Kohout, Martin Donell. *Hal Chase: The Defiant Life and Turbulent Times of Baseball's Biggest Crook.* Jefferson, NC: McFarland, 2001.

Koppett, Leonard. *24 Seconds to Shoot: The Birth and Improbable Rise of the NBA.* Kingston, NY: Total/Sports Illustrated, 1968.

Lancaster, Harry, as told to Cawood Ledford. *Adolph Rupp as I Knew Him.* Lexington: Lexington Productions, 1979.

Lee, Jason W., and Jeffrey C. Lee, eds. *Sport and Criminal Behavior.* Durham, NC: Carolina Academic Press, 2009.

Leonotti, Philip, with Scott Bernstein, and Christopher Graziano. *Mafia Prince: Inside America's Most Violent Crime Family and the Bloody Fall of "La Cosa Nostra."* Philadelphia: Running Press, 2012.

Lester, Robin. *Stagg's University: The Rise, Decline, and Fall of Big-Time Football At Chicago.* Urbana: University of Illinois Press, 1995.

Levine, Mel. *Life in the Fast Lane, Cash, Cars and Corruption: A Sports Agent's True Story.* Plantation, FL: Distinctive, 1993.

Lingeman, Richard R. *Don't You Know There's a War On? the American Home Front, 1941– 1945.* New York: Putnam, 1970.

Luchs, Josh, and James Dale. *Illegal Procedure: A Sports Agent Comes Clean on the Dirty Business of College Football.* New York: Bloomsbury USA, 2012.

Luther, Jessica W. "A List of College Football Sexual Assault Investigations and Cases." *Power Forward,* December 2, 2013. http:// pwrfwd.net/2013/12/02/updated-a-list-of-college-football-rape-cases (accessed December 13, 2013).

Maisel, Ivan. "Autonomy Set to Benefit Athletes." *ESPN.com,* August 7, 2014. http://espn.go. com/college-football/story/_/id/11321434/ autonomy-grants-power-5-more-control (accessed August 13, 2014).

Mandel, Stewart. *Bowls, Polls, & Tattered Souls: Tackling the Chaos and Controversy That Reign Over College Football.* Hoboken, NJ: John Wiley, 2007.

McCloskey, John, and Julian Bailes, *When Winning Costs Too Much: Steroids, Supplements, and Scandal in Today's Sports.* Dallas: Taylor Trade, 2005.

McComb, Jennifer L., and William E. Hanson. "Problem Gambling on College Campuses." NASPA Journal 46, no. 1 (2009), 1–20.

McLaren, Richard H. "Corruption, Its Impact on Fair Play." 19 Marq.Sports L. Review, 2008. http://scholarship.law.marquette.edu/ sportslaw/vol19/iss1/3 (accessed August 25, 2013).

McMillen, Tom, and Paul Coggins. *Out of Bounds: How the American Sports Establishment Is Being Driven by Greed and Hypocrisy— And What Needs to Be Done About It.* New York: Simon & Schuster, 1992.

Mewshaw, Martin. *Short Circuit: The Shocking Exposé of Men's Professional Tennis.* New York: Penguin, 1983.

"Miami Ponzi Swindler Gained Cred with Sports Stars." *Sun Sentinel,* April 25, 2010. http://articles.sun-sentinel.com/2010-04-25/ news/fl-miami-ponzi-20100425_1_sports-dwayne-wade-two-rings (accessed February 21, 2015).

Miles, Thomas J. "Dupes and Losers in Mail Fraud." *77 University of Chicago Law Review,* 1111, 2010. http://chicagounbound.uchicago. edu/journal_articles (accessed May 19, 2014).

Miller, John J. *The Big Scrum: How Teddy Roosevelt Saved Football.* New York: Harper-Collins, 2011.

Miller, Patrick B., Ed. *The Sporting World of the Modern South.* Urbana: University of Illinois Press, 2002.

Miller, Richard I. *The Truth About Big-Time College Football.* New York: William Sloane Associates, 1953.

Millman, Chad "Authorities Expose $50m Betting Ring." *ESPN the Magazine,* October 25, 2012. http://espn.go.com/espn/story/_/id/ 8550476/new-york-issues-25-indictments-50-million-betting-ring (accessed December 23, 2014).

_____. *The Odds: One Season, Three Gamblers and the Death of Their Las Vegas.* Cambridge, MA: Da Capo, 2001.

Moldea, Dan E. *Interference: How Organized Crime Influences Professional Football*. New York: Morrow, 1989.

Moore, William Howard. *The Kefauver Committee and the Politics of Crime, 1950–1952*. Columbia: University of Missouri Press, 1974.

Morris, Willie. *The Courting of Marcus Dupree*. Garden City, NY: Doubleday, 1983.

Morrison, Samuel Eliot. *Three Centuries of Harvard, 1636–1936*. Cambridge, MA: Harvard University Press, 1936.

Mortensen, Chris. *Playing for Keeps: How One Man Kept the Mob from Sinking Its Hooks Into Pro Football*. New York: Simon & Schuster, 1991.

Munzenrieder, Kyle. "Nevin Shapiro's Gambling Claims Won't Be Part of NCAA Investigation." *Miami New Times*, June 12, 2013. http://blogs.miaminewtimes.com/riptide/2013/06/nevin_shapiros_new_gambling_cl.php (accessed December 23, 2014).

Myler, Thomas. *The Sweet Science Goes Sour: How Scandal Brought Boxing to Its Knees*. Vancouver: Greystone, 2006.

Nathan, Daniel A. *Saying It's So: A Cultural History of the Black Sox Scandal*. Urbana: University of Illinois Press, 2003.

"NCAA Pushes Cosmetic 'Fix' to Illegal Gambling Problem." *RGT Newspaper*, April 4, 2001. http://www.rgtonline.com/newspaper2/detail.psp.q.All.e.(!00018fe3!).a.htm (accessed May 27, 2014).

Nelli, Bert. *The Winning Tradition: A History of Kentucky Wildcat Basketball*. Lexington: University Press of Kentucky, 1984.

Noll, Roger G. "The Business of College Sports and the High Cost of Winning." *Milliken Institute Review* (1999), 25.

Nye, James. "UNC Football Player's Shocking Term Paper Is Released by Whistleblower Who Alleges Widespread Academic Fraud." *Renaissance*, March 28, 2014. http://www.amren.com/news/2014/03/unc-football-players-shocking-term-paper-is-released-by-whistleblower-who-alleges-widespread-academic-fraud/ (accessed November 12, 2014).

Omalu, Bennett, MD. *Play Hard, Die Young: Football Dementia, Depression, and Death*. Lodi, CA: Neo-Forenxis, 2008.

Oriard. Michael. *Bowled Over: Big-Time Football from the Sixties to the BCS Era*. Chapel Hill: University of North Carolina Press, 2009.

"Out of Bounds: College Athletes and Crime." *CBS News*, March 2, 2011. www.cbsnews.com/8301-18563_162-20038475.html (accessed April 10, 2013).

Pallette, Philip. *The Game Changer: How Hank Luisetti Revolutionized America's Great Indoor Game*. Bloomington, IN: AuthorHouse, 2005.

Parasuraman, Vishnu. "Miami Football Seeks Closure in Indy." *Page Q Sports*, June 17, 2013. (http://www.pageqsports.com/2013/06/after-media-conviction-miami-hurricanes-head-to-indy-for-closure-from-nevin-shapiro-case/ (accessed May 23, 2014).

Patton, Phil. *Razzle Dazzle: The Curious Marriage of Television & Football*. Garden City, NY: Dial, 1984.

"Penn State's Crimes and the NCAA: How Big Money Boosters Corrupt College Sports." *HillBuzz*, November 14, 2011. http://hillbuzz.org/penn-states-crimes-and-the-ncaa-how-big-money-boosters-corrupt-college-sports-69444 (accessed January 4, 2014).

Peterson, Robert. *Cages to Jump Shots: Pro Basketball's Early Years*. New York: Oxford University Press, 1990.

Pileggi, Nicholas. *Casino: Love and Honor in Las Vegas*. New York: Simon & Schuster, 1995.

Pope, Edwin. *Football's Greatest Coaches*. Atlanta: Tupper and Love, 1956.

Pope, S. W. *The New American Sport History: Recent Approaches and Perspectives*. Urbana: University of Illinois Press, 1997.

Popper, Nathanial. "Committing to Play for a College, Then Starting 9th Grade." January 26, 2014. http://www.nytimes.com/2014/01/27/sports/committing-to-play-for-a-college-then-starting-9th-grade.html?-r=1 (accessed March 5, 2014).

Porter, David. *Fixed: How Goodfellas Bought Boston College Basketball*. Dallas: Taylor Trade, 2000.

Porto, Brian. *The Supreme Court and the NCAA: The Case for Less Commercialization and More Due Process in College*. Ann Arbor: University of Michigan Press, 2012.

Posnaski. Joe. *Paterno*. New York: Simon & Schuster, 2012.

Powers, Ron. *Supertube: The Rise of Television Sports*. New York: Coward-McCann, 1984.

Putnam, Pat. "Another View of Gambling: It's Good for You." *SI.com*, March 10, 1986. http://www.si.com/vault/1986/0310/638304/another-view-of-gambling-its-good-for-you (accessed September 10, 2013).

Rammelkamp, Charles Henry. *Illinois College: A Centennial History, 1829–1929*. New Haven: Yale University Press, 1928.

Rampersad, Arnold. *Jackie Robinson: A Biography*. New York: Alfred A. Knopf, 1997.

The Red Grange Story: An Autobiography, as told to Ira Morton. Urbana: University of Illinois Press, 1993.

Reid, Bill, and Ronald A. Smith. *Big-Time Football At Harvard, 1905: The Diary of Coach Bill Reid.* Urbana: University of Illinois Press, 1994.

Rhoden, William C. "College Level Gambling Growing All Across the Country; the New Major?" *New York Times,* May 10, 1992, Sports, 3.

Ribock, J. Adam. "The NCAA: Enabling Cheating Since 1910 by Inadequately Punishing Cheating Coaches." *Mississippi Sports Law Review* 1 no.2 (2012), 389–409.

Rice, Grantland, *The Tumult and the Shooting: My Life in Sport.* New York: A. S. Barnes, 1963.

Rice, Robert. *The Business of Crime.* Westport, CT: Greenwood, 1956.

Rice, Russell. *Adolph Rupp: Kentucky's Basketball Baron.* Champaign, IL: Sagamore, 1994.

Ridpath, B. David, *Tainted Glory: Marshall University, the NCAA, and One Man's Fight for Justice.* Bloomington, IN: iUniverse, 2012.

Ritchie, Michael. *Please Stand By: A Prehistory of Television.* Woodstock, NY: Overlook Press, 1994.

Robinson, Charles. "Hurricanes Coach Al Golden's Staff Used Booster Associate4 in Potential Recruiting Violations." *Yahoo Sports,* July 20, 2012. http://sports.yahoo.com/news/ncaaf-hurricanes-coach-al-golden-s-staff-used-booster-s-associate-in-potential-recruiting-violations.html (accessed September 9, 2014).

Robinson, Ray. *Rockne of Notre Dame: The Making of a Football Legend.* New York: Oxford University Press, 1999.

Rogers, Rex M. *Gambling: Don't Bet on It.* Grand Rapids, MI: Kregel Publications, 2007.

Rose. Kenneth D. *Myth and the Greatest Generation: A Social History of Americans in World War Two.* New York: Routledge, 2008.

Rosen, Charles. *Barney Polan's Game: A Novel of the 1951 College Basketball Scandals.* New York: Seven Stories Press, 1998.

_____. *Scandals of '51: How the Gambling Scandals Almost Killed College Basketball.* New York: Holt, Rinehart and Winston, 1978.

Rudolph, Frederick. *The America College and University: A History.* New York: Alfred A. Knopf, 1962.

Russell, Bill, and Taylor Branch. *Second Wind: Memoirs of an Opinionated Man.* New York: Random House, 1979.

Sack, Allen L. *Counterfeit Amateurs: An Athlete's Journey Through the Sixties to the Age Academic Capitalism.* University Park: Pennsylvania State University Press, 2008.

Sack, Allen L., and Ellen J. Staurowski. *College Athletes for Hire: The Evolution and Legacy of the NCAA'S Amateur Myth.* Westport, CT: Praeger, 1998.

Sagendorph, Kent. *Michigan: The Story of the University.* New York: E. P. Dutton, 1948.

Sarandis, Ted. *Boston College Basketball Point-Shaving Scandal of 1978–1979.* Memphis, TN: Books LLC.

Sasuly, Richard. *Bookies and Bettors: Two Hundred Years of Gambling.* New York: Holt, Rinehart and Winston, 1982.

Savage, Howard J., Harold Woodmansee, Bentley, John T. McGovern, and Dean Franklin Smiley. *American College Athletics.* New York: Carnegie Foundation for the Advancement of Teaching, 1929.

Schlichter, Art, with Jeff Snook, *Busted: The Rise & Fall of Art Schlichter.* Wilmington, OH: Orange Frazier Press, 2009.

Schmidt, Raymond. *Shaping College Football: The Transformation of an American Sport, 1919–1930.* Syracuse, NY: Syracuse University Press, 2007.

Schrotenboer, "Brent. Digging into the Past of NCAA President Mark Emmert." *USA Today Sports.* April 3, 2013. http://www.usatoday.com/story/sports/college/2013/04/02/mark-emmert-documents-ncaa-president-lsu-uconn/2047725/ (accessed May 2, 2014).

Schulman, James L., and William G. Bowen. *The Game of Life: College Sports and Educational Values,* Princeton, NJ: Princeton University Press, 2001.

Schwartz, David G. *Roll the Bones: The History of Gambling.* New York: Gotham, 2006.

Scott, Jack. *Bill Walton: On the Road with the Portland Trail Blazers.* New York: Crowell, 1978.

Seidel, Larry R. *College: Investing in Basketball.* Indianapolis, IN: AuthorHouse, 2004.

Seymour, Harold. *Baseball.* New York: Oxford University Press, 1990.

"Shady Football Boosters Can Now Fear Federal Prosecutors." *Lubbock Avalanche-Journal,* February 6, 2005. http://lubbockonline.com/stories/020605/col_020605036.shtml (accessed July 5, 2013).

Sheehan, Jack. *The Players: The Men Who Made Las Vegas.* Reno: University of Nevada Press, 1997.

Smith, Curt. *Voices of the Game: The Acclaimed Chronicle of Baseball Radio & Television Broadcasting—From 1921 to the Present.* New York: Simon & Schuster, 1987.

Smith, John L. *Running Scared: The Life and Treacherous Times of Las Vegas Casino King Steve Wynn.* New York: Thunder Mouth Press, 2001.

Smith, John Matthew. *The Sons of Westwood: John Wooden, UCLA, and the Dynasty That Changed College Basketball.* Urbana: University of Illinois Press, 2013.

Smith, Ronald A. *Pay for Play: A History of Big-Time College Athletic Reform.* Urbana: University of Illinois Press, 2011.

_____. *Play-By-Play: Radio, Television, and Big-Time College Sport.* Baltimore, MD: Johns Hopkins, 2001.

_____. *Sports and Freedom: The Rise of Big-Time College Athletics.* New York: Oxford University Press, 1988.

Smith, Shelley. "The Shark Attacked Jerry Tarkanian: Succumbing to the Las Vegas Heat, Says He'll Call It Quits After Next Season." *SI.com,* June 17, 1991. http://www.si.com/vault/1991/06/17/124400/the-shark-attacked-jerry-tarkanian-succumbing-to-the-las-vegas-heat-say-he'll-call-it-quits-after-next-season (accessed July 25, 2013).

Snelling, Dennis. *The Greatest Minor League: A History of the Pacific Coast League, 1903–1957.* Jefferson, NC: McFarland, 2012.

Soderstrom, Robert M. *The Big House: Fielding H. Yost and the Building of Michigan Stadium.* Ann Arbor: Huron River Press, 2005.

Sokolove, Michael, Y. *Hustle: The Myth, Life, and Lies of Pete Rose.* New York: Simon & Schuster, 1990.

Sperber, Murray A. *Beer and Circus: How Big-Time College Sports Is Crippling Undergraduate Education.* New York: Henry Holt, 2000.

_____. *Onward to Victory: The Crises That Shaped College Sports.* New York: Henry Holt, 1998.

_____. *College Sports, Inc.: The Athletic Department Vs. the University.* New York: Henry Holt, 1990.

Stagg, Amos Alonzo, and Wesley Winans Stout. *Touchdown!* New York: Longmans, Green, 1927.

Standen, Jeffrey. *Taking Sports Seriously: Law and Sports in Contemporary American Culture.* Durham, NC: Carolina Academic Press, 2009.

Strohl, Nick. "Big-Time Football and Big-Time Scandals: What History Can Tell Us About the Future of College Sports and the NCAA." *The Education Optimists.* July 22, 2012. http://eduoptimists.blogspot.com/2012/07/big-time-football-and-big-time-scandals-htm (accessed August 17, 2014).

Stuhldreher, Harry A. *Knute Rockne: Man Builder.* New York: Grosset & Dunlap, 1931.

Sullivan, John L., and Gilbert Odd, eds. *I Can Lick Any Sonofabitch in the House.* New York: Proteus, 1980.

Tarkanian, Jerry, and Dan Wetzel. *Runnin' Rebel: Shark Tales of Extra Benefits, Frank Sinatra, and Winning It All.* Champaign, IL: Sports Publishers, 2006.

Tarkanian, Jerry, and Terry Pluto. *Tark: College Basketball's Winningest Coach.* New York: McGraw-Hill, 1988.

Thelin, John R. *Games Colleges Play: Scandal and Reform in Intercollegiate Athletics.* Baltimore: Johns Hopkins, 2004.

_____. *History of American Higher Education,* 2d ed. Baltimore: Johns Hopkins University Press, 2011.

Trope, Mike, and Steve Delsohn. *Necessary Roughness.* Chicago: Contemporary, 1987.

Tuohy, Brian. *Larceny Games: Sports Gambling, Game Fixing and the FBI.* Port Townsend, WA: Feral House, 2013.

_____. "Should U.S. Leagues Be Worried About Match Fixing?" *SportsonEarth.com.* December 5, 2013. http://www.sportsonearth.comarticle/64398178/ (accessed December 24, 2013).

Tygiel, Jules. *Past Time: Baseball as History.* New York: Oxford University Press, 2000.

Underwood, John. *The Death of an American Game: The Crisis in Football.* Boston: Little, Brown, 1979.

Underwood, John, et al. "The Biggest Game in Town." *Sports Illustrated.* March 10, 1986, 30.

"UW Suspends Quarterback Hobart." *The Oregonian,* November 6, 1992, C01.

Veblen, Thorstein. *The Higher Learning in America: A Memorandum on the Conduct of Universities by Businessmen.* New York: Sagamore, 1957.

Vecchione, Joseph J. *The New York Times Book of Sports Legends.* New York: Times Books, 1991.

Veysey, Laurence R. *The Emergence of the American University.* Chicago: University of Chicago Press, 1965.

Vincent, Ted. *The Rise and Fall of American Sport: Mudville's Revenge.* Lincoln: University of Nebraska Press, 1994.

Voight, David Quentin, *Vol. 1. American Baseball: From the Gentlemen's Sport to the Commissioner System.* University Park: Pennsylvania University Press, 1983.

Wasserman, Howard M., ed. *Institutional Failures: Duke Lacrosse, Universities, the News Media, and the Legal System.* Burlington, VT: Ashgate, 2011.

Watterson. John Sayle. *College Football: History, Spectacle, Controversy.* Baltimore, MD: Johns Hopkins, 2000.

Weissberg, Ted. *Breaking the Rules: The NCAA*

and Recruitment in American High Schools. New York: Franklin Watts, 1995.

Wells, Joseph P., and Dick Carozza. "Corruption in College Sports: U.S. University Athletic Programs Vulnerable to Devastating Fraud." *Fraud Magazine,* May/June 2000 (accessed January 3, 2013).

Wetzel, Dan, and Don Yaeger. *Sole Influence: Basketball, Corporate Greed, and the Corruption of America's Youth.* New York: Warner Books, 2000.

Whannel, Garry. *Fields in Vision: Television Sport and Cultural Transformation.* New York: Routledge, 1992.

Whitford, David. *A Payroll to Meet: A Story of Greed Corruption, and Football At SMU.* New York: Macmillan, 1989.

Whitney, Stu, and Bob Kourtakis. *Behind the Green Curtain: The Sacrifice of Ethics and Academics in Michigan State Football's Rise to National Prominence.* Grand Rapids, MI: Masters Press, 1990.

Whitt, Rich. *Behind the Hedges: Big Money and Power Politics At the University of Georgia.* Montgomery, AL: New South, 2009.

Wieland, Paul. *The Father ... The Son ... And the Sweet Sixteen: A College Basketball Disaster.* Great Valley, NY: Brown Hill, 2011.

Wiggins, David K., ed. *Sport in America: From Wicked Amusement to National Obsession.* Champaign, IL: Human Kinetics, 1995.

Wind, Herbert Warren. *The Gilded Age of Sport.* New York: Simon & Schuster, 1961.

Witosky, Tom. "Former Michigan, NBA Star Rumeal Robinson Sentenced to Prison." *Des Moines Register,* January 1, 2011. http://usatoday/30/usatoday.com/sports/basketball/2011–01-07-rumeal-robinson-prison_N.htm (accessed May 4, 2013).

Wolf, Dave. *Foul! The Connie Hawkins Story.* New York: Holt, Rinehart and Winston, 1972.

Wolfe, Alan, and Erik C. Owens, eds. *Gambling: Mapping the American Moral Landscape.* Waco, TX: Baylor University Press, 2009.

Wolfe, Alex, and Pete Thamel. "How the NCAA Mishandling of the Miami Case Exposed an Enforcement Department Seemingly Powerless to Do Its Job." *SI Special Report,* June 12, 2013. http://insidesportsillustrated.com/2013/06/12/si-special-report-ncaa-miami/ (accessed September 24, 2014).

Wolfers, Justin. "Blow the Whistle on Betting Scandals." *New York Times,* July 27, 2007. http://www.nytimes.com2007/07/27/opinion/27wolfers.html?_r=0 (accessed October 21, 2014).

Wolff, Alexander. "In Jailhouse Interviews, Nevin Shapiro Still Talking about Miami, NCAA." *SI.com.* May 18, 2014. http://www.si.com/college-football/2013/06/12/nevn-shapiro-miami-ncaa (accessed May 28, 2014).

Wolverton, Brad. "Confessions of a Fixer: How a Former Coach Perpetuated a Cheating Scheme." *SI.com,* December 30, 2014. http://Www.Si.Com/College-Basketball/2014/12/29/College-Athletes-Fixer (accessed January 1, 2015).

_____. "NCAA Proposal Would Give New Powers to Biggest Leagues." *Chronicle of Higher Education,* January 10, 2014. www.Collegeathleticsclips.Com/Index.Php/Arcchive/Ncaa/8605-Ncaa-Proposal-Would-Give-New-Powers-To-Biggest-Leagues-) (accessed March 23, 2015).

Woodburn, James Albert, and D. D. Banta. *History of Indiana University.* Bloomington: Indiana University Press, 1940.

Yaeger, Don. *Undue Process: The NCAA'S Injustice for All.* Champaign, IL: Sagamore, 1991.

Yeager, Don, and Jerry Tarkanian. *Shark Attack: Jerry Tarkanian and His Battle with the NCAA and UNLV.* New York: HarperCollins, 1992.

Yeager, Don, and Jim Henry. *Tarnished Heisman: Did Reggie Bush Turn His Final College Season Into a Six-Figure Job?* New York: Pocket Books, 2008.

Yiannnakis, Andrew, and Merrill J. Melnick, eds. *Contemporary Issues in Sociology of Sport.* Champaign, IL: Human Kinetics, 2001.

Yoder, Matt. Yahoo's "Miami Investigation Is Their One Shining Moment." *Awful Announcing,* August 17, 2011. http://awfulannouncing.com/2011-articles/yahoos-miami-investigation-is-their-one-shining-moment.html (accessed October 1, 2014).

Yost, Mark. *Varsity Green. A Behind the Scenes Look At Culture and Corruption in College Athletics.* Stanford, CA: Stanford University Press, 2010.

Zinn, Dave. "The NCAA-Poster Boy for Corruption and Exploitation." March 26, 2013, *The Nation.* http://portside.org/2013–03-26/ncaa—poster-boy-corruption-and-exploitation (accessed March 25, 2014).

Reports

Big Ten Conference and University of Michigan, "Joint Enquiry Report to the NCAA in Response to Allegations Involving the Men's Basketball Program," March 4, 1997, Athletic Department, Box 7B, University of Michigan Archives.

Cabot, Anthony. "The Absence of a Comprehensive Federal Policy Toward Internet and Sports Wagering and a Proposal for Change," *Villanova Sports & Entertainment Law Journal* 17 (2010), 271–294.

Corruption in Boxing: The Ike Williams Testimony, *U.S. Congress Senate Judiciary Committee: Professional Hearings Before Subcommittee on Antitrust and Monopoly*, 86th Cong., 2d. sess., Pursuant to S.Res. 238, December 5–14, 1960 (Washington: Government Printing Office, 1961), 664–677. Steven A. Riess, *The American Sporting Experience: A Historical Anthology of Sport in America*. Champaign, IL: Leisure Press, 1984, 348–364.

Goldstein, Jason. "Take the Money Line: PASPA, Bureaucratic Politics, and the Integrity of the Game," *Virginia Sports & Entertainment Journal*, 11, no. 2 (spring 2012), 362–376.

Muehle, Michael. "Paving the Way for Legalized Sports Gambling," *Rutgers Law Review Commentaries*, October 22, 2012, 1–24.

Reib, E. N. "Ante Up or Fold: What Should Be Done About Gambling in College Sports?" *Marquette Sport Law Review*, 2011, 621. http://scholarship.law.marquette.edu/sportslaw/vol/21/iss2/7, 2011 (accessed January 4, 2015).

"Testimony of Eduardo Gonzales Before the United States Senate Committee on Governmental Affairs—The Asset Forfeiture Program—A Case Study," Forfeiture Endangers American Rights. http://fear.org/gonzalez.html (accessed September 29, 2014).

"University of Michigan Infractions Report," *NCAA Infractions Committee*, March 25, 1991.

"University of Michigan Redacted Report of Self-Investigation of Alleged NCAA Rules Violations in the University's Men's Basketball Program." Freedom of Information Act Office, University of Michigan, October 9, 1997.

Cases

Attorney General Eugene Cook's Butts-Bryant Report, Part One (1963), O. C. Aderhold Collection 1920–1975, Box 97–100:2. in David Sumner, "Libelous—But True: Another Look at Butts V. Curtis."

Curtis Publishing Company, Appellant and Cross-Appellee Vs Wallace Butts, Appellee and Cross-Appellant, United States Court of Appeals for the Fifth Circuit, No. 8311, United States District Court Northern District of Georgia Atlanta Division, February 19, 1964.

Mark D. Hall V. University of Minnesota, 530 Fed. Supp., Case 104, 1982, U.S. District Court, District of Minnesota, 104–111.

NCAA V. Board of Regents of the University of the University of Oklahoma. 468 U.S.85 (1984).

New York Times Co. V. Sullivan. 376 U.S. 967 84. Ct. 1130 12L. Ed. 2d 83 (1964).

62 F. 3d 1144, 95 Cal. Daily Op. Serv.6114, 95 Daily Journal, D.A.R. 10,474 ... in the Matter of the Grand Jury Subpoena Issued to David Z. Chesnoff, Esq, Las Vegas Nevada (Two Cases). United States of America, Plaintiff-Appellee, V. David Z. Chesnoff, Defendant-Appellant. Goodman and Chesnoff, Appellant, V. United States of America, Appellee (Parties), Nos. 94–15412, 94–15547. United States Court of Appeals, Ninth Circuit. Submitted July 12, 1995. Decided August 3, 1995.

State of New Mexico V. Norman Ellenberger, 983, 1980, Court of Appeals of New Mexico, 109.

United States District Court, Eastern District of Michigan, Southern District, the United States of America, Plaintiff, Vs D-1 Eddie L. Martin, Hilda Martin, and Clarence Malvo, Defendants, March 22, 2002.

United States of America, Eastern District Court of Michigan, Southern Division, the United States of America, Plaintiff, Vs Mayce Christopher Webber, 111, A/K/A Chris Webber, A/K/A C Webb, Mayce Webber, Jr., A/K/A Deacon Webber, and Charlene Johnson, Defendants, September 9, 2002.

United States of America, Plaintiff, V. Benjamin Barry Kramer, Et. Al. Defendants, No. 87–879-cr. 957 F. Supp. 223.United States District Court of Florida, S.D. Florida, March 20, 1997.

United States of America V. Michael Gilbert 244 3rd 888 (11 Cir. 2001).

U.S. V. Burke, 700, F .2nd 70 (C.A. 2 N.Y.), 1983.

U.S. V. Walters, 711, F.Supp. 1435, 1989.

Wallace Butts, Plaintiff V. Curtis Publishing Company Defendant, Civ. A, no. 8311 225 F. Supp. 16-Dist Court, ND Georgia, 14, January 1964.

Written Statements from LeRoy Pearce to James H. Terrell, Assistant Attorney General; Wyatt Posey to Terrell, John Tillitski to Terrell, John W. Gregory to Terrell, Bobby Proctor to Terrell, and Frank E. Inman to Terrell (March 26, 1963).

Index

Numbers in ***bold italics*** indicate pages with illustrations.

175